GW00786663

# IMRE VASS
# ÉPÉE FENCING

# CORVINA

IMRE VASS

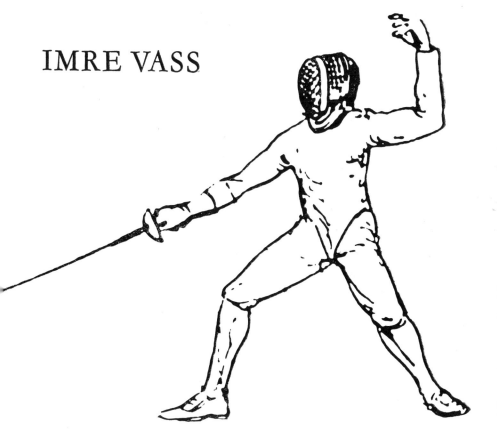

# ÉPÉE
# FENCING

Title of the Hungarian original:
*Párbajtőrvívás*
Sport. Budapest, 1965
Hungarian edition © Imre Vass, 1965

Translated by István Butykai
Translation revised by Charles Coutts
Technical supervision by János Hajdu
Line-drawings by Csaba Gaál
Jacket and cover by Károly Pogány

© Imre Vass, 1976
ISBN 963 13 3703 0
Printed in Hungary, 1976
Athenaeum Printing House, Budapest

# CONTENTS

7

# FOREWORD

In discussing the theoretical and practical aspects of épée fencing this book draws on over a quarter of a century of practical experience. Although the author's approach is a very individual one, the material will be easily understood by the fencing expert. It establishes a system of the material disclosed up to the present day, starting out from the fundamentals and incorporating gradually exercises of the highest standard. Those characteristic aspects of épée fencing which rely on the material of the related weapon: the foil, are duly pointed out. In addition, it specifies the forms that demand extension of existing knowledge, and includes material of a novel character as required by the special features of the weapon.

The chapter entitled "The Fencing Lesson" contains the basic exercises on which the whole system of épée fencing is built up. The individual chapters provide the detailed analysis essential for the elaboration of basic instruction both in attacks and in defence. Each action contains all the possible variations of starting an attack, the system of parrying the attack concerned, all the actions of the riposte following a parry and counter return thrust as well as every possible stop thrust that can be carried out in the course of the attack in question.

In accordance with the classification of feints the book discusses the system of simple and double feint attacks, extending from the fundamental exercises up to fencing lesson exercises of the highest level. In addition, the types of actions that can be carried out from renewals of attack and second intention attacks and constitute part and parcel of the exercises considered so far are also discussed.

Each chapter is completed with examples and figures.

The methodical description of the exercises is given along the lines of the well-tested and checked three-year curriculum of the Faculty of Training Coaches at the Hungarian School of Physical Education.

# INTRODUCTION

Any review, however brief, of literature on fencing leaves no doubt about the fact that the specialized literature on épée fencing is meagre and scanty compared to the huge, appropriately systematized and rich material on sabre and foil fencing. This is all the more surprising if we consider the history of the weapon, the remarkable development and results, on which its international prestige is based. For this reason the material used in the course of instruction in épée fencing and during actual combat conditions needs to be analysed and systematized in detail, so that essentials that serve as a basis of systematic coaching can be appropriately recorded. The elements currently encountered in practical instruction are, for the time being, like a mass of uncorrected pieces for a mosaic, handed down, like a tradition, from generation to generation or from coach to coach. This mass of material lies ready at hand waiting to be fashioned into a uniform whole. I have attempted to perform this task, above all, within the framework of the three-year course at the Hungarian School for Training Coaches where favourable conditions have been provided for importing systematic instruction.

The knowledge I acquired at the Budapest Institute for Training Sport Teachers and Fencing Coaches from 1934 to 1939 above all from Italy's Eduardo Alajmo, a man with brilliant technique, and from the French coach André Gardêre, who worked in Hungary during the same period is the principal basis of my work in this field.

During the period following the liberation in 1945 of Hungary from under fascist rule I concentrated my attention, in the first place, on observing the technique adopted by my most outstanding pupils (Sákovits and Rerrich, and Győző Kulcsár of the younger generation of épéeists). Abroad I found the elements that I regarded as examples to follow in the establishment of the classical school in the fencing of Italy's Eduardo Mangiarotti, Pavesi, Bertinetti and Delaunois of Belgium. The above remarks show that my aim has been, working within the limits of the available material, to select the best and most valuable experiences and acquired knowledge, and forge them into a coherent whole. I am well aware of the fact that the fencing generation of today can observe and control the original features of the different technical solutions only as long as the great competitors I mentioned are on the piste. I also know that my ideas are bound to undergo certain changes in the future, and that these will reveal unmistakable marks of distortion as has been the case in the sabre fencing schools founded by Hungary's Borsodi and Santelli of Italy.

My overriding objective has been to create a firm foundation for future development in terms of both technique and criticism.

When examining the question from a practical aspect it must be made clear as a principle of instruction that the number one requirement is to teach the épéeist to fence well with the foil so that the fundamental skills necessary for fencing, the rapid and correct execution of the movements in the bout with foil can be developed to a stage at which they can be applied most effectively.

In the second phase of development the fundamental features

that distinguish the épée from its related weapon, the foil, should be pointed out. The exercises with the feet and hand as well as the different positions and transitions should be executed as required by the special characteristics of the weapon.

In the course of a fencing lesson the coach should rely on foil fencing as a basis, yet he should deviate from it concerning the system. While retaining the unities of action the pupil should carry out every attacking movement by moving the weapon apart from his body and towards an enlarged target area from every distance. This exercise should be performed in three stages: first as in foil fencing, then with "opposition" and finally with "angular thrust". Instruction should be given simultaneously with the teaching of attacking movements in all the possible parries of an attack. The individual actions should be composed of three successive moves: thrust, parry and thrust. The pupil should practise the stop thrusts of counter-attacks that can be applied during the opponent's attacking movements as early as the initial stages of his training.

It is characteristic of épée fencing that it contains movements both in attack and defence that constitute the elements of foil fencing. These movements can be directed to and executed against the adversary's whole body including his arms, head and legs, in accordance with the special features of the épée and the rules governing épée fencing. The enlarged target area compared to foil fencing and the advantage for the fencer hitting first (priority of hits) led to the formation of special épée fencing movements that are necessarily different from those used in foil fencing in terms of the methods of execution. In this sense, the épée must be regarded as a completely independent weapon; and the foil considered as what might be described as its "training weapon". During the decisive period of development the special épéeist skills must be formed on the basis of the individual's suitability. The pupil must be taught the method of applying the movements and his relevant reflexes must be developed but without destroying the essential technical basis acquired in foil fencing, which is indispensable in épée fencing as well. In several cases even what are termed as conventional action units cannot be dispensed with, for they must be considered as a basis vital for development.

As I mentioned earlier the épée fencing schooling is founded on the foil, it necessarily returns to this foundation several times to draw the overwhelming majority of its material from this source, yet it relies on new elements, too, even in the early stages. If a foilist takes up the épée and enters an épée competition straight away the bank of movements on which he will draw will be 100 per cent those common to foil fencing. However, with the passage of time this ratio will gradually change as his assets increase under the influence of his training in épée fencing and practice bouts. In six months' time the ratio will be 15 per cent épée, 85 per cent foil. In one year the share of épée movements will have risen to some 25 per cent and will increase to some 35 or 40 per cent in two or three years' time. A fifty–fifty position can be achieved in about five years.

The coach should refrain from any attempt to accelerate this process. He should never make his pupil develop ahead of "schedule" by forcing him to acquire épée movements at the expense of those foil movements that are established as though they were reflexes. The competitor should be encouraged to take advantage of the material from his own arsenal, to use those which appear to be most effective at the given moment in the bout. While training, the pupil should naturally practise and experiment ignoring for the time being the question of his powers of hitting, so that he can constantly enrich his knowledge and skills.

# I. FUNDAMENTALS

## 1. Preparatory exercises

This term covers all the gymnastic exercises designed to provide for the general and specific physical preparation of the fencer. The relevant material should be planned according to the stage of development and the period in question so that it corresponds to the requirements of what can be termed as "the gradual building up of a pyramid", with the correct proportions and the available possibilities appropriately taken into consideration. Special attention must be paid to the characteristics and movement of épée fencing when determining the contents of these exercises. General training should be completed with special exercises. The coach should make a point of setting exercises designed to strengthen the leg muscles and develop their speed and elasticity.

## 2. Foot exercises without the weapon

*(a)* Initial position: Identical with that of foil fencing.
*(b)* Taking up on guard position:
    – the fencer should take a step forward with his right foot just like in foil fencing,
    – he should take a step back with his left foot.
The distance separating the two feet is somewhat shorter than

in foil fencing, with the body's point of gravity slightly inclined towards the left foot.

(c) Taking a step forward:
- starting the movement with the right foot as in foil fencing,
- starting the movement with the left foot so that it is placed close to the right foot or in front of it, and then the right foot is moved a step forward.

(d) Taking a step backward:
- starting the movement with the left foot as in foil fencing,
- starting the movement with the right foot so that it is placed close to the left foot or behind it and then the left foot is moved a step backwards.

(e) Appel: as in foil fencing.

(f) Lunge:
- short (or half) lunge, or
- full distance lunge as in foil fencing.

(g) Transition:
- into on guard position and initial position as in foil fencing.

(h) Step forward and lunge: as in foil fencing.

(i) Reprise (renewed lunge): as in foil fencing.

(j) Flèche:
- from medium distance,
- from long distance.
The execution of the flèche should be practised without the weapon, with the body inclining forward but without turning round the horizontal axis. A step forward should be taken smoothly with the foot in the rear (cross feet) and then the swing of the body should be slowed down smoothly.
- Flèche carried out from lunge.

This is an indispensable foot exercise at a higher stage of development (especially in the event of renewed attacks). In the case of this foot exercise there can be three kinds of execution, depending on the fencer's muscles, physique, and abilities. They are as follows:

1. From lunge; the dead centre is bridged over merely by the pronounced forward inclination of the body and the centre of gravity is transferred smoothly past the foot in the front.

2. The foot placed in front of the fencer in the lunge should be withdrawn to a distance of one foot-length from the rear foot; meanwhile the upper part of the body should incline forward. In this manner it is easier to bridge over the dead centre.

3. Following the withdrawal of the foot in the front the inclination forward of the body should be assisted with a short, appel-like step taken with the rear foot in order to accelerate the flèche movement.


## 3. Grips

Competitors invariably pose questions concerning the grip to be used.

There are two types of grips to be distinguished in épée fencing: the straight or French grip and the pistol grip. It is not a decisive issue which of the two is more general or widespread. The question of which of them is more successful frequently arises. Of course, success depends on the individual using the weapon and not on the grip. It is the muscles and the limits of the movement of his joints that determine which grip is most suitable for the individual fencer. For example, the finer hand with longer than average fingers will more easily adjust to the French grip, facilitating the conducting of the blade and rapid changes in gripping the weapon. With the French grip the direction of the blade is determined by the thumb and the fore-finger, and this gives a wider scope of action especially in attack and in counter-attack. The principal weakness of the French grip lies in the fact that it is comparatively easy to be rendered loose in the direction of the fingers in the event of an attack by the opponent on the blade and in particular in the case of beats and attempts at disarming the opponent. It is noteworthy that both Italy's Eduardo Mangiarotti, regarded as the most techni-cally accomplished épéeist fencing most effectively over the widest possible range, and József Sákovits of Hungary, whose technical brilliance won world-wide admiration, used the French grip. This, of course, cannot be a decisive factor in the debate for and against the French grip since there have been and will be a number of top-class épéeists who prefer the pistol grip. For example, Pavesi of Italy, the Melbourne Olympic champion, and Delaunois of Belgium, a fencer with most classic movements and Balthazár of Hungary, all favoured the pistol grip.

The question arises: to which fencer should we recommend the pistol grip? In my opinion it is most convenient for fencers with broad hands, short fingers and possessing in general less flexible muscles and hand joints. The épéeist with a weak wrist and so loose a hold on the French grip that he is unable to direct the blade appropriately should also be recommended to use the pistol grip.

There are few if any problems with the use of the pistol grip the form of which determines the position of the fingers and the palm. The handle lies completely within the palm and the wrist joint has the job of conducting the blade.

With the French grip the thumb is accommodated to the handle from on top, lying about half an inch behind the guard in order to prevent the thumb or its nail from being injured in the event of the two fencers clashing following a collision. The forefinger is adjusted to the handle from below, gripping it with the first joint, and lying opposite to the thumb. The fore-finger and the thumb have the task of conducting the blade, thus the direction of the weapon is effected from the front of the hand. The third, middle and little fingers embrace the handle to hold it tight against the palm.

## 4. Position of readiness with the épée

In the position of readiness the fencer should have all his fenc-ing equipment: the weapon and mask as well as appropriate clothing ready for a fencing lesson, a bout or a competition. The position of readiness can thus be described as a state of standing by on the part of the fencer.

## 5. Initial position with the épée

The pupil must have been made familiar with this exercise (of course without the épée) long before, and so he will encounter no new elements concerning the initial position and the position of the body associated with it. The only thing that is, to a certain extent, different from foil fencing is that the plane of the blade is somewhat lower than the horizontal line. The extent of low-ering can be checked by allowing the point of the blade to sink to the lower plane of the guard held in the competitor's hand with the arm straightened shoulder high.

## 6. On guard position with the épée

Correct and expedient determination of the on guard position to be taken up by the fencer is of paramount importance because it simultaneously determines the technical and tactical basis on which the competitor will rely throughout his fencing future. Recognition of this fact followed prolonged observation and research work. There had been no definite position on this question prior to 1955. The experiences of the top Hungarian competitors abroad were often diametrically opposed to one another.

Practice came to the aid of fencers and coaches in finding a solution to this problem. In addition to observing the most successful Hungarian competitors attention was focused on the Italian épéeists in an effort to find an answer to the problem. Extensive observation revealed that what is known as the classical style used by the Italian fencers, the fist was held fairly high even in the initial or on guard position.

Analysis of the positive and negative features of this high position supplies the answer to the problem, especially a comparison is made with the so-called foil fencing on guard position in which the fist is held comparatively low. From the point of view of épée fencing the forearm in the foil fencing on guard is left open and is thus vulnerable from every direction. The fact is that in the foil fencing arm position the competitor does not have to reckon with the constant threat represented by the point of the opponent's blade in épée fencing.

Provided the fist is held high and the forearm and elbow are positioned correctly the guard of the weapon will offer complete protection for the upper and outer surface of the arm and the one area left open to attack on the inner side is easy to defend. At first sight the lower part of the forearm from the wrist to the pit of the elbow may seem to be an open target, however, the protection afforded by the advanced foot is augmented by lowering the point of the blade to run parallel with the plane of the pit of the elbow. When fixing the blade it should be slightly bent at the section in front of the guard so that it is sunk to the depth of the plane of the lower edge of the guard. In on guard position the point of the blade should incline outwards at an angle of 45 degrees pointing to the opponent's wrist. A fist held high enough offers excellent possibilities for carrying out

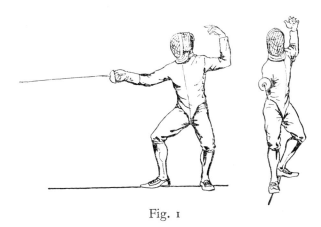

Fig. 1

an attack, counter-attacking in any direction, or for parrying the adversary's moves. It has proved to be a very advantageous initial position for carrying out a thrust, or disengagement of counter-attack. However, it would be unwise to generalize because there always are competitors who adopt different methods. For instance Lajos Balthazár allowed his fist to sink very low in on guard position (the plane of his weapon was thus well below the line). He lifted his arm at the very moment the action commenced and it was only then that the position of his weapon corresponded to that shown in figure 1.

## 7. Foot exercises with the épée

One of the commonly known definitions of fencing is this: "Fencing is an aggregation of movements executed with the arm and feet."

It follows from the above definition that in giving instruction in fencing and during the fencing lessons the coach's activities must extend to the training of both arms and feet. It is fairly common at the basic stage of training for the coach to confine teaching almost exclusively to the development of arm technique. As a result the pupil often performs the foot exercises instinctively; such movements will have an incorrect rhythm and are bound to be out of harmony with the build-up of the body. Even where the coach is aware of the fault, he may not try to eliminate it because he is convinced that the key to speedy results lies in the acquisition of hand and arm technique. Undoubtedly, this approach is basically unsound. The work directed towards achieving technical perfection can only bear fruit if in the course of the fencing lessons the coach gives maximum attention to the development of footwork so as to ensure harmonious co-ordination with the arm movements.

It is both advisable and desirable for the coach to hold regular group sessions not only for footwork exercises, but for collective concentration of attention on a limited section of épée fencing. His pupil can then analyse every fault in detail.

Strengthening of the foot and leg muscles, correct timing of the movements and correct acquisition of the rhythm and mechanism of the compound foot exercises are of no small importance. In this stage of instruction the pupil should have a weapon in his hand; this emphasizes the necessity of harmony between the arm and the feet.

Fig. 2

Figure 2 illustrates the first stage of taking a step forward, the straightening of the arm with the weapon and the straightening of the leg in the front from the knee.

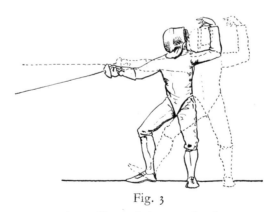

Fig. 3

Figure 3 shows the pulling of the rear leg in on guard position and the re-loosening of the arm with the épée.

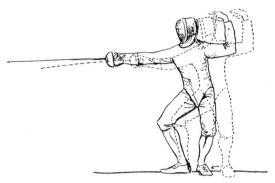

Fig. 4

Figure 4 shows the first stage of taking a step forward when the movement is begun with the rear leg.

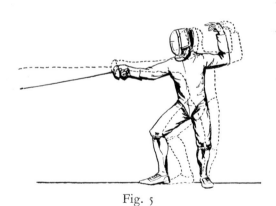

Fig. 5

Figure 5 illustrates the movement performed with the leg in the front at the moment on guard position is resumed.

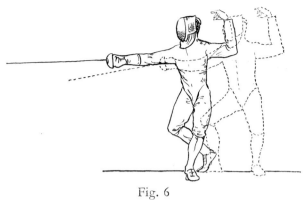

Fig. 6

Figure 6 demonstrates the first stage of taking a step forward (cross feet) at the moment one foot passes in front of the other.

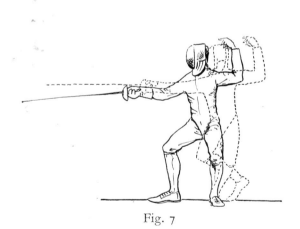

Fig. 7

Figure 7 shows the resumption of on guard position with the foot left behind placed in position again.

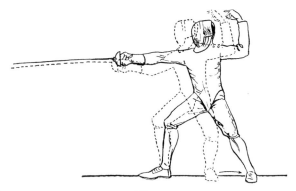

Fig. 8

Figure 8 shows the first stage of taking a step backward in the usual manner (as in foil fencing); the leg is straightened and moved backwards.

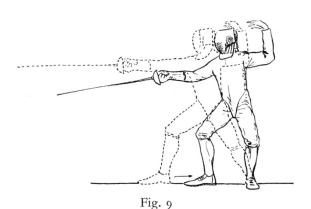

Fig. 9

Figure 9 illustrates the closing stage of taking a step backward; the leg in the front is moved backwards for resuming on guard position.

26

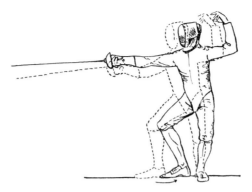

Fig. 10

Figure 10 shows the first stage of taking a step backward; the movement is started with the leg in the front. The two feet are close to each other.

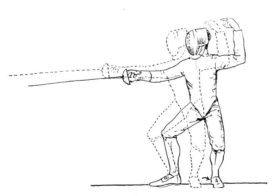

Fig. 11

Figure 11 demonstrates the movement backward of the rear leg for the resumption of on guard position.

27

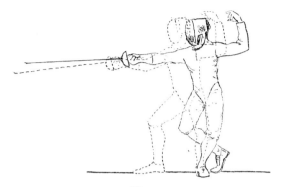

Fig. 12

Figure 12 presents the first stage of taking a step backward with the foot in the front (cross feet) at the moment the foot is moved past the other one.

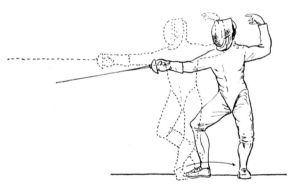

Fig. 13

Figure 13 illustrates the second stage of taking a step backward (cross feet) when the foot left in front is withdrawn for the taking up of on guard position.

Fig. 14

Figure 14 shows the short (half) lunge from on guard position (the fencer's original position is illustrated by the dotted line).

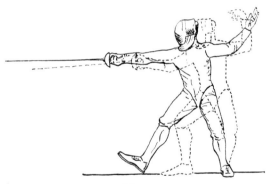

Fig. 15

Figure 15 demonstrates the first element of a full-length lunge from on guard position; it illustrates in particular the straightening of the arm with the weapon, a slight movement forward of the body's point of gravity and the moment at which the leg in the front is moved forward.

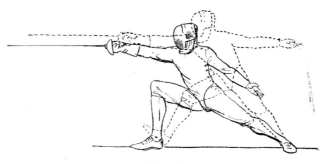

Fig. 16

Figure 16 shows the final position of the lunge; the dotted line illustrates the moment at which the fencer hit his opponent prior to assuming final position.

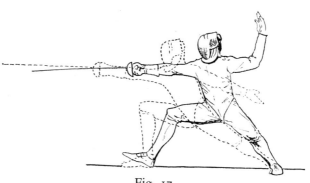

Fig. 17

Figure 17 shows the first stage of returning to on guard position from lunge; this is the moment of take-off with the foot in the front (the dotted line illustrates the fencer's original position in the lunge).

30

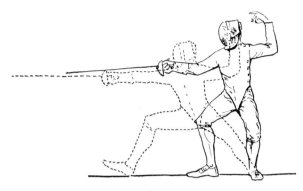

Fig. 18

Figure 18 illustrates the final position of returning to on guard position from lunge (the preceding [take-off] position is shown by the dotted line).

Fig. 19

Figure 19 demonstrates in complex figures the phases of renewed lunge carried out from lunge.

31

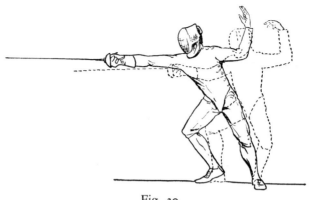

Fig. 20

Figures 20 and 21 present in complex figures the flèches from
on guard position.

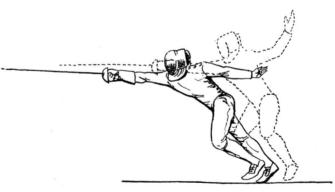

Fig. 21

Fig. 22

Figure 22 shows in complex figures the flèche from lunge; the flèche is performed exclusively with the forward inclination of the trunk.

Fig. 23

Figure 23 illustrates the flèche from lunge. The flèche is performed so that the body's point of gravity is moved forward as the foot in the front is withdrawn slightly.

33

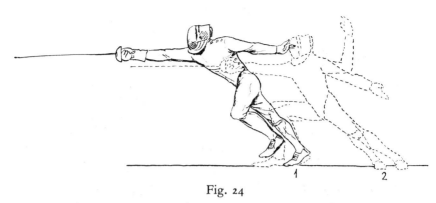

Fig. 24

Figure 24 demonstrates the flèche from lunge. The flèche is performed after the foot in the front has been pulled backward and with the rear foot brought into almost on guard position.

## 8. Fencing distances

*Closed or short distance*

When giving instruction in positions, final positions and thrusts aimed at the opponent's body, the coach should make his pupils practise from distances learned and applied in foil fencing, that is when the fencing target can be reached with the straightening of the arm. When it comes to practising thrusts to the enlarged fencing target (the arm), the distance should naturally be made longer. The distance should always be judged in relation to the given point of the target to be hit. Thus depending on the character of the weapon and on the evaluation of the given point in the target area, if the two opponents stand at what is described in foil fencing as "long distance" (that is when the two weapons make contact with one another at the foible of the blade),

34

in épée fencing this is called closed or short distance in relation to the wrist, or medium distance in relation to the elbow, or long distance in relation to the body. Medium distance is to be interpreted accordingly.
Long distance is also to be interpreted accordingly.


## 9. Fencing line

In épée fencing the concept of the fencing line is identical with the use of the same term in foil fencing, that is the imaginary straight line connecting the heels of the adversaries as they stand facing one another.


## 10. Relations between the two blades and positions of the blade

During the process of instruction it is possible to describe or explain the individual actions used in fencing only in case the pupils have first been made acquainted with the positions in which the weapons of the two opponents can be evaluated from the point of view of fencing actions. This applies to both the final positions and the movement that is in progress. These positions can be the following:
  – in line,
  – in on guard,
  – in invito,
  – the fencer's own and his opponent's engagement,
  – blade relations that follow from the position of the two fencers' blade.

## 11. Line of the blade

In foil fencing the terms upper and lower line mean the position of the blade in which the point of the fencer's blade is directed towards his opponent's target area, with the arm straightened out. In fencing with conventional weapons this position of the blade involves not only positional but also conventional advantage. For example, where other weapons are concerned, the opponent is forced to carry out an attack on the blade, because when the fencer ignores the line when carrying out his attack and a double hit would be the result, the hit is awarded in favour of the opponent and not the attacker.

In épée fencing, however, the line has no more than positional advantage to offer, for the decisive factor is: who is the first to hit his opponent.

In épée fencing the idea of the line of the blade cannot be simplified to holding the blade on the upper or lower plane. Here it is essential to distinguish two types:

*(a)* the straight line formed with the arm straightened out, which can point in the direction of any part of the fencing target, that is the opponent's head, shoulder, body, arm, hand, thigh, knee or foot;

*(b)* the diagonal line which generally means that the weapon is held at an angle with its point directed against the opponent's forearm. Its direction can be the following:

outer (with fourth position of the hand)
low (with third position of the hand)
inner (from second position of the hand to opposition position or with fifth position of the hand)
high (with fourth and supine position of the hand).

In attack or defence the action of both *(a)* and *(b)* lines are on an extremely active character. In attack they determine the form, depending on the fencer's own decision. In defence they enable the fencer to divert the attacking blade off the target or to anticipate the opponent's action in good time.

*Variations of the straight and diagonal line*

They are as follows:
– straights,
– angles,
– straights combined with straights,
– straights combined with angles,
– angles combined with angles.

# 12. On guard positions

In upper and lower positions the line separates and at the same time connects the four fields of action that are grouped around the sixth, fourth, second and eighth positions which follow from the blade positions outside the line.

If the blade moves out of line positions or it is in a position outside the line even in the fencer's original position with the weapon pointing to or moving within the target area the fencer is in on guard position. Depending on the direction of the movement, the on guard position can be of sixth, fourth, second and eighth.

The on guard position fails to provide conventional advantage even in the case of conventional weapons. In épée fencing the position of the blade is of paramount importance since attacks, counter-attacks and parries are carried out most frequently from this position.

Fig. 25

Figure 25 illustrates the upper line, and the final positions of the fourth on guard position and the fourth invito.

## 13. Invitos

Invito can be defined as the position of the blade with which an opening is made on the fencing target conspicuously with the purpose of stimulating the opponent to carry out an attack on the opening that has been apparently left undefended.

We speak of invito when the weapon exceeds the outer limits of on guard position and its point is moved into a position outside the fencing target.

## 14. Transitions

The fencer takes up a new position from a certain position of the blade with the aid of "transitions". Depending on the preceding position and on the direction in which the fencer wishes to establish the new position the direction of the transitions can be:

- straight (that is: simple),
- semicircular,
- circular.

## 15. Equipment

The requirements concerning equipment are laid down in the Rules issued by the International Fencing Federation.

## 16. Parries

Parries considered as final positions are given the same denomination in the system of épée fencing as in that of foil fencing. Practically, the parry can be defined as the deflection of the attacker's weapon from the target in due time and with a definite movement either with the middle or forte of the blade or the guard of the parrying fencer's épée.

According to the ways in which the parry is carried out, simple, semicircular, counter, ceding (or yielding) parries and parries with opposition can be distinguished. They are termed as fourth, third, second and eighth parries. As has been pointed out in the preceding passage the primary objective of the parry is to deflect the opponent's thrust. To this end the first requirement is to adopt a parry of appropriate strength. Therefore the fencer must, in consideration of the character of his weapon, apply a tight hold on the handle of his épée at the moment the attack is started, and only minimum movement should be allowed from the wrist. As a result of applying a tight grip on the handle, the movement will be shifted backwards primarily on to the elbow joint and the blade will thus be conducted by the forearm.

It is a secondary yet very important requirement that the parry should offer a favourable and safe concluding opportunity for the carrying out of a riposte. This purpose is served by the weapon and forearm forming an inseparable unit, with the point of the blade conducted within striking distance from the fencing target and moved well within the line.

What is known as "parry with the point" plays a very important part in the defensive system of épée fencing. The essence of the defensive system will be discussed in detail in the chapter on counter-attacks. Here we only wish to point out the fact that two different methods of parry not only supplement one another but can substitute one another in certain cases. The fencing distance and the given relation of the two blades determine the type of parry to be preferred.

### Simple parries

The simple parry is the shortest method of parrying the opponent's attack.

It can be executed from
– invito,
– line,
– the fencer's own engagement,
– the opponent's engagement.

### Fourth parry

It can be performed from
– sixth invito,

– the fencer's own sixth engagement and
– high line.

It defends the inner part of the arm and the inner upper opening of the target. When giving instruction in the technique of carrying out this parry the coach is advised to start out from foil fencing and emphasize the requirements discussed during the general definition of the parries.

As the first stage of the movement the shoulder and elbow joint should be loosened completely and the movement proper should commence with the fencer moving his whole forearm obliquely downwards to the left. The weapon must be held firmly, with a tight grip applied by the palm. Only as much movement should be allowed from the wrist as is necessary for turning the plane of the blade from the outer supine position into the fourth position. The point of the blade is displaced only horizontally to the height of the opponent's shoulder.

The opponent's thrust is met with the middle of the blade. The plane of the weapon should move continuously from fourth

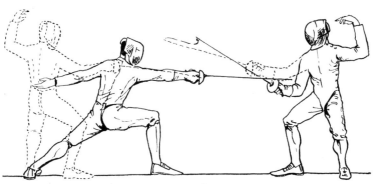

Fig. 26

Figure 26 shows the final position of the usual fourth parry performed from the sixth position.

to the fifth position. This movement will cause the adversary's blade to slide to the forte of the fencer's own weapon. At this point the side position should be firmly established.

The opponent's blade must be dominated during the whole process of the parry and subsequent riposte in order to avoid collision with his guard as a result of reflex resistance. Collision rules out the possibility of scoring a hit for both fencers.

The lower limit of the parry is the second position, while its upper limit extends to the line.

### *Thrust riposte carried out from the fourth parry*

*(a)* The riposte can be directed, as in foil fencing, to the inner upper opening as well as to the upper arm down to the bent elbow.

It should be performed with the blade conducted straight forward. During the process of the thrust the fist should proceed at the height and in front of its corresponding shoulder, and does not follow the direction of the point of the blade. At the moment the thrust is completed the forearm rises above the shoulder simultaneously with the bending of the blade. The forearm and the forte of the blade should be on the same plane.

*(b)* The riposte can be carried out with opposition into the inner upper opening as well as on to the upper arm down to the elbow.

It should be performed in the following manner: immediately after catching the adversary's blade the fencer should temporarily move the point of his own blade away from the attacker's weapon along the shortest route and complete his thrust by lifting his fist high.

*(c)* The riposte can be carried out with an angular thrust on to the adversary's upper arm, forearm or wrist. The parry can

be a very brief grazing or beat parry which is followed straight away by the direction of the riposte thrust or the formation of the angle at which it is to be performed. The point should be conducted on to the target so that it travels along the shortest route; simultaneously the fist is moved outwards to the right and placed in an oblique high position. The movement should be completed with a foot exercise that depends on the distance.

*(d)* The riposte can be carried out with a bind thrust into the inner upper opening as well as on to the upper arm down to the elbow bent.

It should be performed as follows: from the moment the fencer makes contact with his opponent's blade to the completion of the thrust the attacker's weapon should be constantly engaged. As a result, scoring a hit is ruled out after reaching the fencer's guard simultaneously with the termination of the thrust. In the closing stage the fist is held high on the left-hand side.

*(e)* It can be carried out with a flanconade which is actually a thrust directed on to the opponent's side. When performing it the adversary's blade should momentarily be held firmly in the final position of the parry and then pressed deep and held down with the forearm. With a semicircle to the left the point of the fencer's blade should be directed from his wrist towards the opponent's side, and the thrust should be completed either on his side or on his thigh placed in front, following a vigorous push forward of the arm.

*(f)* The riposte can be carried out by adopting a feint, that is, depending on the opponent's parry, with a simple or circular, or with a single, double or multiple feint.

*The sixth parry*

can be carried out from
- fourth invito,
- second invito,
- the fencer's own fourth and second engagement,
- the high and low line.

It protects the outside of the arm and the outside upper opening of the fencing target.

From the positions described above the fencer conducts his weapon in the direction of his own right shoulder to protect the opening of the fencing target threatened by the adversary's thrust. He should carry out the parrying movement as follows:
- upwards and to the right from fourth position,
- horizontally to the right from the high line,
- upwards from the low line and
- upwards from the second position by describing a small semicircle.

During the parrying movement the upper arm slightly sinks in the direction of the right hip, and the elbow is bent somewhat. The forearm rises in front of the right shoulder along with the rising plane of the épée. The wrist has the job of moving the plane of the opponent's blade outwards along the longitudinal axis and into a supine position by applying a vigorous hold on the weapon. The point of the fencer's blade should be positioned in line in front of the adversary's right shoulder. If possible, the fencer should master the thrusting weapon of his opponent with the middle of his own blade and put it out of striking range on the side.

*Thrust carried out from the sixth parry*

*(a)* As in foil fencing the riposte can be directed to the out-side lower opening, the thigh and the foot placed in the front. The method of execution is as follows: right after making contact with the opponent's blade the fencer should direct the point of his blade towards the target he has chosen as he is moving it outwards to the left with a semicircular movement. The thrust should be completed with a foot exercise chosen according to the distance separating the fencers. The blade should be conducted along a straight line throughout the movement.

*(b)* The riposte can be performed with opposition only to the lower part of the adversary's hand or wrist. It is necessary to choose one of these two targets because in the event of performing a thrust directed to the other low openings of the target, the fencer is bound to move apart from his opponent's blade during the process of thrusting. As to the performance of the thrust, while directing the point of his blade on to the lower edge of the opponent's guard the fencer should move his weapon forward by letting it literally glide on the guard as long as the point hits the target. In the closing stage opposition should be slightly upwards with the fist.

The method described here is not a general one and the coach is advised to give instruction in it only to pupils of exceptional talent.

*(c)* The riposte can be carried out with an angular thrust onto the outside surface of the forearm, with the target extending to the wrist.

When executing it the fencer should allow his fist to drop fairly low immediately after parrying the attacker's thrust and direct the point of his blade towards the target along the shortest possible route. The thrust should be performed with the angular position thus taken up, and the foot exercise to be adopted in support of the angular movement is dependent on the distance between the two fencers.

*(d)* The riposte can be carried out with an upper bind thrust to the outside upper opening or to the upper arm.

When performing it, the fencer should move the point of his blade towards the opening he selected along the shortest possible route. The riposte movement should be started right after contact has been made with the opponent's weapon either without any interruption or from a fixed final position. Engagement with the opponent's blade should be maintained throughout the movement as long as the target is reached.

In épée fencing, the riposte described above is most common from sixth parry.

*(e)* The riposte can be carried out with feint. Here, too, it is possible to adopt a simple or circular, single, a double or multiple feint dependent on the type of parry the opponent has applied.

*Third parry*

The third parry is adopted to protect the same parts of the target that are covered by the sixth parry. The only difference between them is that the third parry has to protect a larger surface of the target. It is more difficult to acquire and execute the third parry, but it is worth the effort in view of its inherent practical value.

The third parry should be executed from the positions described in the case of the sixth so that the plane of the weapon should be moved into second position of the fist following a semicircular launching of the movement. With the elbow slightly bent and the plane of the weapon being raised along with the forearm obliquely upwards and in the direction of the thrust, contact should be made of the opponent's blade with the forte.

46

Fig. 27

Figure 27 shows the final position of the third parry carried out from sixth invito.

Fig. 28

Figure 28 illustrates the final position of the third parry performed from high line position.

The side position thus achieved should be maintained. Simultaneously with the straightening of the arm and the sinking of the fist below the plane of the shoulder, the point of the blade should be raised to the height of the fencer's own head.

Two kinds of riposte are performed from third parry. In the

first case the fencer pushes his weapon forward with his fist in the direction of his adversary's chest, the hand held in second position as in the parry. The thrust should be completed to the outside upper opening of the target, with the opponent's weapon held engaged and pressed downwards throughout the movement.

In the second case the fencer should conduct the point of his weapon (with the opponent's blade engaged) towards the outside upper opening or the adversary's upper arm after "screwing" his fist from second into fourth position. In most cases the foot exercise adopted is the flèche.

*Second parry*

It can be carried out from
– seventh and sixth invito,
– the fencer's own seventh and sixth engagement,
– high line.
The second parry protects the outside lower opening and the foot placed in front. It is related to the third parry with regard to the low plane. A hold and position of the blade based on the second position of the arm enables the parry to be appropriately firm.

With his elbow held loose, the fencer should turn the plane of his blade around the longitudinal axis of the forearm with a minor semicircular movement into the second position of the hand from the positions described above. The épée should be pushed downwards to the right obliquely, and the fist sunk some four inches below the plane of the shoulder. The opponent's blade should be mastered firmly with the forte of our blade. The point of the fencer's weapon should remain within the limits of the target area at the height of his adversary's front thigh.

Fig. 29

Figure 29 shows the final position of the second parry performed from high line position.


*Eighth parry*

The eighth parry protects the same openings as those covered by the second parry. Its advantage over the second parry is in the fact that it can be performed with a brief and rapid move-

Fig. 30

The final position of the eighth parry is illustrated in figure 30.

ment of the forearm, wrist and blade. It has an important role in parrying the so-called "false attacks".

It has the disadvantage that in the fourth position of the hand it fails to provide appropriate firmness for the parry, and in this manner the thrust executed by a firm-fisted adversary might succeed in the closing stage. In general, the eighth parry is applied as a brief gliding or beat parry.

### *Riposte carried out from the second (eighth) parry*

*(a)* The riposte can be performed, as in foil fencing, to the body (inside upper opening), to the forearm and upper arm and to the wrist.

It should be executed in the following manner: immediately after performing a parry the fencer should direct the point of his weapon to the fencing target following a semicircular movement to the left and a thrust along the plane of the arm shoulder high. The supporting foot exercise depends on the distance between the two fencers.

The moment the target is hit only the bending of the blade should lift the fencer's fist.

*(b)* In case of an opposition parry the thrust can be performed to the same targets as in the case of point *(a)*. Even the way the blade is directed is similar except for the fact that the fencer's fist is positioned lower already at the moment the weapon is given its direction. During the closing stage of the thrust the fencer's fist should be defended against the threat of the adversary's épée from below.

The above method of finishing the thrust is far from being one intended for general application. The coach is advised to give instruction in this method only in exceptional cases.

*(c)* The riposte can be carried out with an angular thrust in

which case the surfaces to be hit are identical with those described above. When conducting the blade the fencer should endeavour to hit the target along the shortest possible route. The fencer's fist moves as far from the opponent's blade as is allowed by the limits within which the wrist can be moved. Conducting of the blade or completion of the thrust must be supported by the foot exercise most convenient to the distance.

*(d)* The riposte can be carried out with bind thrust to the opponent's side and to the outside low opening. It can be executed from second parry with the second position of the hand so that the point of the blade is directed to the adversary's side along the shortest possible route and with a position established during the parry. The thrust must be completed without any change in the hold of the weapon.

If the other type of execution is adopted, the point should hit the same areas of the target, but in the course of thrusting the fencer should screw his fist from second into fourth position, and in the closing stage he should offer opposition upwards.

Bind thrust from the eighth position must be performed with the fist in fourth position taken up during the parry.


*Seventh parry*

It can be carried out from
– second (eighth) invito,
– the fencer's own second (eighth) engagement,
– low line.

It defends the inside low, and, to a certain extent, the inside upper opening. While turning the plane of his blade into fourth position of the hand, the fencer should lift his weapon from the right to the left in front of his left shoulder, with his elbow held loose. The point of the blade, which is held in line, should be

Fig. 31

Figure 31 presents the final position of the seventh parry taken up from second position.

allowed to dip some four inches below the horizontal plane. The opponent's blade should be met by the fencer moving his weapon across from below and it should be held firm in this position with the forte of our blade.

Riposte carried out from the seventh parry

*(a)* As in foil fencing, the riposte can be performed to the adversary's body (inside lower opening) or to the thigh placed in the front.

The fencer should conduct the point of his blade along the shortest possible route towards the selected target. The movement is made from the parry. The thrust is completed independent of the opponent's blade.

*(b)* The riposte with opposition can be performed into the same opening as in point *(a)*, in the direction of the adversary's blade throughout the process of thrusting.

*(c)* The riposte can be carried out with bind thrust to the adversary's side, inside low opening or thigh. After catching the opponent's weapon, it should be held bound from below to facilitate the completion of the riposte. The point of the blade

52

should be allowed to dip comparatively low while being directed, within the limits of the target, to the point selected beforehand. The thrust should be executed with the bind upheld; in the closing stage of the movement the fist is held high to the left and the opponent's weapon deflected from its course.

*(d)* The riposte can be performed with a flanconade. In this case the fencer should turn his blade into high engagement position from low engagement position after making contact with his opponent's weapon. In this manner the adversary's blade can be kept engaged and pressed downwards by the action of the forearm. The épée should be directed on the opponent's side outside and from below, and the thrust should be performed as a flanconade.

*(e)* The riposte can be carried out to the inside of the upper arm with angular thrust. It should be executed so that after parrying the opponent's attack with the middle of the blade the fencer should lift his fist out of the parrying position slightly sideways to the right and while doing so he should direct the point of his weapon straight to the fencing target. The thrust should be performed with the arm and weapon held in the angular position.

*(f)* The riposte can be carried out with a feint. In this case, as after any kind of parry, the feint can be a simple or circular one, or a single, double or multiple one.


### Semicircular parries

*Semicircular fourth parry*

It can be carried out from
- second (eighth) invito,
- the fencer's own second (eighth) engagement.

It defends the inside upper and inside lower openings. It can be performed from the positions listed above so that the fencer moves his forearm–with the elbow held loose–outside to the right in a small semicircle. The blade then is brought into fourth position with its full plane in front of the fencer's body by means of a semicircular movement–as is described in the simple parry. This position should be maintained as long as the fencer controls with the middle of his blade the adversary's weapon in front of the threatened opening. The épée should then be held firmly between the fourth and fifth positions of the hand and the thrust should be completed continuously in the same manner as described in the case of simple parries.

*Semicircular second (eighth) parry*

It can be performed from
– fourth invito,
– the fencer's own fourth engagement.
This movement has more theoretical than practical value. However, it can occur in the event of manipulations with the blade, designed to prepare a movement or close an area of the target temporarily. The type of situation envisaged cannot be taken as a starting-point for the basis of a solid defensive system.

*Semicircular seventh parry*

It can be performed from
– sixth (third) invito,
– the fencer's own sixth (third) engagement.
It defends the inside upper and inside lower opening. Starting out of sixth or third position and with the point of the blade

moving outwards, the fencer turns the plane of his blade around the horizontal axis into the fourth position of the hand. Contact with the attacking weapon is made with the strong part of the fencer's blade which is moved upwards and to the left from below by describing a complete semicircle. At the moment the two blades meet, the fencer's épée is in seventh position–as described in the case of simple parries.

The side position should be fixed and the thrust completed in the same manner as that of a simple parry. Complementary though it is, the semicircular seventh parry is indispensable to the defence of the upper plane.

*Semicircular sixth (third) parry*

It can be performed from
– seventh invito,
– the fencer's own seventh engagement.

It defends the outside of the arm and the outside upper opening. When executing it from the above-listed positions, the fencer should bend his arm slightly at the elbow and hold his upper arm closer to the body in the direction of the corresponding hip. The plane of the blade should be moved by the forearm outwards to the right and then further outwards to the right and around the longitudinal axis into position of opposition in the same way as described in the case of the simple sixth parry.

In the event of a semicircular third parry, simultaneously with the loosening of the elbow the semicircular movement should be started from seventh position outwards to the left. While doing so the fencer should move the plane of his weapon from the eighth position of the hand into the second, with the weapon turning around the longitudinal axis of the forearm. After contact has been made with the opponent's épée, the arm should be straightened at the elbow and the fist allowed to sink below the level of the corresponding shoulder. At the same time the point of the blade rises head high to defend the opening exposed to threat.

The riposte should be carried out in the same way as described in the case of the simple third parry.

*Circular parries*

The essence of a circular parry is that the fencer describes a complete circle around his opponent's weapon with the point of his blade, moving from invito and back into the initial position. Here, too, the end-point of the movement is the fencer's elbow, and so the parry is performed principally by the forearm, with the loosening of the wrist necessarily having a lesser part to play.

*Change parries*

Change parries can be performed

*From the high line:*

– instead of a simple fourth parry a change sixth (or third) parry,
– instead of a simple second parry a change seventh parry.

*From the low line:*

– instead of a simple seventh parry a change second (or eighth) parry,
– instead of a simple sixth parry a change fourth parry.

All change parries should be executed in the following manner:

Instead of applying a simple parry the fencer makes contact with the attacking weapon after rounding it with a semicircular movement. The rounding movement starts out from the given line position and, in accordance with the direction of the parry, the plane of the fencer's épée begins to go round the adversary's weapon from above or from below. The fixing of the blade and the riposte should be carried out in the same manner as in the case of simple parries.

The objective (and inherent advantage) of a change parry lies in the element of surprise which allows the thrust to be completed from a side on which the opponent has not foreseen it.

## Ceding (yielding) parries

*First ceding parry*

This kind of parry can be used to good advantage against attacks made from sixth bind thrust and directed to the outside upper opening. When performing it the point of the parrying weapon should be allowed to sink as the fencer yields to the opponent's thrust. Simultaneously with a moderate bending of the elbow, the blade should be turned to the left into the first position of the hand, and withdrawn near to the body.

The riposte should be performed along the low line with the hand in the second position. It should primarily be directed to

Fig. 32

Figure 32 presents the final position of the first ceding parry performed from a high line position.

the opponent's leg in front, or it should be executed high, with the weapon swung across the opponent's blade as though it were a cutover hit (coupé). In the closing stage of the movement the adversary is virtually disarmed.

*Fourth ceding parry*

It is used to parry the second bind thrust directed to the outside low opening and the fourth flanconade. While performing it the fencer should move his elbow close to the corresponding hip and allow his forearm to sink as he yields to his adversary's thrust. The plane of the épée should be moved around the opponent's blade (with the point kept high) and then the fourth position, which was described in the case of simple parries, should be taken up. In this manner the adversary's weapon will be blocked in its attempt to hit the target. As a rule, the closing stage of the thrust is performed in the manner of opposition described in the case of simple fourth parries.

With thrusting weapons the value of every parry in the build-up of the particular system of defence is in direct ratio with the extent to which it can be applied. The applicability of a parry is dependent, above all, on the position from which the movement is started prior to the parry, on whether or not the opponent's weapon can be caught safely in the course of parrying, thus creating favourable conditions for a riposte either from a final position or from a momentary parrying position.

Judged from this point of view neither the fourth nor the seventh parry semicircular can be regarded as a firm basis for a defensive system. Instead, the "destructing" seventh parry should be adopted from fourth position, with the semicircular second ignored. From the seventh position the "distructing" fourth parry can be adopted and the semicircular sixth dispensed with.

"Destructing" seventh parry can be used to the best advan-

Fig. 33

Figure 33 presents the final position of the "destructing" seventh parry performed from the fourth position.

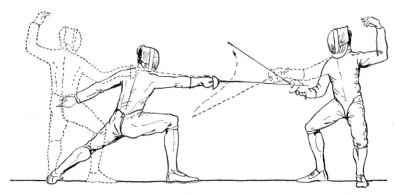

Fig. 34

Figure 34 illustrates the final position of the "destructing" fourth parry performed from the seventh position.

tage in countering attacks directed against the fourth position or invito and against the fencing target lying below the on guard position. The manipulation of the blade is composed of a movement pointing outside and to the right and carried out continually upwards from below by describing a semicircle. It terminates in the final stage of the seventh position. The thrust can be completed in the same way as a riposte performed following a parry based on the seventh position.

"Destructing" fourth parry from the seventh final position should be adopted when the opponent's blade threatens the target lying above the seventh on guard position or invito. When performing it the fencer should conduct his weapon from the seventh position into the final position described in the case of the fourth parry. The movement should be started outwards to the right and completed by the blade describing a semicircle as it moves upwards from below. Meanwhile the point of the weapon should be allowed to lie comparatively low as the fencer sinks his forearm and draws his elbow close to his body. The thrust should be completed in the same way as in the case of thrusts executed from the fourth position taken up after any of the positions.

## Parrying systems

The chapter on Parries contains the description and detailed analysis of all the parrying possibilities that can be adopted in both a fencing lesson or during actual bouts.

Practical observations have supplied ample evidence to the effect that the totality of the individual parries comprises a perfect, coherent system enabling the fencer to parry every kind of attack at the moment it is launched by his opponent–independently of the position of the blade the fencer took up prior to the attack–provided the fencer otherwise satisfies all the requirements the parry is expected to meet.

This applies most effectively if the fencer consciously adopts the parries that occasionally occur from the given position of the blade.

If the observation is confined to the narrow field of what is termed as the usual positions of the blade, that is the ones adopted most frequently by and adjusted to the individual concerned, experience shows that the overwhelming majority of competitors using the thrusting weapons prefer the sixth and eighth positions. This means that they tend to select one or the other of these positions to act as a starting basis from which their own attacking or defensive movement, as the case may be, can be carried out.

In épée fencing, the sixth position has come to be established in a more definite form than in foil.

Since in épée fencing the whole body of the competitor constitutes the fencing target, the question automatically arises whether or not the whole target can be defended from the sixth position, or perhaps it would, in certain cases, be more advantageous (for instance, in case the opponent's intention of performing an attack has been detected in advance) to take up a more favourable position (of the blade) from which the attack about to be made is safer to parry. The answer to this question is definitely negative, because each position or invito together with the corresponding parries that can automatically be adopted in the given cases constitutes an independent and complete system of parrying. Thus it can be stated that

the sixth parrying system includes:
– the simple fourth, simple second, semicircular seventh and the circular sixth parries;
the second parrying system includes:
– the simple seventh, the simple sixth, the semicircular fourth and the circular second parries;
the seventh parrying system includes:
– the simple second, the semicircular sixth, the circular seventh and the "destructing" fourth parries;
the fourth parrying system includes:
– the simple sixth, the semicircular second, the circular fourth and the "destructing" seventh parries;
the high line parrying system includes:
– the simple fourth, the simple second, the change seventh and the change sixth parries;
the low line parrying system includes:
– the simple seventh, the simple sixth, the change second and the change fourth parries.

A second question automatically follows from what has been said so far. Once the fencer's individual parrying system has been established, a system with which the range of parries has been narrowed down and its application has been facilitated, why is it forbidden to ignore the substantial surplus that appears to be lying outside the individual's particular parrying system? Because every movement involving technique and the objective of which is either attack or defence creates a new position of the blade. This is of paramount importance even if it is beyond any doubt that the final point of the parrying system, the basis on which the fencer relies, can be established for good. It follows that the fencer is obliged to operate, temporarily, on the terrain of a different parrying system before he returns to the usual basis. To return to this basis costs the fencer the loss of a tempo that naturally rules out the possibility of performing immediate action.

If the épéeist crosses the boundaries of his usual parrying system to temporarily operate in the domain of a neighbouring system, the laws that apply to the parrying system concerned will obviously govern the possibilities of continuous action.

Every parrying system has its own positive and negative characteristics as viewed from the vantage point of fencer or his adversary. These characteristics decide the question of applicability in practice.

For example, conditions are extremely favourable for launching attacks from the sixth position of the high line, and the direction of related parries is natural and easy to find.

The conditions provided by the eighth position or the low line for performing an attack are less favourable especially if the fencer intends to launch the attack in the direction of the high plane; nevertheless the related parrying system is highly effective and quite safe.

The fourth position fails to give appropriate safety either for launching an attack or for carrying out parries. Its most vulnerable part is the undefended outside low opening of the fencing target.

The seventh is the most unnatural, oblique position. It gives little support for carrying out an attack or performing parries.

Both the fourth and seventh positions should be regarded as temporary and emergency positions from which the fencer should return to his original or usual basis after the initial moves.

## 17. Tempo

Before discussing the idea of counter-attacks the question of tempo, a term used in foil fencing, must be considered briefly. The definition used in foil fencing applies to épée fencing as well so the discussion of tempo will be confined here to a brief definition of the idea.

Tempo can be defined as the most suitable point of time (moment) necessary for carrying out any fencing movement. This means in practice that in the course of bout fencing or of the competition the fencer should co-ordinate his own physical and psychological readiness with the momentary unpreparedness of his opponent and carry out his movement (action) in the given point of time (moment).

## 18. Relations between tempo and technique

No doubt both factors are of immense importance but the fencer must be able to recognize which is the more important at the different stages of the competition.

In the early stages of a competition when the fencers' ability to concentrate is at its maximum, tempo dominates on the piste. This statement is verified by the fact that during the initial phase of a contest, such as the preliminary rounds, fencers generally of a low standard and relying, above all, on tempo (thrust and stop thrusts) are likely to cause quite a few unpleasant surprises. They tend to ignore even the least technical preparation, fail to react to feints, concentrate all their attention merely on the action they are accustomed to and carry out the usual counter-attack at the moment the movement commences.

As the competition progresses fatigue increasingly tells and the tempo slows down. This is the vital stage at which technique comes very much into the picture. Skill gradually gains the upper hand during the phase dominated by fatigue and this is attributable to constant exercises and drilling. This explains why a fencer of rather inferior technical standards may defeat even épéeists of world class in the preliminary rounds, may even reach as far as the final, only to play a quite insignificant role in that ultimate test. One lesson to be drawn is that even a fencer of the most outstanding technical standards cannot rely exclusively on his technical superiority. It is true that most épéeists of a higher technical skill possess a good sense of tempo as well, but they tend to underrate the part it plays. In general they tend to concentrate on persuading their opponents to perform movements based on technique and tend to forget that the fencer of high technical standards who relies exclusively on tempo, on straightforward fencing movements consciously and patiently performed can establish absolute dominance of the piste.

While in the initial stages the intensive development of technical standards must continue to be a principal objective, it is necessary to make the fencer aware of the fact that tempo movements cannot be ignored. Such movements are the major factors especially during the initial stages (preliminary rounds) of a competition against which counter movements (second intention attacks) or more frequently counter tempo actions must be adopted instead of superfluous movements or even sometimes parries.

It is observable that foil fencing into which mechanization was introduced at a later stage than in épée succeeded in preserving the beauties of the sport as long as the fencers were not overinfluenced by the aid of the scoring machine. The machine accurately and mercilessly records the moment at which the hit is scored, independent of the action. This has created the perception of priority in hitting also among foil fencers. It quite often happens that apparently insignificant yet decisive hits are scored with some simple movement by a technically brilliant world class fencer while executing spectacular actions. It may also happen that a top class competitor, well adjusted to the electric scoring machine but employing wrong tactics, overlooking or ignoring the need for a correct relationship of tempo and technique, finds himself fencing well below his standard and form in some part of a contest. If he fails to recognize the underlying reasons for his loss of form then the result can be a serious crisis. It must be emphasized that in épée fencing where conventions are ignored and the main question is priority in hitting the much larger fencing target, then the need for greater pace of technique than in foil fencing and increased consideration for fencers of tempo and tempo actions are vital factors.

## 19. Counter-attacks

In contrast to foil and sabre fencing in which conventions must be taken into consideration, épée fencing is governed by the principle of priority in hitting. That is why counter-attacks are of greater importance than in fencing with the other two weapons. As has already been mentioned, the electric scoring device indicates a hit, scored independently of the fencing action. It can show accurately who hit or who was hit first, and indicates a double hit if the difference between the two hits does not exceed the interval of time between one-twenty-fifth–one-fifteenth of a second. For the reasons outlined above the mechanism of épée fencing is different from that of foil fencing in the case of attacks, while with regard to defence, every kind of counter-attack has a distinct role to play in addition to the parries.

The attacker is constantly aware of the fact that he has an extended target to hit, the front parts of his opponent's body are fairly close to him and that they are vulnerable. At the same time, however, he must also reckon with a counter-attack that can be launched by his adversary at any time. Thus when he is about to start an attack, he has to divide his attention between his own attacking movement and the counter-attack that is likely to be the adversary's reaction.

The rules of épée fencing lay down no particular convention as to the right to carry out a counter-attack. This means that the fencer has the right to counter-attack during any type of attack on the part of his opponent.

A convenient method of building up the theoretical structure of counter-attacks is to take as a basis the definitions adopted in foil fencing. Accordingly, counter-attacks can be divided into the following categories:
– time degagement thrusts, *(cavazione in tempo)*
– stop thrusts, *(coup d'arrêt)*
– feint counter-attacks *(finta in tempo)* that can be made as a combination of the above two kinds of thrusts,
– counter-tempo (counter-time), that is a counter-attack performed during the opponent's counter-attack.


*Time degagement thrusts*

These can be carried out against any attack made with the blade including every kind of bind and beat so that the fencer avoids making contact with his adversary's blade as it is advancing in the attack and a thrusts to the part of the target left open.

*Stop thrusts*

Their primary objective is to act as substitutes for parrying a given attack. The close relationship between parries and counter-attacks were pointed out in the chapter on Parries. Here it is sufficient to note that any attack can be parried either with the usual parry or the corresponding one of the parrying system or with a stop thrust that acts as a substitute for the given parry.

Stop thrusts can be carried out
– in the first cadence of all the single feint attacks,
– in the second cadence of all the double feint attacks,
– in the last cadence, that is in the closing cadence of any of the simple or feint attacks.


*Stop thrusts carried out in the first cadence*

Stop thrusts in the first cadence can be performed on all the single feint attacks so that instead of parrying or reacting to the feint, a thrust is executed to the upper or lower opening of the target.

According to the theory of foil fencing:
– If the stop thrust is adopted instead of a simple fourth or second parry, it must be performed to the upper part; when it is used instead of the simple sixth and seventh parry, it must be carried out to the lower part.
– If the stop thrust is adopted instead of a circular or change fourth or second parry, it must be carried out to the lower part; when it is used instead of a circular or change sixth parry, it must be performed to the outside low section, and when it is applied instead of a circular change seventh parry, it must be carried out to the upper section of the adversary's target.

The theory described above corresponds to the practice of épée fencing in the event of stop thrusts performed in both the first and second cadences.

## Stop thrusts carried out in the second cadence

Stop thrusts in the second cadence can be executed against any of the double feint attacks so that the fencer reacts to the first feint with the corresponding parry and this is followed by the stop thrust proper instead of the second parry.

## Stop thrusts carried out in the last cadence

Stop thrusts in the last cadence can be performed against:
– every direct attack,
– every change or time degagement thrust,
– every attack on the blade: binds and beats,
– thrusts concluding every feint attack.
They are denoted by the term: contractio.
In foil fencing, counter-attacks can be divided into three categories:
– inquartata,
– imbroccata,
– passata di sotto.
In the event of concluding thrusts aimed by the adversary at the inside upper opening of the target the inquartata being a movement of a single cadence fits favourably into the parrying system, and since its direction is identical with that of the fourth parry, it acts as a substitute for the fourth parry.
Imbroccata is carried out in a direction identical with that of the second parry and so it acts as a substitute for the second

parry in the event of thrusts aimed at the outside lower opening of the target.

Passata di sotto performed by ducking can be adopted above all as a tactical move when the opponent's thrust is directed towards the upper sections of the fencing target. Thus it does not act as a substitute for any definite parry.

The fundamental principle of the theory of stop thrusts analysed in detail in foil fencing cannot be challenged; nevertheless it can be supplemented with new elements in the case of épée fencing.

In the event of stop thrusts carried out in the first and second cadences the fencer's movement is based on a given parry, instead of which the stop thrust is performed so that the adversary is prevented from elaborating the closing stages of his attack. In this case we block the path of the opponent's blade to the target by holding the defending weapon in an appropriate plane. This movement should be performed by the fencer while the feint is in progress and the adversary's blade is about to round the confronting weapon.

In the event of stop thrusts carried out in the final cadence, the closing stage (the thrust proper) of an attack that has been built up completely must be parried, whatever action is being performed by the adversary.

In the case of defence performed with parry, the fencer being attacked must base himself on a definite parrying system, and take up position accordingly. The choice will depend on the relative position of the blades. Four types of parries can be carried out from the parrying system. It follows that stop thrusts in the final cadence can be executed instead of any of the parries in a direction identical with that of the parry concerned. Thus they can substitute not only the fourth and second but also the sixth and seventh parries. The so-called time thrust makes possible the utilization of the fourth (inquartata) and of the sixth in the upper plane and of the second (imbroccata) and of the seventh in the lower plane.

These tempo actions discussed above must be completed with stop thrusts that can be carried out with the point of the blade and in a direction identical with the given parry, above all, on to the opponent's hand and arm holding the weapon.

### Stop thrusts carried out on ripostes

The theoretical material of foil fencing contains only one such action: the appuntata. It is actually a stop thrust carried out in the first cadence into a straight feint riposte.

The theory of foil fencing omits the discussion of stop thrusts that can be carried out on single or double feint ripostes. This is attributable to the fact that, according to the conventional rules, the possibility of performing a stop thrust can only be sensed distinctly in the first cadence. But even in this case the only type of thrust considered is a thrust directed to the same point of the target; in this movement the fencer performing the counter-attack to the riposte has a cadence in hand.

The practice of épée fencing has developed well beyond this theory. In épée stop thrusts can be carried out practically on every kind of riposte including single and double feint ripostes in the same way as on attacking actions of the same type and cadence.

For example, a stop thrust of the first or final cadence can be executed on a feint riposte.

Depending on the direction of the closing thrust the stop thrust can be adopted instead of the parries normally employed against the riposte.

Practically, inside upper inquartata can be carried out on high ripostes and a sixth time thrust can be performed to the outside upper section. If the riposte happens to be a low one, imbroccata should be executed to the outside low and a seventh time thrust should be performed to the inside low section of the fencing target.

The stop thrusts listed above can be carried out as stop thrusts in the final cadence on the closing movement (the riposte proper) of any of the feint ripostes.

Appuntata or stop thrust in the first cadence in hand can be carried out on every straight feint riposte instead of parrying it.

A stop thrust in the second cadence can be carried out on every double feint riposte so that the fencer reacts to the first feint with the appropriate parrying movement (simple, semi-circular, circular, change parry, ceding or opposition parry as the case may be), and instead of performing the second parry a stop thrust must be carried out according to the scheme analysed in detail in the case of attacking actions.

As in the case of stop thrusts executed on attacking actions, stop thrusts carried out in the first or second cadence on ripostes can be used as substitutes for the corresponding parries. On the other hand, stop thrusts in the first or final cadence in hand are performed as substitutes for all the parries that can be carried out from the given parrying system, and they should be executed with a movement corresponding to the direction of the parries.

# II. THE FENCING LESSON

## 1. The concept of the fencing lesson

In the foil the fencing lesson is interpreted as: "Regular and thorough drilling of all the fencing activities that occur in attacks, defence and counter-attacks in bout fencing". This definition applies to épée fencing as well.

There are differences between the foil and épée lesson. These are in the systematization and execution of the material as well as in the ways its elements are related to one another.

There are quite a few similarities in the systematization of the material because the definition of the individual actions in épée fencing is also based on the way of introduction, the quality and number of parries.

The characteristic feature of the ways in which the elements are related to one another is that in the course of instruction the pupil should carry out all possible parries as movements designed to counter the adversary's action, along with the counter-attacks or stop thrusts that can be performed on the attack. All this should be executed parallel with the attacking movement selected for the purposes of practice.

The forms and practical variations of execution have already been considered in the chapter on Parries. Here it is pointed out specially that the thrust as a conclusive movement stemming from any kind of fencing activity including attacks, counter-attacks and parrying can be of the following three types:

*(a)* Execution as in foil fencing.
*(b)* Execution with opposition.
*(c)* Angular thrust.

(a) *Execution as in foil fencing*

The fencer takes advantage of his opponent's split-second inability in appropriate tempo and from a given situation. He conducts the point of his blade along the shortest route so that the plane of the weapon and the arm that should be stretched out completely form a straight line in the final cadence of the action. It can be performed any time the fencer is able to make a realistic judgement that he has a full cadence in hand over the probable counter-action of his adversary.

(b) *Execution with opposition*

Opposition can be described as resistance displayed by the fencer in the process of a thrust performed by his opponent, above all in the crucial moment of concluding the adversary's movement. This opposition takes the form of a position taken by the fist or guard in relation to the adversary's blade.

(c) *Angular thrust*

As has already been mentioned the foil is the practice weapon of épée fencing, and the material of foil fencing constitutes the basis of the technical know-how of épée fencing. Certain movements commonly used in foil can be adopted highly successfully in épée, but the special characteristics of the latter weapon that

74

arise, above all, from the priority of hits and the extended fencing target call for the extension of the arsenal of movements and the inclusion of new elements in the technical material of épée fencing.

One of the new elements is the angular (or diagonal) thrust, unknown in what is described as classic foil fencing. The practical possibility of attacks ending in a sure hit on the parts of the opponent's body situated in front, first of all on the arm, with a thrust performed at an angle instead of along a straight line gave rise to the concept of angular thrusts.

The other important viewpoint in addition to the increased likelihood of a hit is that during the process of thrusting the fencer's own fist and his whole arm will move apart from the point of his adversary's blade that involves the immediate menace of a counter-attack. Thus while in opposition, the fencer's fist remains well within striking distance of the opponent and the dangers of the exposed position are reduced by blocking the path of the menacing point of the opponent's. In the case of angular thrusts the fencer's fist will be positioned wide of the line as a result of the formation of an angle favourable for the thrust. In short, in the latter case the immediate target is moved out of the adversary's striking range.

Angular thrusts can be performed on different on guard positions and invitos, but above all on the arm and fist that hold the blade in line.

## 2. Fundamental exercises of the fencing lesson

### (a) *Thrust*

The thrust, the objective of which is to hit the opponent, is the closing stage of attacking and defensive movements.

## (b) *Parry*

The object and forms of the parry have been considered in detail in a separate chapter.

## (c) *Parry and thrust*

This is a compound exercise composed of two technical elements (parry and thrust) in which the fencer on defence meets the thrust started or executed by his opponent with a parry fixed in the final position. He continues to remain in this position for a period corresponding to the objective of the exercise and then executes his own thrust as required by the fencing lesson.

## (d) *Riposte*

Like the exercise discussed in point *(c)* the riposte also comprises two technical elements. The only difference between point *(c)* and point *(d)* is that in the latter case the fencer carries out his thrust without a pause, that is right after the parry so that the period that elapses between the performance of the parry and the subsequent thrust cannot exceed the length of a fencing cadence.

## (e) *Thrust and parry*

An exercise made up of two technical elements (thrust and parry) which is introduced by a thrust performed by the attacker. The adversary's response from a parry should be parried by fixing the parry in a final position so that the ultimate objective of the movement is the parry itself. Exercises of this kind are termed as groups of incomplete exercises.

### (f) *Thrust, parry and thrust*

A complex exercise comprising three technical elements. In accordance with the object of instruction the pupil can be permitted to pause in the ultimate position of the thrust or the parry for more than the length of a fencing cadence. Whether he pauses in the parry or thrust depends on the purpose of the exercise.

### (g) *Counter-riposte*

Like the exercise in point *(f)* this is also made up of three technical elements. However, the pause held in the ultimate position of either the thrust or the parry cannot exceed the length of a fencing cadence.

## 3. The build-up of instruction in straight thrusts

### (a) *Thrust*

It can be performed
– from on guard position on the opponent's body or arm,
– with lunge on the opponent's body or arm,
– from long distance on the opponent's body or arm.

(b) *Parry*

It can be performed
– in on guard position (simple, semicircular and circular parries),
– by taking a step backward (simple, semicircular and circular parries).

(c) *Parry and thrust*

This compound movement can take the form of
– parry in on guard followed by a thrust from on guard position,
– parry in on guard followed by a thrust with lunge,
– parry performed with a step backward followed by a thrust from on guard position,
– parry performed with a step backward followed by a thrust with lunge.

(d) *Riposte*

It can be carried out as follows:
– parry performed in on guard position followed by a riposte from on guard position,
– parry performed in on guard position followed by a riposte with lunge,
– parry performed from on guard position followed by a riposte with flèche,
– parry performed with a step backward followed by a riposte from on guard position,

78

– parry performed with a step backward followed by a riposte with lunge,
– parry performed with a step backward followed by a riposte with flèche.

## (e) *Thrust and parry*

This compound movement should be performed as follows:
– thrust with lunge followed by a parry performed in lunge,
– thrust with lunge followed by a parry performed in on guard position.

## (f) *Thrust, parry and thrust*

This compound movement should be executed as follows:
– thrust with lunge followed by a parry in lunge and a thrust in lunge completes the movement,
– thrust with lunge followed by a parry in lunge and a thrust with flèche completes the movement,
– thrust in lunge followed by a parry in on guard position and a thrust with flèche completes the movement,
– thrust with lunge followed by a parry in on guard position and a thrust with lunge completes the movement.

## (g) *Counter-riposte*

Should be performed as described in point *(f)* above.

(h) *Stop thrust*

It can be performed
– as in foil fencing,
– with opposition,
– with an angular thrust.

# III. STRAIGHT THRUST ON EVERY KIND OF INVITO

*Straight thrust performed on sixth (third) invito*

It can be executed at close quarters on the opponent's body, on the inside upper section of the target.

It can be carried out

*(a)* as in foil fencing,

*(b)* with opposition,

*(c)* with angular thrust.

*(a)* The pupil should be instructed to perform the exercise merely by straightening his arm. The coach should see that his pupil conducts the point of his blade along a straight line which is the shortest distance to travel along. The plane of the weapon which inclines outwards to the right in on guard position should retain its original position even in the course of the thrust. The forte of the blade should remain in the same plane as the straightened arm even at the moment the thrust is concluded. In this way any bending of the blade will cause the weapon as a whole to move upwards along with the fencer's arm so that there will not be a loosening of the grip nor the deformation of the position of the wrist that generally coincides with such loosening.

In case the thrust is to be performed on the opponent's upper arm the distance between the two fencers should be slightly lengthened. The method of execution is exactly the same as when the thrust is aimed at the body. When conducting the blade care must be taken that the button travels along the shortest possible route in order to hit the target. The fist does not follow the direction of the point of the blade. Instead, it closes down the outside upper opening along a completely straight line in front and at the height of the corresponding shoulder.

*(b)* The thrust with opposition can be performed on the body, the inside upper section of the target and the upper arm of the adversary.

The opposition position taken up by the fist or guard is high on the left. Whether or not the extent of the opposition is correct can be checked to an accuracy of a millimetre so that the coach makes sure that his pupil's thrust lies–at the moment the thrust is being concluded–along a straight plane connecting his own and his pupil's eyes. The pupil should make sure that he sees his coach's eyes lying along the right-hand side edge of the guard of his own weapon. Meanwhile the coach should see that his pupil does not distort the position of his body either with his trunk or with his head.

*(c)* When the thrust is an angular one the opponent's upper arm and forearm form the fencing target.

Practising at close quarters, it should be primarily an exercise of manipulating the blade during which the coach should demonstrate the correct method of forming an optimum angle with the parts of the opponent's body and the different sections of the fencing target that can be hit with an angular thrust. The coach should demonstrate very clearly to each pupil that the angle formed by the weapon and arm facilitates the hitting of those parts of the target that are covered by the guard of the opponent's blade and are therefore blocked to his own line of vision. Naturally the hit can only be made if the blade is conducted appropriately. The pupil's attention should be drawn to the correct method of executing the movement. The coach should emphasize that the point of the fencer's blade should still travel along a straight line (the shortest route).

The advantages involved in this movement and the magnitude of the angle formed are most evident in the case of an action performed in sixth invito. The fist should be held high on the right. The plane of the blade is identical with that in the initial position. Fencers of exceptional quality can be encouraged to perform the thrust with the hand in the second position.

The straight thrust can be executed with lunge from medium distance:

### (a) *As in foil fencing*

It should be performed in the same manner as in the case of thrusting at close quarters. In the early stages the pupil should execute the movement in parts following the commands of the coach. He should straighten his arm and imitate thrusting on separate signals. The coach should make sure that there is appropriate harmony between the hand and the feet, that both the sequence of the movements and the position of the body are correct, that shoulder and hips are adequately loose and that the foot in front and the one in the rear start moving rhythmically.

Once the coach has made sure that the individual movements of his pupil's feet and arm have been adequately drilled in the correct sequence, he can embark on establishing the continuity of the movement followed by the pupil practising the movement in appropriate tempo from different positions.

When the attack is directed to the upper arm the distance between the fencers should be longer.

## (b) *With opposition*

It should be executed so that simultaneously with the indication of the thrust the fencer's fist should gradually follow the path of the point of the épée. The opposition is made complete (which means at the same time complete blocking of the path of the adversary's blade) at the moment the thrust is concluded. This sequence emphasizes that the thrust is of primary importance.

Fig. 35

Figure 35 illustrates the thrust (with lunge) carried out with opposition, as in foil fencing, on the sixth on guard position or invito.

## (c) *With angular thrust*

The principal distance from which this type of thrust should be practised is medium distance. The longer the distance, the more difficult it is to carry out the thrust and what are its essential parts: the manipulation and direction of the blade. Special attention should be devoted to establishing appropriate harmony between the fencer's hand and feet. Direction of the blade or appropriate formation of the angle should always precede the lunge. If the weapon is conducted appropriately a lunge is

Fig. 36

Figure 36 shows a thrust to the opponent's hand (inside) carried out with angular thrust on the sixth on guard position or invito.

Fig. 37

The angular thrust from below performed on the sixth on guard position is shown in figure 37.

necessary only to drive the button forward until it makes contact with the target.

From long distance the straight thrust can be executed with a step forward and lunge:

### (a) *As in foil fencing*

The manner of execution, the sequence of the parts of the movement and the method of instruction are identical with those described in the corresponding passage on thrusts carried out from medium distance.

The pupil should be instructed to concentrate his attention on conducting his weapon and arm in perfect harmony along a straight line to the target throughout the whole process of execution. The fist is allowed to be raised to the height corresponding to the extent of the bending of the blade only after the thrust has been completed. The wrist is not allowed to take up any distorted position.

### (b) *With opposition*

The blade should be conducted in accordance with the principles described in the event of carrying out straight thrusts from medium distance. The only difference lies in the fact that the first movement with the feet is aimed at narrowing the distance (approach work) during which the arm is slightly straightened out to move forward in a position of safety. From this stage the concluding thrust should be performed in the same manner as when it is executed from medium distance.

(c) *With angular thrust*

While taking a step forward, that is during the process of the approach work, the blade should be conducted along a straight plane. The fencer should start forming the angle at the moment his left foot makes contact with the piste. The blade should be aimed at the target so that when the lunge is performed it helps the weapon to forge ahead in the adopted position.
From long distance the straight thrust can be executed with flèche:

(a) *As in foil fencing*

At this stage of instruction the exercises should be confined to the so-called short flèche, the essence of which is that following indication by the pupil of the action to be practised (which is the straight thrust introduced by taking a step forward), he should incline forward with the upper part of his trunk in the direction of his straightened arm instead of performing a lunge. Then he should push his weapon forward in the direction of the target he has selected by virtually rolling forward over the knee of the front leg. Simultaneously with scoring a hit the foot left in the rear should be moved forward lightly across the other one, to serve as a brake gradually slowing down the forward movement.

(b) *With opposition*

The footwork is identical with that described in point *(a)* above, while the technique of execution is much the same as in a thrust with opposition from medium and long distance.

## (c) *With angular thrust*

Viewed from the aspect of épée fencing, this is one of the most convenient actions because the button of the attacker's weapon threatens virtually the whole fencing target. An attack launched in good tempo and combined with appropriate control of the blade always promises success.

The flèche should be introduced with a step forward during which the weapon is positioned in the required direction. The movement started with a step is completed with a rapid flèche performed at a fast pace.

The parries to be adopted are the following: simple fourth, circular sixth (third) and semicircular seventh parry.

When instruction is given in the parries, the coach should perform the thrust or indicate it. His pupil is left with the job of carrying out the parries from the sixth invito. In this case the exercises are confined strictly to checking that the parry has been carried out correctly from a technical point of view and to fixing the parrying blade in the final positions taken up following the parries. Each parry should be practised first in on guard position and then with a step taken backward.

*Parry and thrust exercises*

### First exercise

| Coach | Pupil |
|---|---|
| Performs a straight thrust | Parries the thrust with a simple fourth parry in on guard position and then takes a step backward; he should then fix the parry in the final position |

| Coach | Pupil |
|---|---|
| Checks and corrects the execution | On a command or signal from the coach he should complete the thrust to the coach's body or upper arm from on guard position or with lunge, as in foil fencing, or in opposition or with an angular thrust |

*Second exercise*

| Coach | Pupil |
|---|---|
| Carries out a straight thrust to the inside upper opening of the target | Parries the thrust in on guard position or by taking a step backward with circular sixth parry |
| Checks and corrects execution | On a command or signal from the coach he should complete the thrust to the coach's body or upper arm from on guard position or with lunge, as in foil fencing, with opposition or an angular thrust |

| Coach | Pupil |
|---|---|

*Third exercise*

| | |
|---|---|
| Performs a thrust to the inside upper opening of the target | Parries the thrust with a semicircular seventh parry in on guard position or by taking a step backward and then fixes the parry |
| Checks and corrects the execution | Completes the concluding thrust to the inside lower opening of the target, or the inside part of the upper arm or wrist from on guard position or with lunge as required by the distance, as in foil fencing, with opposition or with an angular thrust |

Note. In this group of exercises the pupil should hold a pause in the final position of every parry. The length of the pause corresponds to the objective of the exercise but it should exceed that of a fencing cadence (tempo).

*Riposte exercises*

This series of exercises is built up on that of Parry and Thrust Exercises. The relevant exercises from simple fourth, circular sixth and semicircular seventh parries are identical with the respective exercises of parry and thrust. During execution the pupil must meet the requirement of continuity and he is not permitted to pause longer in between two elements than the duration of a cadence. The thrust can be completed from on guard position, with lunge or with flèche.

## Thrust and parry exercises

This is a group of incomplete exercises because the parry performed by the pupil is not followed by a thrust. The characteristic feature of the exercise lies in the pause between the thrust and the subsequent parry. The length of this pause between the two elements performed by the pupil will correspond to the special purpose of the exercise, but in any case it should exceed the duration of one fencing cadence.

| Pupil | Coach |
|---|---|

### First exercise

| Pupil | Coach |
|---|---|
| Performs straight thrust with lunge to the outside upper opening of the target or to the upper arm | Parries the thrust with a simple fourth parry and performs a riposte to the inside upper opening of the target |
| Performs the parry with a simple fourth or change sixth parry in the lunge or while taking up on guard position from the lunge and fixes the parry in the ultimate position | |

| Pupil | Coach |
|---|---|

*Second exercise*

| Pupil | Coach |
|---|---|
| Performs a straight thrust with lunge | Parries with circular sixth and performs a thrust to the outside low opening of the target after the parry |
| Performs simple second or change seventh parry in lunge or simultaneously with the resumption of on guard position from lunge and the parry is fixed in the final position | |

*Third exercise*

| Pupil | Coach |
|---|---|
| Carries out a straight thrust with lunge to the outside upper opening of the target or the upper arm | Performs semicircular seventh parry and executes a thrust to the inside low opening of the target |
| Performs simple or change seventh parry in lunge or while resuming on guard position from lunge and the épée is then fixed in the final position | |

92

## Exercises of thrust, parry and thrust

Actually this group of exercises is a more complex version of the previous thrust and parry exercise. All the exercises that figured in the previous group are applied here in exactly the same form. The only difference between this and the previous group is that here the exercises are completed by the closing thrust executed by the pupil.

In the case of this group of exercises the pupil should pause in between two technical elements, that is after the thrust or the parry that follows the thrust, or perhaps on both occasions. The length of the pause should correspond to the particular objective of the exercise, but in any case its duration should exceed the length of a fencing cadence.


## Counter-riposte exercises

The counter-riposte is composed of the two preceding groups of exercises of the fencing lesson, or more exactly, it is built up on them. The related exercises are identical with those of the previous two groups. There is a difference, however, in respect of the execution, because in the counter-riposte exercises the "thrust, parry and thrust" are performed from lunge, from flèche carried out from lunge, or with flèche executed from temporary resumption of the on guard position from lunge. In the course of execution the pause in between two component elements must not exceed the length of a cadence. The final action, as in foil fencing, with opposition or with an angular thrust.

The counter-attack can be a stop thrust performed in the first and at the same time ultimate cadence.

– Instead of the fourth parry, inquartata carried out to the inside upper opening of the target, to the opponent's upper arm, or an angular thrust to his forearm or wrist.

– Instead of a circular sixth parry, a time thrust can be performed on the sixth side, or an angular thrust from below to the opponent's wrist, with the hand held in third position.

When the opponent is in the sixth on guard position or invito, an attack can be carried out not only to the upper but also to the lower opening of the target. In this case the defending fencer should adopt the seventh or eighth stop thrust (imbroccata) instead of either of the parries used to defend the low-lying sections of the target.

*Performing thrusts on the fourth invito*

The thrust can be carried out at close quarters to the opponent's body from outside and high.

*(a)* As in foil fencing,
*(b)* with opposition,
*(c)* with angular thrust.

*(a)* The blade should be conducted in the same manner as described in the case of attack on the sixth invito. The fencer should pay special attention to protecting his own right-hand side from where there is the immediate threat of a counter-attack. The plane of the fencer's blade is allowed to rise above the plane of his shoulder only at the moment of completing the thrust. This is essential in order to prevent the very likely possibility of counter-attack from below.

The thrust to the shoulder should be executed in the same manner as when the thrust is performed to the body.

When instruction is given in thrusting to the upper arm, the distance should be widened.

The fencer must possess exceptional ability to conduct his blade if he is to perform his thrust to the opponent's wrist. It should be noted that this kind of attack is of immense practical value.

*(b)* The fencing target is the same as when the thrust is carried out in foil fencing. The holding of the fist–opposition–is displayed high on the right-hand side. In this case the pupil should make sure that he sees the coach's eyes lying behind the left-hand side edge (inside) of the guard of his own weapon. Technically there is little if any difference between this type of thrust and its counterpart in foil fencing. Only the fact that the fencer's fist is placed high up on the right-hand side outside the line reveals that there is opposition involved in this movement. It does not necessarily involve a contact with the opponent's blade. Here the importance of opposition is, in general, one of principle, assuming a concrete technical form only in certain cases. This movement results in engagement of the blades or the possibility of scoring a hit is ruled out if the opponent's weapon reaches the extreme limit of opposition.

*(c)* When the thrust is carried out with angular thrust, the opponent's forearm and wrist serve as the fencing target. The fencer should conduct his weapon from on guard position along the shortest possible distance in the direction of the point he has selected to hit. When performing this movement, his fist will be raised above the plane of the shoulder simultaneously with the straightening of the arm. If the weapon is manipulated in the manner described above, the fencer will find it possible to hit even the relatively small target lying behind the guard of his adversary's épée.

*Performing thrusts from medium distance with lunge*

(a) *As in foil fencing*

The parts of the target involved are the same as when the thrust is executed at close quarters. The movement should be carried out and the blade should be conducted in accordance with the principles described in connection with the attacks on the sixth invito or those outlined in the preceding paragraphs.

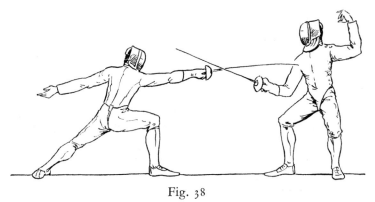

Fig. 38

Figure 38 illustrates the thrust executed as in foil fencing on the fourth on guard position or invito.

(b) *With opposition*

The thrust should be performed so that simultaneously with the indication of the thrust the fencer's fist is moved high up and to the right-hand side. The movement is completed, with the foot exercise corresponding to the given situation, in the same manner as when it is performed at close quarters.

96

Fig. 39

The thrust carried out with opposition on the fourth on guard position or invito is shown in figure 39.

(c) *With angular thrust*

It should be executed and the correct angle formed in the same manner as described in the case of the same type of thrust

Fig. 40

Figure 40 shows the high angular thrust executed on the fourth on guard position or invito.

97

Fig. 41

The high angular thrust performed to the outside on the fourth on guard position or invito is illustrated in figure 41.

performed at close quarters. The weapon about to make the angular thrust is carried forward towards the target by a lunge only.

*Performing thrusts from long distance with a step forward and lunge*

(a) *As in foil fencing*

The fundamental principle of instruction and the method of conducting the blade are identical with those described in the corresponding paragraph on attacks from medium distance.

(b) *With opposition*

The appropriate position of the fist is adopted during the approach work. The blade should be directed to the target

98

simultaneously with the closing of the distance. The thrust should be completed in the same manner as described in the corresponding paragraphs on attacks at close quarters and from medium distance.

(c) *With angular thrust*

When taking a step forward which means the actual process of approach the blade should be conducted along a straight plane. The fencer's arm stretches out slightly and the angle is formed parallel with the concluding stage of the step forward. The final movement of the thrust should be performed in the same manner as described in the case of performing an attack with angular thrust from medium distance.

*Performing thrusts from long distance with flèche*

(a) *As in foil fencing*

As in the event of attacks on the sixth on guard position or invito this exercise should be drilled with a short flèche only. Emphasis during training should be laid, above all, on conducting the blade and the developing rhythm of the movement.

(b) *With opposition*

The action should be introduced along the same lines as described in the preceding paragraph. It is a form adopted quite frequently for the purpose of acceleration.

(c) *With angular thrust*

The opponent should be approached and the angle should be formed in the same manner as when the movement is performed with lunge. In this case the thrust that completes the action is carried out with the usual type of flèche.

The following parries can be adopted:
simple sixth (or third), circular fourth, destruction seventh and semicircular second parry.

The execution of parries in on guard position or while taking a step backward should be practised in the same manner as in the case of attacks on the sixth invito.

The exercises should be of the following types:
– parry and thrust,
– riposte,
– thrust, parry and thrust,
– counter-riposte.

The above exercises should be built up on the parries listed below.

– Simple sixth,
– circular fourth,
– destruction seventh,
– semicircular second.

The methods of execution are identical with those described in detail in the case of attacks on the sixth invito.


*Counter-attacks*

Stop thrust performed with the first and, at the same time, ultimate cadence.

– Instead of a simple sixth parry a straight time thrust can be performed from outside and to the opponent's shoulder or upper part of his trunk, or an angular thrust can be executed from below to the adversary's wrist.

– Instead of a circular fourth parry either inquartata can be carried out in a direction identical with that of the parry and to the upper part of the opponent's trunk or shoulder, or an angular thrust to his wrist.

In the former case the blade is conducted high and inside, in the latter, it moves forward inside.

The following counter-attacks can be adopted when the adversary's attack is directed to the lower opening of the target:

– Instead of a destruction seventh parry; in this case the thrust should be a straight or angular one directed to the inside low opening of the target or to the upper part of the adversary's hand following a circular movement the direction of which is identical with that of the parry the thrust substitutes.

– Instead a of semicircular second parry; thrust (imbroccata) performed outside and low to the opponent's body or thigh, or an angular thrust can be carried out from upside to his hand or wrist.


*Against the second (eighth) invito*

At close quarters to the opponent's body or to the high and low opening of the target.

*(a)* As in foil fencing,

*(b)* with opposition,

*(c)* with angular thrust.

*(a)* Thrusts directed to the body should be carried out in the same manner as in the case of attacks on sixth invito. The plane along which the blade is conducted should lie below that of the fencer's corresponding shoulder, and so prevent the counter-attack from below.

When the attack is to be made to the shoulder, arm and wrist, the distance between coach and pupil should be increased to correspond to the fencing target. The thrust should be performed along a straight line, with the fencer's arm allowed to sink relatively low.

(b) The principal target for this type of thrust is the arm. The blade should be conducted along the shortest route and with the fencer's fist allowed to lie low in order to block with the guard of the weapon the path of a possible counter-attack from below.

(c) The forearm and wrist act as the fencing target. The position of the adversary's blade offers an ideal opportunity to the fencer to carry out the exercise. The first stage of the execution is to direct the weapon so that it travels the shortest distance to the selected target. Simultaneously with the straightening of the fencer's arm his fist, while retaining its original supine position, is raised above the plane of the shoulder. In this manner the fencer's arm moves apart from the opponent's blade as it threatens from below in the course of the thrust. The formation of the maximum angle makes it possible for the fencer to hit anywhere between his opponent's elbow and wrist.

*Performing thrusts from medium distance with lunge*

(a) *As in foil fencing*

The principles of instruction are, in general, much the same as those of attacks carried out on the fourth and sixth invito.

Fig. 42

Figure 42 illustrates a thrust executed as in foil fencing on the second on guard position or invito.

(b) *With oppositon*

The attacking blade should be conducted in the same manner as when the thrust is carried out at close quarters. The only difference is that here the thrust is supported by a lunge.

Fig. 43

The oppositional thrust performed on second on guard position or invito is illustrated in figure 43.

## (c) *With angular thrust*

The blade should be conducted and the angle should be formed in the same manner as described in the case of angular thrust performed at close quarters. The only difference is that here a lunge supports the thrust in its forward movement.

Fig. 44

Angular thrust executed on the second on guard position or invito is illustrated in figures 44 and 45.

Fig. 45

*Performing thrusts from long distance with a step forward and lunge*

(a) *As in foil fencing*

This type of thrust should be carried out in a manner similar to that of thrusts on the fourth and sixth invito, except for the fact that here the blade should be conducted along the plane of the low line.

(b) *With opposition*

The direction of the blade should start during the approach work with the fist held low. The closing stage of the direction of the épée is when the rear foot is placed on the piste as the concluding movement of the step forward. From this position the weapon is moved forward by lunge only.

(c) *With angular thrust*

The fencer should straighten out his arm loosely in the course of the approach work. The formation of the angle should terminate as the rear foot is placed on the piste to end the step forward. Once this position is reached the épée should be moved forward in the direction of the target by lunge only.

*Performing thrusts from long distance with flèche*

At the present stage of épée fencing a thrust with a short flèche should be executed only to the opponent's body. It should be borne in mind that safety takes priority over the form of the action.

The following parries can be adopted: simple sixth (third), simple seventh, semicircular fourth and circular second.

As in the case of attacks carried out on other invitos the execution of simple, semicircular and circular parrying as well as the fixation of final positions should be included in the exercises.

The exercises of the fencing lesson can be built up on the types of parries given above and on the basis of the examples provided in detail in the paragraphs on attacks on the sixth invito.

*Counter-attacks*

The counter-attack can take the form of a stop thrust in the first and, at the same time, final cadence.

– Instead of a sixth parry either a straight time thrust can be performed from outside and high or a straight or angular thrust directed to the opponent's hand from below.

– Instead of a semicircular fourth parry inquartata can be carried out in the direction of the fourth position inside and high to the adversary's body or shoulder.

In case the opponent's attack is directed to the low opening of the target:

– Instead of a simple seventh parry an angular thrust can be carried out inside and low to the opponent's body and thigh with the fencer's fist held high, or to the hand or wrist, with the blade conducted inside and from below.

– Instead of a circular second parry either an imbroccata can be performed outside and low to the adversary's body or thigh, or a straight or angular thrust can be executed inside and high.

At close quarters to the opponent's body and to the outside low opening of the target.

*(a)* As in foil fencing,

*(b)* with opposition,

*(c)* with angular thrust.

*(a)* At close quarters, this action is used primarily as an exercise designed to facilitate the pupil in conducting and directing his weapon.

The method adopted when performing the thrust to the thigh, foot or the forearm of the opponent from below is identical with that used when the attack involves the body. When practising, the pupil should be instructed to do no more than indicate the direction of the thrust. At this stage it is advisable to omit completion of the thrust from the material to be drilled.

*(b)* There is no real fencing target available for carrying out a thrust of the opposition type. If the fencer finds that his adversary has positioned himself in this type of on guard or invito, he is advised to adopt either the kind of thrust used in foil fencing and discussed in the preceding paragraph, or the angular thrust that is considered below.

*(c)* While it is true that the fencing target displayed is rather small, nevertheless it is quite vulnerable, for neither the forearm nor the wrist of the opponent is defended adequately. When performing the exercise the fencer should turn the plane of his blade from the right-hand side supine position to the left and into the second hand position. After allowing his fist to sink low the fencer directs the point of his weapon along the shortest path to his opponent's wrist situated behind the guard of his weapon. From the position thus formed the épée is moved forward as long as its button makes contact with the target.

*Performing thrust on the seventh invito with lunge from medium distance*

(a) *As in foil fencing*

The thrust should be carried out to the opponent's body, to be exact, to the outside lower opening of the target. The thrust can only be successful if the upper part of the fencer's body is withdrawn sideways from the line position threatened by the adversary, simultaneously with the execution of the thrust. To this end the fencer should incline the upper part of his trunk sideways outwards and downwards parallel with the performance of the lunge. The knee and thigh of the opponent's leg placed in front constitutes the nearest and most convenient target. The adversary's right foot (if he is a right-handed fencer) is the deepest lying and most extreme target. This type of thrust is recommended only if the opponent's attention has been deceived into concentrating his attention on a sham preparation.

Thrusts to the forearm can be performed without the immediate danger of the adversary executing a counter-attack but with much less certainty of a hit.

(b) *With opposition*

This is an exclusively theoretical definition without practical importance.

(c) *With angular thrust*

The reality of execution can be felt best above all from medium distance. Technically speaking, the weapon should be directed in the same manner as described in point *(c)* of thrusts at

Fig. 46

The thrust carried out as in foil fencing on the seventh on guard position or invito is illustrated in figure 46.

Fig. 47

The thrust performed as in foil fencing to the right thigh of the opponent who has positioned himself in the seventh on guard or invito is shown in figure 47.

close quarters. During the lunge, the fencer should focus his attention on maintaining the angle formed by his weapon and arm. His hold on the grip should be a firm one so that the point of the blade should not slide on the target at the moment a hit is being scored. Following a thrust that has slid on the target (passé thrust) the fencer will find the parts of his opponent's body to be lying at too great a distance to permit a renewal of his thrust.

Fig. 48

The angular thrust performed to the foot of the opponent who is in the seventh on guard or invito by the fencer bending his body very low is shown in figure 48.

Fig. 49

The angular thrust performed with the second position of the hand on the opponent's seventh on guard position or invito is shown in figure 49.

*Performing thrusts from long distance with a step forward and lunge*

(a) *As in foil fencing*

Execution of this kind of attack involves a number of dangers. That is why it is rarely adopted. A straight thrust carried out to the adversary's body carries the risk peculiar to this position of the blade. Execution of the thrust to the thigh or foot are likely to take the opponent by surprise and promise more success. Thrusts to the arm call for superior technical knowledge and very accurate control of the blade.

(b) *With opposition*

This type of thrust is without practical significance.

(c) *With angular thrust*

It is not reasonable to perform this kind of thrust from long distance either with a step forward or with flèche; because of the distance, the angle required for success can only be formed after the distance has been appropriately reduced.

*Performing thrusts from long distance with flèche*

## (a) *As in foil fencing*

The recommended movement is to the outside low opening of the target, above all to the knee or thigh according to the method described in the preceding paragraphs, that is, with the fencer's fist held high and the point of the blade allowed to point downwards. Fencers of exceptional ability are capable of performing thrusts gliding on the lower edge of the opponent's guard and directed towards the lower part of his hand with flèche. Naturally, a great deal of exercise and repeated drilling are needed to ensure successful mastery of this technique.

Oppositional and angular thrusts are rarely performed in practice.

The following parries can be adopted: simple second (eighth), circular seventh, destructing fourth and semicircular sixth.

The pupils should practise the above-listed parries in on guard position as well as with a step backward. The coach should check that the parries are carried out correctly from the technical point of view both during the parrying process and in the final position.

Here too the exercises of the fencing lesson can be built up on the types of parries mentioned in the foregoing.

## *Counter-attacks*

Stop thrusts in the first and, at the same time, final cadence. – Instead of a simple second parry either an imbroccata can be performed from outside and low to the opponent's body and thigh, or a high straight or angular thrust can be executed to his hand.

– Instead of a circular seventh parry an angular thrust can be carried out to the opponent's body and thigh inside and low in the direction of the seventh invito, or to the hand and wrist, with the blade conducted inside and high.

If the attack is aimed at the adversary's head:

– Instead of a destructing fourth parry, either inquartata should be performed inside and high or from below an angular thrust directed to the hand.

– Instead of a semicircular sixth parry, either a straight stop thrust should be executed outside and high to the body and shoulder or from below an angular thrust.

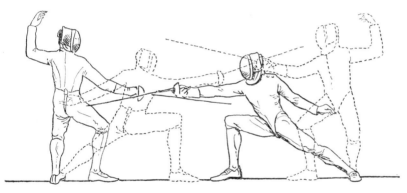

Fig. 50

Every exercise of the material of the fencing lesson considered so far has been discussed in detail, with all the distances and forms analysed at length. Based on the fundamental exercises of the fencing lesson detailed analysis of the exercises has been made along with the method of building them up into complex movements such as thrust followed by parry and thrust or the performance of counter-riposte.

113

Fig. 51

Figures 50, 51 and 52 illustrate both the "thrust, parry and coun-ter-riposte" which is the fundamental exercise of the highest level of the fencing lesson and the stop thrust carried out on the opponent's concluding thrust in the final cadence.

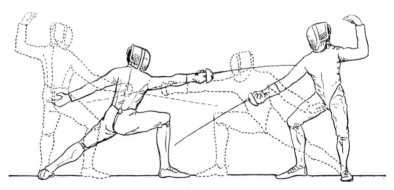

Fig. 52

In the chapters that follow the medium distance which is the principal distance of instruction will be regarded as the standard for the discussion of every exercise. Although exercises performed at close quarters will be retained as a form of instruction and method, the technical description of the individual exercises will be confined to the "standard" distance. Where co-ordination of the movements of the hand and feet is necessary because of the long distance, the correct method of execution will be considered separately. The forms of the conclusion of both the attacking (thrust) and defensive (parry) movements will be discussed simultaneously in order to facilitate, through the exercises, the establishment of the most general forms that can be carried out in the different situations along with the formation of a wide range of abilities to perform movements.

# IV. THE CONCEPT OF BINDS

In foil fencing the bind is defined as "the movement with the blade with which the adversary's weapon held in line is removed from this line; in doing so the forte of the fencer's blade makes contact with the weak part of the opponent's arm".

This definition applies to épée fencing too, but it must be completed with the following remarks. Engagement in épée fencing plays no part other than the change in the prevailing relations between the two blades; the only positive feature lies in the fact that it has changed a line position that had constituted a threat for the fencer. As long as neither one nor the other fencer attempts to initiate an immediate attacking movement on the engagement, the relation between the two blades brought about by the bind must be regarded a final position from which either fencer can embark on an attacking movement.

Binds are denominated according to the invito on which they are performed. There are fourth, sixth (third), second (eighth) and seventh (first) binds.

According to another classification the binds can be divided into two groups depending on whether the fencer has engaged his opponent's weapon or vice versa.

In addition, there are some other types of binds to be distinguished such as simple, semicircular, circular and change binds, the fencer's own bind of the blade already engaged, etc.

# V. CHANGE THRUSTS

Before turning to the discussion of actions performed by the fencer with his own bind (as attacks on the blade), the change thrust, which is the simplest type of attack that can be performed from the opponent's engagement, will be considered.

The change thrust can be defined as an attacking action performed by the fencer from his adversary's engagement. After freeing his weapon from the binding blade and going round the guard of the opponent's weapon the fencer carries out a thrust to the opening of the target lying nearest to him. While rounding the adversary's weapon the point of the blade about to execute the thrust forges ahead as though it were a screw powered from behind.

*Change thrust performed from the sixth (third) engagement*

Change thrust from the sixth engagement can be carried out from medium distance.

*(a)* As in foil fencing,
*(b)* with opposition,
*(c)* with angular thrust.

*(a)* After releasing the point of his blade and rounding the guard of the opponent's weapon from below the fencer should

conduct his épée in the direction of the inside high opening of the target. The thrust should proceed with a spiral-like movement as the fencer's arm is straightened out with his wrist held loose. In the early stages of instruction the thrust should be directed toward the adversary's body shoulder high. Later on, however, the thrust should be carried out gradually to the upper arm and finally to the inside of his elbow. The final stage of direction, the straightening of the arm, should be combined with lunge that will bring the point of the blade into contact with the target. At the moment of finishing the movement the hand holding the weapon rises somewhat along with the forte of the blade, but the plane of the arm and épée should virtually be retained during this process. The fencer's fist is positioned high on the left-hand side.

*(b)* In this case the attack should be launched and the change (rounding the guard of the opponent's weapon) should be per-

Fig. 53

The change thrust performed with lunge from the opponent's previous sixth bind in a manner similar to foil fencing is given in figure 53. The dotted line indicates the attacker's position prior to the movement.

formed in the same manner as the thrust in foil fencing (see point *(a)*). Following the direction of the blade toward the target the closing stage of the thrust and the holding of the fist are identical with that described in Straight thrust performed with opposition.

*(c)* The first move is to release the foible of our blade from the engagement. Then comes the rounding of the guard of the adversary's blade from below. While doing this the fencer should position his fist high on the right-hand side and outside the line so that the plane of the blade is inclined by the straightened arm outside to the right (supine position). At the same time the point of the blade should be aimed at the inside of the opponent's arm with an angle formed by the fencer's wrist. The target should be the inside of the opponent's arm but the section to be hit depends on the distance separating the two fencers. In certain cases the thrust can be directed toward the adversary's body or head. The thrust should be aided in its forward movement by lunge.

*Change thrust from long distance with a step forward and by lunge*

The exercises of change thrust from long distance should be carried out as follows: while taking a step forward the fencer should move his blade forward along the plane of the opponent's weapon until it reaches the level of his guard, and the change should be performed simultaneously with the fencer's rear foot stamping on the piste.

*Change thrust from long distance with flèche*

The flèche should be introduced with a step forward in the course of which the fencer conducts his blade until it reaches the level of the guard of his opponent's weapon in the same manner as described in the preceding paragraph. The finish should be a flèche executed at a fast pace instead of a lunge.

The following parries can be adopted: simple fourth, semi-circular seventh, circular sixth and simple second.

*Exercises of parry, thrust and riposte*

Pupil                                                    Coach

*First exercise*

Binds with sixth the coach's blade held in high line

Carries out change thrust to the inside upper opening of the target

Performs a simple fourth parry in on guard position or with a step backward and executes a thrust from on guard or with lunge; this is followed straight away by a riposte to the inside upper opening of the target. The general form of the closing thrust (riposte) is one in opposition

| Pupil | Coach |
|---|---|

## *Second exercise*

| | |
|---|---|
| Binds with sixth the coach's blade held in high line | Performs change thrust to the inside upper opening of the target |

Executes a circular sixth parry in on guard position or with a step backward and carries out a thrust as in foil fencing from on guard or with lunge; this is followed by a riposte directed to the outside low opening of the target or the opponent's foot. In some cases the riposte can be an angular one performed to the adversary's hand from below

## *Third exercise*

| | |
|---|---|
| Binds with sixth the coach's blade held in high line | Performs change thrust to the inside low opening of the target |

Performs a simple second parry in on guard position or with a step backward and then carries out a thrust followed by a riposte to the

| Pupil | Coach |
|---|---|

inside upper opening of the target or the opponent's arm from on guard position or with lunge. Today, the general form of the riposte is a thrust similar to what is used in foil fencing, or an angular thrust

*Fourth exercise*

| Pupil | Coach |
|---|---|
| Binds with sixth the coach's blade held in high line | Performs change thrust to the inside low opening of the target |

Performs a semicircular seventh parry in on guard position or with a step backward and then carries out a thrust followed by a riposte to the inside low opening of the target from on guard position or with lunge. The general form of the riposte is in opposition

*Exercises of thrust, parry and thrust and counter-riposte*

*First exercise*

| | |
|---|---|
| Binds with sixth his pupil's blade held in high line | Performs change thrust with lunge to the inside upper opening of the target |
| Parries the thrust with a simple fourth parry and indicates a thrust directed to the inside upper opening of the target | Parries with a simple fourth or change sixth in lunge or while resuming on guard position from lunge and carries out a thrust (counter-riposte) in accordance with the objective of the exercise; from fourth a high thrust and from sixth a low thrust should be executed in the form best suited to the purpose |

*Second exercise*

| | |
|---|---|
| Binds with sixth his pupil's blade held in high line | Performs change thrust with lunge to the inside upper opening of the target |
| Carries out a circular sixth parry and indicates a thrust directed to the outside lower opening of the target | Adopts a simple second or change seventh parry from lunge or while resuming on guard position. After the |

| Coach | Pupil |
|---|---|
|  | parry he performs, according to the objective of the exercise, either a thrust or a counter-riposte; from the second parry the thrust should be directed high, while from the seventh into the inside lower opening of the target; the form best suited to the purpose should be adopted |

## *Third exercise*

| Coach | Pupil |
|---|---|
| Binds with sixth his pupil's blade held in high line | Performs change thrust with lunge to the inside low opening of the target |
| Carries out a simple second parry and indicates a thrust to the inside upper opening of the target | Parries the thrust in lunge or while resuming on guard position with a simple sixth or change fourth. According to the purpose of the exercise he can adopt a thrust or counter-riposte from the parry; from the sixth parry the thrust should be performed outside and low, while from the fourth one to the inside upper opening of the target |

| Coach | Pupil |
|---|---|

*Fourth exercise*

| | |
|---|---|
| Binds with sixth his pupil's blade held in high line | Performs change thrust with lunge to the inside low opening of the target |
| After carrying out a semicircular seventh parry he indicates a thrust to the inside low opening of the target | Parries the thrust in lunge or while resuming on guard position with simple seventh or change second. He should execute a thrust or counter-riposte from lunge with a tempo allowed to elapse. From the seventh parry the thrust should be directed to the inside low opening and from second to the upper section of the target. The most suitable form of thrust should be adopted |

*Counter-attacks*

The counter-attack can take the form of a thrust instead of a parry.

– Instead of a simple fourth parry either inquartata can be performed inside and high or an angular thrust inside and high directed to the opponent's forearm or wrist.

– Instead of a circular sixth parry the sixth time thrust can be adopted outside and high.

In case the thrust is directed toward the lower part of the target:

– Instead of a semicircular seventh parry either a thrust can be carried out inside and low to the inside low opening of the target or to the adversary's thigh or an angular thrust inside and high to his hand.

– Instead of a simple second parry either an imbroccata can be executed outside and low to the adversary's body or a high angular thrust to his hand.

*Change thrust performed from the fourth engagement*

From medium distance.
*(a)* As in foil fencing,
*(b)* with opposition,
*(c)* with angular thrust.

*(a)* In this case the guard of the opponent's weapon should be rounded from below. The technique of execution is the same as when change thrust is carried out from the sixth engagement as in foil fencing. The inside part of the outside target including the adversary's arm (the right one if he holds the weapon in his right hand) down to his elbow act as the fencing target. At the moment the movement is completed the fist is positioned high on the right-hand side.

*(b)* The practical and methodological principles described in the corresponding paragraph of thrust from the sixth engagement should be adopted here too, in both starting and concluding an attack.

*(c)* In general, the methods of launching an attack, rounding the opponent's blade and forming the angle are much the same as those described in the paragraph concerning performing thrusts from the sixth engagement. Even the fencer's fist should be positioned high on the right-hand side. In certain cases, however, a different solution has to be selected. When the thrust is

Fig. 54

Change thrust carried out with opposition and with a lunge from
the opponent's fourth engagement is illustrated in figure 54.
The dotted line indicates the attacker's position prior to the
attack.

directed toward the outside surface of the adversary's wrist the
angle at which the thrust is to be executed should be formed with
the fist held on the left-hand side. This kind of thrust has the
inherent disadvantage of leaving the fencer's own outside upper
part wide open to attack and his arm is also defenceless.

*Performing change thrust from long distance out of fourth engagement
with a step forward and lunge*

When the distance is being reduced (that is while the step
forward is being taken), the fencer should glide his weapon along
the plane of his opponent's blade and in the direction of the engagement. The adversary's blade should be rounded and the concluding thrust performed at the moment the distance has been reduced, when the fencer's rear foot is stamping on the piste. The
blade is held unchanged and driven forward only by the lunge.

*Performing change thrust from long distance out of fourth engagement with flèche*

The action should be introduced in the same manner as described in the preceding paragraph. The only difference is that in this case the fencer is recommended to dispose of his opponent's blade earlier.

Naturally, the coach should refrain from generalizing what has been said above in connection with the different actions. The method best suited to the individual competitor will be found by the fencer himself during bout fencing.

The following parries can be adopted: simple sixth (third), circular fourth, destructing seventh and semicircular second.

*Exercises of parry, thrust and riposte*

These exercises are built up on the parries listed above. The system of the exercises are completely identical with the corresponding exercises of change thrust performed from sixth engagement.

*Exercises of thrust, parry and thrust and counter-riposte*

These exercises should be based on those of a parry followed by a thrust and riposte and they are recommended to be conducted in the same manner as described in the corresponding group of exercises in the case of change thrust performed from the sixth engagement.

*Counter-attacks*

The counter-attack can take the form of a stop thrust instead of a parry, carried out in the first and, at the same time, final cadence.

– Instead of a simple sixth parry either a sixth type of time thrust can be executed high and outside, or an angular thrust conducted outside and low to the opponent's hand or wrist.

– Instead of a circular fourth parry either inquartata can be performed inside and high, or an angular thrust conducted outside and low to the adversary's hand or wrist.

In case the thrust is directed toward the lower parts of the target:

– Instead of a destructing seventh parry either a thrust can be carried out inside and low to the adversary's body or thigh or an angular thrust conducted outside and high to his hand and wrist.

– Instead of a semicircular second parry either an imbroccata can be executed outside and low, or an angular thrust conducted outside and high to the opponent's hand and wrist.

*Change thrust performed from the second (eighth) engagement*

Change thrust from the second engagement can be performed from medium distance.

*(a)* As in foil fencing,

*(b)* with opposition,

*(c)* with angular thrust.

*(a)* The guard of the blade keeping the fencer's weapon engaged should be rounded from above. The fencing target covers the inside upper part of the body and the whole surface of the opponent's arm down to the wrist. The attacking blade should

be conducted along the middle plane. In the moment of the hit the position of the fist is irrelevant, but that is exceptional.

*(b)* Opposition plays a most important part when the thrust is aimed at the body (inside upper opening of the target) or the leg placed in front. The thrust performed to the forearm and upper arm is much the same as the method used when the thrust is executed in the manner of foil fencing. (In this respect it bears certain similarities with thrusts performed on on guard position and invito.) The only difference is that in this case the fist should be conducted along a lower plane in order to prevent possible counter-attack from below.

*(c)* This position allows the formation of the widest possible angle because the opponent's weapon is positioned along the plane of the low line. Immediately after disengagement the fencer and the angle formed with his fist are further from the point of the adversary's épée than in the case of any other type of thrust. The opponent's arm from his wrist upwards, his shoulder and head act as the fencing target.

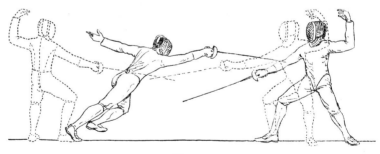

Fig. 55

Change thrust performed with angular thrust and flèche from the opponent's previous second engagement is presented in figure 55. The attacker's position prior to the movement is shown by the dotted line.

*Change thrust from the second engagement from long distance with step forward and lunge*

*Change thrust from the second engagement with flèche from long distance*

In both cases during the reduction of the distance and/or the step forward, the direction of the blade, the rounding of the opponent's guard and the aiming of the thrust should be set on the basis of the principles described for change thrusts performed from the sixth and fourth engagement.

The parries to be adopted are as follows: simple seventh, simple sixth (third), semicircular fourth and circular second.

The exercises of parry, thrust and riposte and thrust, parry, and thrust and counter-riposte are based on the parries listed above and carried on in the same manner as described for change thrust performed from sixth engagement.

*Counter-attacks*

Stop thrust in the first and, at the same time, final cadence can be performed instead of the parries adopted according to the method described in the exercises for change thrust carried out from the sixth and fourth engagement. Naturally, the movements with which the thrusts are executed should be of a direction identical with that of the parries they substitute.

*Change thrust performed from the seventh engagement*

Change thrust from the seventh engagement can be carried out from medium distance.

*(a)* As in foil fencing,

*(b)* with opposition,

*(c)* with angular thrust.

*(a)* The guard of the adversary's weapon should again be rounded from above. The opponent's body as a whole is vulnerable from outside and low and the leg placed in front as well as the lower surface of his forearm are part of the fencing target. The fencer is recommended to carry out his thrust to the forearm, wrist or front leg, that is the target closest to him. It is vitally important to take the given situation into account in order to determine the extent to which a hit can be scored.

*(b)* This type of thrust is virtually without practical importance. The only difference between this and the type discussed in the preceding paragraph (concerning foil-like execution) is

Fig. 56

The angular thrust performed with change thrust with half lunge (and with the fencer's hand in second position) from the opponent's preliminary seventh engagement to the lower section of his forearm is illustrated in figure 56. The attacker's position prior to the movement is indicated by the dotted line.

the opposition tendency. Since it is of no significance, it does not merit detailed discussion.

*(c)* Immediately after disengagement the point of the blade should describe a minor semicircle and move right under the guard of the adversary's weapon. In the case of second and third position the fist should be moved outside to the left into low position. This type of thrust is a highly rational and effective movement.

Change thrust from the seventh engagement can be adopted very rarely from long distance either with a step forward and lunge or flèche. An infrequent and unrealistic action.

The parries to be adopted are as follows: simple second, circular seventh, destructing fourth and semicircular sixth.

The exercises of parry, thrust and riposte as well as those of thrust, parry and thrust and counter-riposte should be built up on the types of parry listed above.

## Counter-attacks

Counter-attacks that can take the form of stop thrust can be carried out in the first and, at the same time, final cadence instead of the above types of parry.

# VI. BINDS

The bind as a final position has already been defined with emphasis placed on the fact that its technical execution brings about a new position of the blade (s) from which either opponent can initiate an attacking movement with equal chances. If the engagement is followed straight away by the concluding thrust, that is engagement and thrust constitute a continuous movement with no cadence in hand left for the adversary, the bind takes the form of attack on the blade and as such it is regarded as an attacking action.

The denomination of attacks introduced by engagement is based on the same systematization as was defined in the case of final positions with bind. The intensity of and extent to which the adversary's blade is engaged depend on a number of factors including the given situation, the knowledge or estimate of the opponent's reflexes, the fencing distance, the fencer's own intention and the co-ordination of tempo and cadence. Based on these factors and considerations the extent of engagement can range from a slight friction to an extremely powerful bind. Accordingly, a bind attack can be adopted not only against an épéeist holding his blade rigidly in line, but also against one standing with his weapon quite loose. Binds commonly adopted in foil fencing should be used against the blade held rigidly. This applies, in particular, in the event of straight attacks.

In the case of feint attacks very often even a momentary contact with a most rigidly held weapon is sufficient to deflect the blade, thus creating favourable conditions for carrying out an attack.

The majority of thrusts following engagement and directed toward the adversary's body and upper arm are bind thrusts or those with opposition. As in foil fencing conclusion is adopted to the opponent's body and arm if the fencer feels he has a full cadence in hand. When the attack is directed toward the adversary's arm and wrist, an angular thrust is preferable.

## 1. Simple binds from invito on the blade held in line

*Bind on the blade held in high line*

Bind can be carried out on the blade held in high line from medium distance.

*(a)* As in foil fencing,
*(b)* with opposition,
*(c)* with angular thrust.

*(a)* Fourth bind and thrust from the sixth (third) invito.

The related fencing targets are as follows: the inside upper opening, the whole inside surface of the arm and, in the event of drop thrust, the inside low opening and the leg placed in front.

In order to engage the opponent's weapon the fencer should make contact with the blade held in high line (the binding movement being the same as described in the case of parrying with the fourth parry). The contacting surface should be the middle of the fencer's blade and the hand should be in fourth position during the binding movement. The blade that is appropriately fixed from the fencer's elbow, forearm and wrist and bordered

135

by the left-hand side plane of his body should be pushed forward and to the left continuously as long as the fifth position of the hand is assumed. The point of the blade should be brought in front of the right shoulder along a straight plane so that the point of the weapon and the full arm form an unbroken straight line. The movement should be a continuous one, and performed from the forearm and elbow, with the button of the épée pointing to the fencing target. This movement should be combined with lunge. At the moment the hit is scored the plane of the blade rises along with the corresponding arm.

*(b)* The opponent's blade should be engaged and the thrust launched in the same manner as described in the preceding paragraph. The blade should be conducted for the finish so that while fixed in position firmly from the elbow and forearm, it is pushed forward along the plane of the bind but without bringing about any change in the position of the blade taken up during the process of bind. The lunge should be made at the moment the thrust is launched. After performing the thrust the fencer's fist is positioned high on the left.

*(c)* When this type of thrust is adopted the opponent's wrist and the inside part of his arm act as the fencing target.

Contact with the adversary's blade should be made and the bind should be performed in the same manner as discussed in point *(a)* of this chapter. In preparation for the thrust the fencer should direct his blade so that the plane of his weapon should be inclined outwards to the right from the fifth position of the hand through the fourth and into supine position. Simultaneously with this the fist should be moved high to the right as the arm is straightened out. Parallel with the change in the position of the hand and the direction of the fist the point of the blade should be directed so that it will travel the shortest distance to the most advantageous point of the inside upper part of the target, the forearm or wrist of the opponent. During the thrust

136

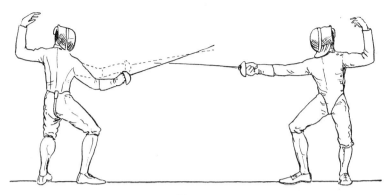

Fig. 57

Figure 57 shows the catching of the blade which is the first element of the simple fourth bind on the opponent's weapon held in high line. It is performed from the sixth invito and from medium distance.

Fig. 58

Angular thrust carried out with lunge from the fencer's own fourth engagement and from medium distance is shown in figure 58.

the weapon should be moved forward with the lunge only; meanwhile, there should be no change in the position of the blade or the hand.

*Bind on the blade held in high line with a step forward and lunge from long distance*

When the engagement is executed from long distance, the bind is preceded, as in foil fencing, by the engagement of the blade. Engagement means that right before the moment the fencer begins to take a step forward with his foot in the front, he catches the foible of his adversary's blade with that of his own weapon. While the opponent's blade thus bound is made to glide towards the middle of the fencer's own blade, he brings it under control when taking a step forward in the same manner as described in the corresponding case of engagement of the blade from medium distance. The thrust should be completed in the same manner as discussed in the case of engagement from medium distance.

*Bind on the blade held in high line from long distance with flèche*

Contact with and catching of the blade should be performed in a manner described in the preceding paragraph. This naturally means that the flèche should be introduced with a step forward, this is essential for both bringing the opponent's weapon under control and reducing the distance to the required extent even if the adversary attempts to withdraw so that he is out of the range of the attack. The step forward is the driving force that sets the body into motion. This initial speed can be accelerated by the flèche as required, and the adversary is unable to evade the attack. Naturally, it is more difficult to conduct the weapon in this case than when the attack is performed with lunge. That is why from every type of bind the thrust should be carried out above all to the body, or to the parts of the target lying in front and comparatively open.

The following parries can be adopted: simple fourth, change sixth (third), change seventh and simple second (eight). The latter can be used in the case of drop thrust.

*Exercises of parry, thrust and riposte*

Coach                                          Pupil

*First exercise*

| | |
|---|---|
| Binds his pupil's blade held in high line and performs a thrust to the inside upper opening of the target | Parries the thrust with simple fourth or change sixth in on guard position or while taking a step backward, and from the parry he executes a thrust followed by a riposte from on guard position or with a lunge; from the fourth type of parry the thrust is directed to the inside upper opening of the target and from the sixth parry to the low opening outside; the general form of the thrust is the one used in foil fencing |

| Coach | Pupil |
|-------|-------|

*Second exercise*

| Coach | Pupil |
|-------|-------|
| Binds his pupil's blade held in high line with fourth and indicates a thrust from the bind toward the inside part of the opponent's arm | Parries the thrust with change seventh or simple second type of parry while taking a step backward; following the parry he performs a thrust from on guard position or with a lunge; from the seventh parry the thrust is conducted low and inside with opposition offered and from the second type the thrust is carried out to the opponent's body or arm in a manner similar to foil fencing |

*Exercises of thrust, parry and thrust and counter-riposte*

| Pupil | Coach |
|-------|-------|

*First exercise*

| Pupil | Coach |
|-------|-------|
| Binds the coach's blade held in high line with the fourth type of engagement. From the engagement he carries out a thrust continuously with a lunge to the inside upper opening of the target | Parries the thrust in lunge or parries the thrust with the fourth type of parry and indicates a thrust directed to the inside upper opening of the target |

| Pupil | Coach |
|---|---|
| while resuming on guard position from lunge with simple fourth type of parry. From the parry he carries out a thrust or counter-riposte in accordance with the objective of the exercise to the inside upper opening of the target | |
| The most usual form of completing the thrust is one of the opposition type | |

## Second exercise

| Pupil | Coach |
|---|---|
| Binds the coach's blade held in high line with the fourth. From the bind carries out a thrust continuously to the inside upper opening of the target | Parries the thrust with the fourth and indicates thrust to the inside upper opening of the target |
| Parries the thrust with the change sixth parry in lunge or while resuming on guard position from lunge. In accordance with the objective of the exercise he performs a thrust and a counter-riposte | |

| Pupil | Coach |
|---|---|

from the parry, to the outside
and low part as in foil fencing
or executes an angular thrust

<br>

*Third exercise*

| Pupil | Coach |
|---|---|
| Binds the coach's blade held in high line. From the bind he carries out a thrust continuously to the inside upper opening of the target | Parries the thrust with simple fourth and indicates thrust toward the inside of the forearm |

Carries out simple seventh
parry in lunge or while resuming on guard position
from lunge. In accordance
with the objective of the
exercise he executes a thrust
with opposition followed by
a counter-riposte to the inside low opening of the target

*Fourth exercise*

| Pupil | Coach |
|---|---|
| Binds the coach's blade held in high line with the fourth. From the bind he carries out a thrust continuously with lunge to the inside upper opening of the target | Parries the thrust with change sixth and indicates thrust to the outside low opening of the target |

| Pupil | Coach |
|---|---|

Adopts simple second or change seventh type of parry in lunge or while resuming on guard position from lunge and, in accordance with the objective of the exercise, executes a thrust followed by counter-riposte. The closing thrust from the second is one like in foil fencing or an angular thrust, while from the seventh parry it is most frequently one of the opposition type

*Fifth exercise*

| Pupil | Coach |
|---|---|
| Binds the coach's blade held in high line with the fourth. From the bind he carries out an angular thrust continuously to the inside of the opponent's arm. | Adopts change seventh parry and indicates thrust to the inside low opening of the target |

Performs simple seventh or change second parry from lunge or while resuming on guard position from lunge. From the parry he carries out a thrust or counter-riposte as required by the particular objective of the exercise

| Pupil | Coach |
|---|---|

*Sixth exercise*

| | |
|---|---|
| Binds the coach's blade held in high line with the fourth and performs a drop thrust from the bind without a pause to the thigh placed in front | Parries the thrust with simple second and indicates thrust to the inside upper opening of the target |

Carries out simple sixth or change fourth type of parry in lunge or while resuming on guard position. The closing thrust from the sixth parry is like that used in foil fencing, or from the fourth it is most often one of the opposition type

*Counter-attacks*

Counter-attacks can take the form of stop thrust of the following three types:

1. *Time degagement stop thrust performed high and outside*

The stop thrust is carried out to the body (outside upper opening of the target) or the upper arm after rounding the binding blade. The foot exercise adopted will depend on the distance separating the two fencers.

## 2. *Change stop thrust performed high and outside*

The stop thrust is executed with a change thrust from the engagement brought about by the opponent. The movement commences with a step backward. The fencer is recommended to direct the thrust to his adversary's forearm or wrist.

## 3. *Stop thrust performed in the final cadence*

This kind of thrust should be performed instead of one of the relevant parries following engagement of the blades by the adversary and before the thrust likely to follow. As in the case of straight thrusts, the movement should be performed from on guard position or with a short step backward. The thrust itself is a time stop thrust, with the blade advancing high or low, and substituting the corresponding parries.

*Sixth (third) bind and thrust performed from the fourth invito*

*Sixth (third) bind and thrust performed from the second invito*

Both movements can be carried out
*(a)* as in foil fencing,
*(b)* with opposition,
*(c)* with angular thrust.
*(a)* In this case the adversary's body, the outside low opening, his thigh and foot (the right foot in the case of a right-handed fencer) constitute the fencing target. Contact with the opponent's blade should be made and bind should be executed from both invitos with the movement of the blade described in the case of the simple sixth parry. Initial contact with the adversary's blade

held in high line should be made with the middle of the weapon of the fencer who should hold his hand in fourth position. Then the opponent's blade should be made to glide until its point is level with the edge of the guard of the fencer's weapon. Meanwhile, the fencer should turn his forearm outwards along the longitudinal axis, and while inclining the plane of his own blade outwards into supine position from the fourth position of the hand, the opponent's blade momentarily is kept engaged.

At the moment of opposition from the adversary, the fencer should break away from the other blade and after going round it from below the thrust should be executed with lunge to the outside low opening of the target, or to the trunk, thigh or perhaps the foot. The lunge should be performed somewhat sideways to the left and while doing so the fencer should withdraw the upper part of his trunk sideways from the direction of the threatening line of his adversary's épée.

*(b)* Thrust performed with opposition from the sixth bind is not at all characteristic of épée fencing. The only difference between this type of thrust and the one discussed in point *(a)* is that in this case the position of the fist is higher both during the process of thrusting and completing the thrust.

*(c)* The adversary's forearm and wrist constitute the fencing target. In general the bind is one of the gliding type of short duration in the course of which the foible of the opponent's blade is allowed to advance during engagement only to the middle of the fencer's own weapon. The fencer should bring his own blade into a momentary final position at the height of his adversary's wrist. From this position he should straighten out his arm, allow his fist to drop well below the line and turn the plane of his blade into the second position of the hand. The point of the weapon should be directed upwards from below and toward the opponent's forearm situated behind his guard and extending to the elbow so that it will travel along the short-

est route. The thrust should be combined and concluded with lunge.

Sixth (third) bind thrust from the second and fourth invito performed from long distance:
 – with a step forward and lunge,
 – with flèche.

The introduction of the attacks, that is the engagement of the opponent's blade, is identical with the method adopted when the bind is carried out from long distance as in foil fencing.

Following the completion of the step forward the blade should be conducted in the same manner as described in the case of carrying out the attack from medium distance.

The parries to be adopted are simple second (eighth) and change seventh.

The exercises of the fencing lesson should be based on and performed from the parries listed above.


*Counter-attacks*

Counter-attacks can take the form of thrusts of the following types:


1. *Time degagement thrust executed high and inside*

It should be carried out in a manner identical with that used when the bind is of the fourth type. The fencer is recommended to perform his thrust to the opponent's body (inside upper opening of the target) or to his upper arm extending from the shoulder down to the bend of the elbow.

## 2. *Change thrust performed high and inside*

This type of thrust should be performed from the sixth (third) engagement completed by the adversary. Simultaneously with a step backward the fencer's blade should be released from the bind upwards; the stop thrust directed toward the forearm is generally of the angular type.

## 3. *Stop thrust performed in the final cadence*

It should be carried out from the adversary's sixth (third) engagement and on his concluding thrust directed toward the low opening of the target.

### *Bind on the blade held in low line*

*Performing second (eighth) bind and thrust from the sixth (third) and seventh invito*

Second (eighth) bind and thrust from the sixth (third) and seventh types of invito can be carried out from medium distance.

*(a)* As in foil fencing,
*(b)* with opposition,
*(c)* with angular thrust.

*(a)* The inside upper opening and the upper arm down to the bend of the elbow constitute the fencing target. The engagement should be executed with the movement of the blade described in the case of the simple second parry so that contact with the adversary's blade held in low line is made with the middle of the fencer's own weapon, with his hand held in second

148

or fourth position respectively in the case of the second or eighth bind.

The opponent's blade is forced to move out of the line by the sideways pressure exercised by the forearm; while exercising this pressure the fencer's fist should be allowed to sink some four inches below the plane of his shoulder. The point of the épée should be directed either toward the inside upper opening of the target or the opponent's upper arm from the shoulder downward. The thrust should be performed along a straight line.

*(b)* The fencing target is identical with that described in point *(a)* of the preceding paragraph. The opponent's blade should be engaged with the same type of blade movement as discussed in the case of engaging the adversary's weapon as in foil fencing. The element of opposition is given prominence especially when the thrust is directed toward the body. In case the thrust is aimed at the opponent's arm, the blade should be directed in the same manner as in the case of foil fencing, and the fencer's fist should be lowered in the direction of the blade threatening from below only after the competitor has assured himself of the security of his thrust.

*(c)* The opponent's arm and wrist constitute the fencing target. Right after the conclusion of engagement the point of the fencer's blade should be rotated from the second into the fourth position of the hand. Breaking the line of the wrist downwards, the straightened arm should be raised so that the fist lies in high position. The thrust should be advanced with lunge.

Second type of bind and thrust from the sixth and seventh invito can be carried out from long distance:
– with a step forward and lunge or
– with flèche.

The process of making contact with the opponent's blade and approach work while keeping it engaged are identical with thrusts from the fourth and sixth engagement. The blade should be directed toward the target and the intended form with which the closing movement is to be accomplished should be assumed at the moment the approach work is concluded, that is simultaneously with the rear foot stamping on the piste after the step forward.

The parries to be adopted are simple sixth (third) and change fourth.

The exercises of the fencing lesson can be performed in the same manner as described in the chapter on the blade held in high line.

*Counter-attacks*

Counter-attacks can take the form of thrusts of the following types:
1. Time degagement thrust executed high.
2. Change thrust performed high.
3. Stop thrust carried out in final cadence.

High: instead of simple sixth, a sixth stop outside and angular thrust below; instead of change fourth inquartata inside and angular thrust should be performed.

*Seventh bind and thrust from the second (eighth) invito*

Seventh bind thrust from the second invito can be carried out from medium distance.
*(a)* As in foil fencing,
*(b)* with opposition,
*(c)* with angular thrust.

*(a)* The inside low opening and the opponent's thigh constitute the fencing target. The adversary's blade should be engaged

so that the plane of the fencer's weapon should be raised from low position to be in front of his shoulder. The hand is in the fourth position, the arm is slightly straightened and the movement is performed from below. The middle of the fencer's blade should make contact with the foible of the opponent's épée, and while the weapon is being raised, the other blade should be made to move toward the forte of the fencer's weapon. The fencer should lower the point of his épée so that it is level with the plane of the low line. The thrust should be carried out to the surface lying between the adversary's right hip and armpit (the right side of his body) or to the thigh. The fist is held high on the left-hand side.

*(b)* The fencing target is identical with the one described in the preceding paragraph. This is the type of thrust applied most generally, because it enables the fencer to keep his opponent's blade under control from right after engaging it up to the moment the thrust is completed. The only difference from the form discussed in the preceding paragraph is that the fist is positioned even more apparently high on the left-hand side.

*(c)* The opponent's forearm and wrist act as the fencing target. His blade is put slightly out of position (is lifted) by a momentary seventh type of bind. The point of the fencer's blade should be directed toward the lower part of the adversary's wrist along the shortest possible route. As in the case of performing the sixth type of engagement, the arm is straightened out and the fist is lowered in the second position of the hand, and the thrust is performed with lunge.

Seventh bind thrust from the second invito can be carried out from long distance:

– with a step forward and lunge or
– with flèche.

Neither the execution of the attack nor the completion of the thrust contains any new element.

The following parries can be adopted: simple seventh and change second.

The exercises of the fencing lesson can be based on and performed from the parries listed above.

*Counter-attacks*

Counter-attacks can take the form of thrusts of the following types:

1. Time degagement in the direction of the outside low opening of the target and of the opponent's hand.
2. Change thrust to the opponent's hand.
3. Stop thrust carried out in the final cadence.

If the attack is performed low, stop thrust directed toward the inside or angular thrust should be carried out instead of a simple seventh, and instead of a change second type, imbroccata or angular thrust should be executed outside and low, or high, respectively.

# 2. Semicircular binds from invito on the blade held in line

The relevant exercises do not need detailed discussion. The systematization given below determines the relation of the two blades to one another in final positions. The direction of the semicircle in which the semicircular engagement is performed follows from the relation of the blades. Every form of finishing the action can be adopted.

The parries and the stop thrusts to be carried out are determined by the direction in which the attacks are designed to be concluded.

*Bind on the blade held in high line*

*Performing semicircular fourth bind and thrust from the second (eighth) invito*

*Performing semicircular sixth (third) bind and thrust from the seventh invito*

*Bind on the blade held in low line*

*Performing semicircular seventh bind and thrust from the sixth (third) invito*

*Performing second (eighth) bind and thrust from the fourth invito from medium distance*

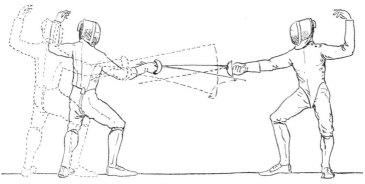

Fig. 59

The first cadence of the semicircular seventh bind carried out from the sixth invito and from long distance on the opponent's blade held in low line (the moment of making contact with the other blade) is presented in figure 59. The figure shows that the fencer stretches out his front leg from the knee at the moment the attack is launched. The second position of the fencer on the

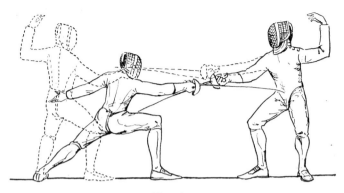

Fig. 60

Figure 60 illustrates the thrust performed with lunge and opposition from the seventh type of engagement indicated by the dotted line.


left shows the engagement after it has been completed and the reduction of the distance.

In the case of every attack the exercises of parry, thrust and riposte and those of thrust, parry and thrust and counter-riposte are dependent on the concluding thrust adopted. These exercises will not be discussed here because only the introduction of the attack contains new elements, the variations have already been considered during the discussion of simple binds.
Performing semicircular seventh and second bind and thrust from the sixth and eighth invito, respectively, from long distance:
  – with a step forward and lunge and
  – with flèche.

The principles, methods and technique of executing the movement are identical with those discussed in the case of simple binds. The only difference is that the direction of the bind is not the same as that of simple binds.

## 3. Circular binds from invito on the blade held in line

All the definitions of principle given in the case of semicircular binds apply perfectly to circular binds too. For this reason discussion is confined to the systematization of the relevant material instead of extending over a detailed description.

*Bind on the blade held in high line*

*Performing circular fourth bind thrust from the fourth invito*

*Performing circular sixth (third) bind thrust from the second (third) invito*

*Bind on the blade held in low line*

Fig. 61

The closing stage of performing the fourth bind thrust from the fourth engagement with the opponent's blade held in high line is shown in figure 61. The attack is carried out from medium distance with a short flèche.

*Performing circular seventh bind thrust from the seventh invito*

*Performing circular second (eighth) bind thrust from the second (eighth) invito*

Fig. 62

The initial cadence of performing the circular sixth bind from the sixth engagement with the opponent's blade held in high line (that is the stage of one blade making contact with the other) is illustrated in figure 62. The movement is carried out from long distance and the introductory stage (the bind) takes place simultaneously with moving the front leg forward. The second position of the fencer on the left of the figure shows the bind after completion and the way in which the fencer's centre of gravity is advanced in order to facilitate the flèche.

The system of performing the parries and counter-attacks is the same in every exercise as in the case of simple and semicircular binds.

156

Fig. 63

Figure 63 presents the thrust proper executed as in foil fencing with flèche. The thrust is performed from preliminary sixth type of engagement and the flèche is carried out after the centre of gravity has been advanced.

## 4. Change binds

The relevant definition used in foil fencing—according to which the "change can be defined as the movement of the blade with which the fencer transfers his weapon from the prevailing engagement (or parry) to the opposite side and into another engagement (or parry) with a circular movement performed from his wrist; during the movement contact is broken between the two blades for a brief period"—applies to the respective material of épée fencing.

The principal objective of a change bind is to take the adversary by surprise from the side he has not expected an attack to come from.

The practical material that follows from the individual relations between the two blades is given in the following system:

*Change bind from the fencer's own engagement on the blade already kept engaged*

Change bind can be performed from medium distance.
(a) *As in foil fencing*

*On the opponent's blade held in high line from the fourth engagement Change sixth (third) bind and thrust*

In case the fencer binds his adversary's blade with the intention of performing a subsequent change, the first bind (which is the fourth bind in the present case) is only a sham-engagement. The overriding objective is to bring the opponent's blade under the fencer's control. This type of bind is more of a simple contact between the two weapons than a bind proper. The actual bind is effected with the second movement of the blade when, following the breaking of contact between the two blades, the fencer rounds his adversary's weapon from below by executing a circular movement and binds it on the sixth (third) side. The bind should be carried out in the same manner as described in the case of the simple, semicircular and circular binds.

The thrust can be executed to the lower part of the target and by adopting any of the three principal kinds of thrust.

Parries in the low line: simple second and change seventh.

*Counter-attacks*

Counter-attacks can take the form of thrusts of the following type:
1. Time degagement thrust carried out high and outside in order to avoid the change bind.
2. Change thrust from sixth bind executed high and outside.

3. Stop thrust in the final cadence on the adversary's concluding thrust. The stop thrust can be a low or a high one, depending on the direction of the thrust.

## Change fourth bind thrust from the sixth (third) engagement

From the technical point of view the movement executed from a preliminary sixth (third) contact follows in the same manner as described in the case of the sixth change bind.
Parries in the high line: simple fourth, change sixth (third) and flanconade, in the low line: simple second and change seventh.

## Counter-attacks

Counter-attacks can take the form of thrust of the following types:
1. Time degagement thrust carried out high and outside on the change.
2. Change thrust performed high and outside on the change.
3. Stop thrust in the final cadence on the opponent's concluding thrust. The stop thrust can be a high one or a low one, depending on the direction of the thrust.

## Change bind on the opponent's blade held in low line
## Change seventh bind thrust from the second (eighth) engagement

The adversary's blade is caught after it has been rounded from below, following a preliminary second (eighth) contact. The attack is performed with the seventh bind.
Parries adopted: simple seventh and change second.

*Counter-attacks*

Counter-attacks can take the form of thrusts of the following types:
1. Time degagement thrust on the change from below to the adversary's hand.
2. Change thrust from the seventh bind; it is a low thrust directed toward the hand.
3. Stop thrust on the opponent's concluding thrust.

*Change second (eighth) bind and thrust from the seventh engagement*

The opponent's blade is engaged after it has been rounded from above. The bind with second (eighth) is performed from the preliminary seventh contact between the two blades.
The following kinds of parries can be adopted: simple sixth (third) and change fourth.

*Counter-attacks*

Counter-attacks can take the form of thrusts of the following types:
1. Time degagement thrust on the change.
2. Change thrust performed from the second bind.
3. Stop thrust in the final cadence on the opponent's concluding thrust.
If the thrust is performed in the high line the stop thrust is carried out high and inside.
The exercises of parry, thrust and riposte and those of thrust, parry and thrust and counter-riposte are dependent on the concluding thrust and are identical with the exercises of bind thrust.

*Performing change second (eighth) bind thrust from the seventh engagement from long distance*

– With a step forward and lunge, or
– with flèche.

In both cases the first contact with the adversary's blade is made from on guard position. This initial bind is followed straight away by the change performed simultaneously with a step forward that is designed to reduce the distance. The movement is completed with a lunge or flèche, with the foot exercise gathering speed as the action gradually progresses.

*Performing change binds from the opponent's engagement on the binding blade*

It frequently occurs that the reaction on the part of the fencer to his adversary's engagement is not one of a bind, or he does not adopt a change thrust in an attempt to liberate his weapon from one completed engagement. Instead, his response is one of re-engagement with the double objective of increasing his own security and creating a new, more favourable position for himself. It is true that re-engagement can be effected on the side where the adversary's bind has been performed, but this is not always a wise step to take. The alternative solution is the change bind when, after giving way to the pressure exercised by the adversary's blade, the fencer executes a circular movement (analysed in detail in the case of change binds) around the plane of the binding weapon and brings it under control by executing a change bind on the opposite side. From the engagement thus carried out the attack can be advanced and completed in the same manner as described in connection with the methods adopted with binds and change binds.

*Change bind from high line*

Change bind carried out from medium distance as in foil fencing.

*Change sixth (third) bind and thrust on the opponent's fourth engagement*

It has been pointed out in the chapter on Binds that this relation between the two blades frequently occurs as a final position from which both fencers can initiate some kind of attacking actions. The most usual method of liberating the blade from engagement is to adopt a change thrust, but in case the plane of the bind is almost line-like, the fencer is advised to use the method of re-engagement as a response. Of the different solutions change bind is the one most frequently applied.

When performing a change bind from the opponent's fourth engagement, the fencer rounds the adversary's blade from below after yielding to the pressure it exerts and then he brings it under control by carrying out a sixth engagement. The attack can be advanced and the thrust can be completed by adopting any of the forms discussed in the chapter on Binds.

The following parries can be applied: semicircular second and destructing seventh.

*Counter-attacks*

Counter-attacks can take the form of thrusts of the following types:
1. Time degagement thrust performed on the change bind.
2. Change thrust performed from the sixth engagement.
3. Stop thrust carried out in the final cadence.

162

The thrusts can be executed low in the opponent's low finish, both outside and inside.

*Change fourth bind thrust on sixth (third) engagement*

So far as technique and methods are concerned this exercise should be carried out in the same manner as the preceding exercise.

The following parries should be adopted: in high line: simple fourth and circular sixth; in low line: simple second and semicircular seventh.

*Counter-attacks*

Counter-attacks can take the form of thrusts of the following types:
1. Time degagement thrust performed on the adversary's change bind.
2. Change thrust carried out from fourth engagement.
3. Stop thrust executed in the final cadence.

The thrusts can be performed high both inside and outside on the adversary's high concluding thrust, or low both outside and inside.

*Change bind from low line*

*Change seventh bind thrust in response to second and eighth*

This exercise should be executed in the same manner as when the attacks are performed from the high line.

Here the system of both the parries and counter-attacks is very much simplified because irrespective of the form adopted the attacks are concluded low.

The following parries should be adopted: simple seventh and circular second.

*Counter-attacks*

Counter-attacks can take the form of thrusts of the following types:

1. Time degagement thrust directed to the opponent's hand in response to his change bind.

2. Change thrust performed from below to the opponent's hand out of the seventh engagement.

3. Stop thrust carried out in the final cadence.

The thrusts can be executed in the low line, both inside and outside, on the adversary's concluding thrust.

*Change second (eighth) bind thrust in response to the seventh engagement*

This kind of attack is recommended for the tall competitor with strong physique against a shorter fencer with a weaker physical build-up; the difference in height offers favourable conditions for the taller épéeist.

The following parries should be adopted: in high line: semi-circular sixth (third) and destructing fourth.

## Counter-attacks

Counter attacks can take the form of the following types:
1. Time degagement thrust in response to the change bind.
2. Change thrust performed from the second engagement.
3. Stop thrust carried out in the final cadence on the adversary's concluding thrust.

### Change second (eighth) bind thrust in response to the seventh engagement, carried out from long distance

– With a step forward and lunge, or
– with flèche.

Taking into consideration the opponent's preliminary attempts at binding the fencer's blade (especially from long distance), this action is regarded as an "attack taken over" from the point of view of both execution and the jury.

This fact is of importance only from the aspect of analysing the actions, and has no part to play in the awarding of hits in épée fencing. Attacks should be concluded following binds and the establishment of momentary final positions on the basis of the principles discussed in the previous chapters.

### Simple and change binds performed from the line on the opponent's blade held in line

The material considered in the chapters on simple and change binds should serve as a basis for practising the movements indicated in the title of this paragraph. The only new element is in the relation between the two blades prior to launching the exercise, but the difference is not of a nature that would have any decisive influence on execution. In the initial stage of simple attacks introduced by bind the different variations of attacks on the opponent's offered line were considered. This was followed by the discussion of special situations in which the fencer's reaction to the bind by his adversary took the form of re-engagement or change bind.

In this section we shall deal with the possibilities of performing attacks when both fencers hold the blade in high or low line (or one in low, the other in high line). Attacks with change bind should be carried out from the different positions figuring in the system given below in the same manner as when they are executed from invito positions in the plane of the given line. The system of performing parries and counter-attacks made from the individual situations is also identical with attacks with simple and change binds, a point discussed in the previous paragraphs.

The system of the material is as follows:

*From high line on a blade held in high line*

When carried out from medium distance it can be of the following types:
- Simple fourth bind and thrust;
- Change sixth (third) bind and thrust.

*From high line on a blade held in low line*

It can be of the following types:
- Simple second (eighth) bind and thrust;
- Change seventh bind and thrust.

*From low line on a blade held in low line*

It can be of the following types:
– Simple seventh bind and thrust;
– Change second (eighth) bind and thrust.


*From low line on a blade held in high line*

It can be of the following types:
– Simple sixth (third) bind and thrust;
– Change fourth bind and thrust.
The parries to be adopted can be of the simple and change types.
The counter-attacks are of the same type as those used on simple and change binds.
Performing attacks from long distance.
– With a step forward and lunge,
– with flèche.
The methods of performing these types of attacks are completely identical with those of bind attacks carried out from invito on the blade held in line.
At the present stage of épée fencing the finish of the attacks can take any form except for feints and bind thrusts.
The exercises of parry, thrust and riposte, and thrust, parry and thrust and counter-riposte are identical with the exercises for simple attacks or those carried out with a change bind.

# VII. BIND THRUSTS

To use the wording common to foil fencing bind thrusts can be defined as those executed so that the two blades remain in contact from the moment they have been bound to the conclusion of the thrust. In respect of the methods of the technique of execution two thrusts of this type can be distinguished: the bind thrust known from foil fencing and the flanconade.

The first type can be carried out from every kind of engagement. Bind thrusts in épée fencing are very similar to those of the opposition type. Their value is enhanced by the fact that they provide for safer finish and that they can deflect the adversary's weapon more effectively than other thrusts. Bind thrusts enable the fencer to come fairly close to or in certain cases to establish active contact with that zone in which a parry from the initial position of engagement can be effected without need of a new transfer.

In practice the following types of bind thrusts can be distinguished: sixth (third), fourth, second (eighth) and seventh.

As its name indicates the flanconade is a thrust on the opponent's side. It is a bind thrust that grew up from the fourth and seventh engagements as such an extreme form in which, at the finish of the thrust, the fencer penetrates the area of the neighbouring parrying zone with his weapon. While he is doing so neither his fist, the guard of his weapon nor his engaged blade crosses the boundary of the zone of the original fourth or seventh engagement. Thus a sharp line of distinction is drawn between the flanconade and the transfers.

Bind thrusts bring us to the conclusion of a very important section of the technical material of épée fencing. The material to be considered in this chapter summarizes the possibilities of concluding thrusts both in attack and in defence.

Depending on the relative position of the blades, the methods of introducing bind thrusts offer possibilities identical with those common to engagements. Therefore it would be unreasonable to discuss them in detail here.

The principal points of executing bind thrusts are given below. They can be performed with
– simple engagement,
– semicircular engagement,
– circular engagement,
– change bind (carried out from the fencer's own engagement),
– change bind on the opponent's engagement,
– from line on a blade held in line.

The discussion in the subsequent paragraphs will be confined to the technical process that follows contact between the two blades.

*Attack on the high line*

*Fourth engagement followed by bind thrust*

From medium distance

The inside upper opening as well as the inside and outside surface of the upper arm constitute the fencing target.

The attack is launched, that is contact is made with the adversary's blade, in the same manner as described in the case of attacks performed with simple, semicircular, circular and change binds.

As a rule, bind thrusts are carried out on a weapon rigidly held in line. Bind is performed by exercising considerable pressure in order to keep the opponent's blade out of the limits of one's own target area throughout the whole action.

To this end the fencer's fist should move along a definite plane on the left-hand side throughout the thrust.
Performing fourth bind followed by bind thrust from long distance.

– With a step forward and lunge,
– with flèche.

This type of attack is initiated according to the same principles as those discussed in connection with attacks performed with simple bind. Following the reduction of the distance the movement should be carried out continuously either with lunge or with flèche in the same manner as described in the preceding chapters.

The following parries can be adopted: simple fourth and change sixth.

The exercises of parry, thrust and riposte are identical with the first exercise of the fourth bind and thrust.

The exercises of thrust, parry and thrust are the same as the corresponding exercises (from the first to the fourth exercise) of the fourth bind thrust.


*Counter-attacks*

Counter-attacks can take the form of thrusts of the following types:
1. Time degagement thrust performed high and outside.

2. Change thrust carried out high and outside.

3. Stop thrust executed in the final cadence. It can be performed high and inside with inquartata or angular thrust, or high and outside with time or angular thrust.


*Fourth flanconade*

From medium distance

The outside low opening (the opponent's side) and the adversary's thigh constitute the fencing target.

After contact has been made with the opponent's weapon it should be held with firm bind in temporary fourth position. This movement is followed by a semicircle performed from the forearm with which the adversary's blade is pressed downwards and to the left. The plane of the fencer's own blade should be lowered into the fifth position and below the horizontal line, with the point directed toward the opponent's side. Meanwhile, the high cross engagement of the blades should be maintained. Then with a powerful movement the fencer should advance his épée in the direction of the opening that has been made vulnerable. The fist is positioned low at the moment of the finish.

Fourth flanconade from long distance with

– a step forward and lunge,

– flèche.

This kind of attack should be performed according to the principles on which the exercises considered in the previous chapters are based.

The parries to be adopted are as follows: ceding fourth, opposition second and change seventh.

| Coach | Pupil |
|---|---|

### Exercise of parry, thrust and riposte

| | |
|---|---|
| Performs a flanconade from the fourth bind, directed to the outside lower opening of the target | Parries with an opposition second, change seventh or ceding fourth parry while taking a step backward in general. The parry is followed by a thrust and a subsequent bind riposte from on guard position either with lunge or flèche |

### Exercises of thrust, parry and thrust and counter-riposte

| Pupil | Coach |
|---|---|

### First exercise

| | |
|---|---|
| Performs fourth flanconade on the coach's blade held in high line | Parries with ceding parry and executes a riposte to the inside upper opening of the target |
| Parries the thrust with a simple fourth or change sixth parry from lunge or while resuming on guard position from lunge. The parry is followed by a thrust | |

| Pupil | Coach |
|---|---|

*Second exercise*

Carries out fourth flanconade on the coach's weapon held in high line

Parries the thrust with a simple sixth, third or change fourth parry either in lunge or while resuming on guard position from lunge. Following the parry he carries out a thrust followed by a riposte carried out with flèche from on guard position. If the thrust is in the high line, it is a sixth bind thrust and if it is in the low line, it is a fourth flanconade

Parries with a simple opposition second and performs a riposte to the inside upper opening target

*Counter-attacks*

Counter-attacks can take the form of thrust of the following types:
1. Time degagement thrust carried out high and outside on the bind.
2. Change thrust performed high and outside from finished bind.
3. Stop thrust in the final cadence on the opponent's concluding thrust.
   When it is performed low, imbroccata or angular thrust should

173

be executed instead of a simple second opposition thrust. If it is carried out high, an angular thrust directed toward the hand should be performed instead of a ceding fourth (inquartata is ruled out because the thrust is directed to the lower opening of the target).

*Sixth and third engagement followed by bind thrust*

From medium distance

The fencing target comprises the outside upper opening and the outside of the opponent's upper arm.

The attack should be launched and contact with the opponent's blade should be made in the same manner as described in the case of the simple sixth bind. If the kind of thrust used in foil fencing or the opposition type is adopted, the thrust is performed low to the outside lower opening of the target. As a result, the fencer's blade breaks away from the adversary's weapon (the contact between them is discontinued) at the moment of the finish. It must be underlined that the opposition type of thrust is by no means a general one from this kind of bind, and it is not at all characteristic of épée fencing, because holding the fist high is no more than the expression of the opposition tendency without opposition proper carried out in practice.

The bind thrust is the most generally adopted proceeding when the fencer seeks to complete his action after dominating his adversary's weapon from the moment contact is made between the two épées up to the point of scoring a hit. The first stage is the performance of engagement and while keeping the opponent's blade firmly under control, the fencer should allow the point of his weapon to sink until it is in line with the fencing target. The thrust should be carried out so that simultaneously

174

Fig. 64

The final stage of the sixth bind thrust to the adversary's upper arm is shown in figure 64. The thrust is carried out from the sixth bind, from medium distance and with half lunge.


with the finish, the adversary's weapon is rendered harmless. At the moment of completion the fist is held high on the right-hand side, but sometimes it occurs that the finish is carried out with a pressing movement the objective of which is to sink the fist under the plane of the corresponding shoulder.

The dotted line indicates the preceding position of the fencers.

From long distance with
  – a step forward and lunge, or
  – flèche.

There is no new element either in the way contact is made between the two blades or in the execution of the movement. It can never be emphasized too often that this is one of the most realistic and effective methods of execution; as such it is regarded as the key movement of épée fencing, one which can be performed successfully from any distance. The parries are: simple opposition sixth, ceding first and change fourth.

| Coach | Pupil |

*Exercises of parry, thrust and riposte*

*First exercise*

| | |
|---|---|
| Performs sixth bind thrust on his pupil's blade held in high line | Parries with a simple opposition sixth while taking a step backward, and after allowing for a cadence to elapse he carries out a bind thrust, then a riposte to the outside upper opening of the target. The thrust is executed from on guard position with a lunge or occasionally with flèche |

*Second exercise*

| | |
|---|---|
| Performs sixth bind thrust on his pupil's blade held in high line | Parries the thrust with a ceding first parry while taking a step backward. Following the parry he carries out a thrust or riposte from on guard position in a manner identical with that described in the case of the ceding parry. The thrust can be performed with a lunge or occasionally with flèche |

176

| Coach | Pupil |
|-------|-------|

### Third exercise

| | |
|---|---|
| Performs sixth bind thrust on his pupil's blade held in high line | Parries the thrust with change fourth while taking a step backward and then executes a thrust or riposte in the usual manner. The form of the finish can generally be one of opposition, bind thrust or flanconade |

### Exercises of thrust, parry and thrust and counter-riposte

| Pupil | Coach |
|-------|-------|

### First exercise

| | |
|---|---|
| Performs sixth bind thrust on the coach's blade held in high line | Parries the thrust with a simple opposition sixth and carries out a bind thrust to the outside upper opening of the target |
| Adopts a simple opposition sixth, change fourth or ceding first parry while resuming on guard position from lunge. After the parry he executes a thrust, a counter-riposte from every position and uses the most general form | |

| Pupil | Coach |
|---|---|

*Second exercise*

Performs sixth bind thrust on the high line

Parries the thrust with change fourth and carries out a riposte to the inside upper opening of the target

Parries with a simple fourth or change sixth while resuming on guard position from lunge, and from the parry he performs a thrust, then a counter-riposte (both of them of the bind type) either from on guard position or with lunge, or occasionally with flèche

*Third exercise*

Performs sixth bind thrust on the coach's blade held in high line

Parries the thrust with ceding first and carries out a riposte to the opponent's thigh placed in front

Adopts a simple second or change seventh while resuming on guard position from lunge. From the parry he executes a thrust then a counter-riposte (both of them of the bind type). The movement is carried out from on guard position or with a lunge

*Counter-attacks*

Counter-attacks can take the form of thrusts of the following types:
1. Time degagement thrust performed high and inside.
2. Change thrust executed high and inside.
3. Stop thrust carried out in the final cadence.

In high line: a sixth type of time thrust or angular thrust instead of a simple opposition sixth, inquartata or angular thrust inside instead of a change fourth;

in low line: a time thrust or angular thrust onto the inside of the opponent's hand inside instead of a ceding first.

*Third bind followed by bind thrust*

Performing third bind followed by bind thrust from medium distance

The outside upper opening, the head, chest and upper arm serve as the fencing target.

Contact with the opponent's blade should be made, the bind should be performed and the thrust should be carried out from the finished bind in accordance with the principles governing the third parry described in detail in the chapter on Parries.

The parries to be adopted and the related exercises are identical with the corresponding exercises of the sixth bind followed by bind thrust.

The system of counter-attacks is also identical with that adopted in the case of the sixth bind followed by bind thrust.

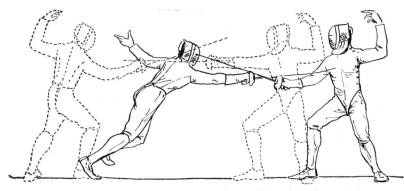

Fig. 65

The closing stage of the third bind thrust performed from the fencer's own third bind and from medium distance with a short flèche is presented in figure 65. The positions of both attacker and defender prior to the action are shown by the dotted lines.

*Attack on the low line*

*Second (eighth) bind and bind thrust*

Performing second (eighth) bind followed by bind thrust from medium distance

The outside low opening and the opponent's thigh placed in front of him act as the fencing target.

After contact has been made with the adversary's blade held in low line (with the fencer's fist held high and his hand lying in the second position), the thrust should be executed by directing the point of the weapon towards the outside lower opening or the opponent's thigh in front. In another practical and highly convenient method of execution the plane of the fencer's own blade is rotated from the second position of the hand into the fourth one simultaneously with the concluding movement. In the event of eighth bind the movement is launched with the hand in fourth position and the thrust is completed in a manner identical with that described above.

Fig. 66

The final position of the second bind thrust performed from the fencer's own second engagement and from medium distance with a lunge is illustrated in figure 66. The positions of attacker and defender prior to the movement are indicated by the dotted lines.


Performing second (eighth) bind followed by bind thrust from long distance with

– a step forward and lunge and
– flèche.

The parries to be adopted are as follows: simple opposition second, change seventh and ceding fourth. The parries used are thus identical with those of the fourth flanconade.

The exercises of parry and thrust and thrust, parry and thrust are the same as the corresponding exercises of the fourth flanconade.

The stop thrust actions are also identical with those of the fourth flanconade.

*Seventh bind followed by bind thrust*

From medium distance

The inside lower opening is the fencing target.

In foil fencing the movement adopted would be a bind thrust transferred into the sixth following a seventh engagement. The application of this form of action in épée fencing will be considered in the chapter on Transfers.

One kind of the seventh bind thrusts emerges on the margin

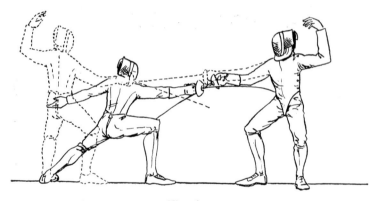

Fig. 67

The final position of the seventh bind thrust performed from the fencer's own seventh type of engagement and from medium distance with a lunge is shown in figure 67. The dotted lines show the position taken up by the attacking and defending fencers prior to the attack.

of the oppositional thrust, assuming the form discussed in the relevant general description. Its essence is that the opponent's blade is kept engaged throughout the whole movement from initial contact to the finish of the thrust. The point of the fencer's blade is lowered and points towards the adversary's armpit. The guard of the weapon is pressed upwards as the fist is being raised high on the left-hand side. The opponent's blade is completely deflected as the closing thrust is performed.

Performing seventh bind followed by bind thrust from long distance with

- a step forward and lunge, or
- flèche.

This is a highly natural, prudent action, and frequently adopted.

The parries to be adopted are as follows: simple seventh and change second.

The exercises of parry and thrust, counter-ripostes and stop thrusts are identical with those of the seventh bind thrust.


*Seventh flanconade*

From medium distance

The form established by the practice of épée fencing in the plane of the low line in the event of the seventh bind thrust is different from that adopted in foil fencing.

After contact has been made the adversary's weapon lying in the upper plane and on top of the fencer's blade is kept engaged with a subsequent upper cross bind and by turning the plane of the épée from the fourth position into the second one, the fencer presses his opponent's blade down to the low plane. The point of the fencer's weapon is directed obliquely upwards from below to point to his adversary's side. The finishing thrust is flanconade-like.

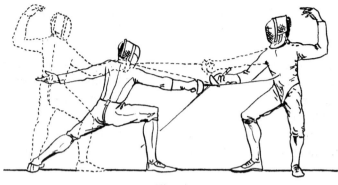

Fig. 68

The final position of the seventh flanconade (pressing down) performed from the fencer's own seventh engagement and from medium distance is presented in figure 68. The dotted lines indicate the positions of the two fencers prior to the attack.


Seventh flanconade from long distance with
  – a step forward and lunge, or
  – flèche.

Technically speaking, the attack with a step forward and lunge should be executed in the same manner as any of the actions introduced by a bind followed by thrust. After bringing the opponent's blade under control and reducing the distance the fencer concludes his attack in accordance with the principles described earlier for medium distance.

Bind thrusts carried out with flèche are rightly referred to as the key actions of épée fencing. That is why the coach should lay special emphasis on the related exercises. As a rule, the opponent's blade is brought under control in the course of taking a step forward, the movement introducing the flèche and forcing the adversary to retreat. If successfully executed the movement compels the opponent to foresake a safe position, and exercises a demoralizing effect. The fencer should take maximum advantage of this moment which is in fact a favourable tempo arising from his own tactics, in order to launch his flèche. The speed of the attack can thus reach its maximum and go hand in hand with the bind thrust that renders harmless any reflex counter-attacks.

Parries and counter-attacks performed on the attack rarely succeed because the attacker dominates the other weapon so powerfully that the opponent usually finds it virtually impossible to break away. Provided the fencer is capable of recognizing the attacker's intention of adopting this kind of attack in good time, it is best to avoid the bind in the very first stage of the movement. If the fencer fails to do so, then the recommended action is to reduce the distance or lengthen it to the extent of making it impossible for his opponent to finish his attack successfully.

In view of the special character of this action we dispense with discussion of the exercises of parry, thrust and counter-riposte.

# VIII. TRANSFERS

Since the concept and practice of transfers are wellknown from foil fencing, discussion will be confined to a brief summary of essentials.

"Transfer can be defined as a movement with the blade with which the opponent's weapon is moved from the fencer's own engagement into another type of engagement so that contact between the two blades is maintained during the whole process."

The methods of conducting the épée in every position following completed engagements have already been considered in connection with the attacks introduced by binds. Thus the only novelty here is the technique of executing the transfer from preliminary engagement.

According to their direction distinction can be made between semicircular and circular transfers.

The direction of semicircular transfers and the execution of the manipulation of the blade from a technical point of view are identical with the movements with the blade connected with semicircular transfers. In other words, there is no difference at all between the two systems.

# 1. Semicircular transfers

*Semicircular transfers of the blade held in high line*

*Second (eighth) transfer from the fourth engagement and thrust*

## From medium distance

The engagement should be performed in the same manner as in the case of attacks with simple binds. The transfer should be carried out without interrupting the contact between the two blades and the movement should be executed from the elbow. This enables the fencer to exercise heavy pressure on the opponent's weapon. Only as much movement should be performed from the wrist as is necessary for fixing the adversary's épée. This applies, above all, to the concluding movement.

Following the completion of the transfer the thrust can be carried out in two directions:

Fig. 69

Semicircular second transfer performed from the fencer's own fourth engagement and at close quarters is illustrated in figure 69.

187

– Low bind thrust and
– high thrust executed in the same manner as though a second
or eighth bind had been performed.
The thrust proper can be executed as in foil fencing, with
opposition and with angular thrust.

Performing the transfer and thrust from long distance with
– a step forward and lunge, or
– flèche.
When attacks are made with transfer from long distance, the
opponent's blade should be engaged simultaneously with the
step forward, that is contact between the two blades should be
made at the moment the foot in front is moved forward, and
the transfer should take place simultaneously with the rear foot
stamping on the piste. The lunge or the flèche is preceded by the
direction of the blade. The blade is advanced and the thrust is
completed with the assistance of the foot exercise only.
The following parries can be adopted:
If the thrust is directed towards the upper opening of the
target, simple sixth (third) and change fourth.
In case of bind thrust on the low line opposition second, ceding fourth or change seventh should be used.


*Exercises of parry, thrust and riposte*

In the high plane they are identical with the exercises given
in connection with the second bind and thrust.
The exercises of the low bind thrust are the same as those of
the second bind thrust and fourth flanconade.

*Exercises of thrust, parry and thrust and counter-riposte*

The exercises performed from the parries executed by the coach and his pupil depend on whether the action carried out from the parry concerned is completed high or low.

In the event of high finish the exercises are identical with those of the second bind and thrust, whereas in the case of low finish the exercises should correspond to those of the second (eighth) bind thrust and fourth flanconade.

*Counter-attacks*

Counter-attacks can take the form of thrusts of the following types:

1. There is no time degagement thrust.
2. Change thrust should be performed high and outside to the whole surface of the arm from shoulder to wrist.
3. Stop thrust carried out in the final cadence.

In high line: sixth time and angular thrust instead of the simple sixth thrust, inquartata and angular thrust instead of the change fourth; in low line: imbroccata or high angular thrust instead of the opposition second thrust, inquartata and high angular thrust instead of a ceding fourth thrust, time thrust performed inside instead of the change seventh thrust.

*Seventh transfer and thrust from the sixth engagement*

From medium distance

Engagements of the sixth are key épée-fencing movements. Both the efficiency of the engagement and the safety of the finish can be enhanced if the opponent's blade is transferred from

189

such engagement positions into the seventh position with a semicircular movement. The transfer from preliminary sixth bind should be performed so that the adversary's blade already brought under control is held engaged by the forte of the fencer's blade and the guard of his weapon as his arm with his elbow straightened out slightly is raised above the plane of the fencer's left shoulder. This follows a powerful semicircular movement executed by the wrist.

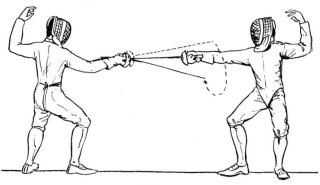

Fig. 70

The semicircular seventh transfer performed from the fencer's own sixth engagement and at close quarters is shown in figure 70.

The finish of the thrust can take the form of a thrust as in foil fencing, one of opposition, angular and bind thrust.

Performing seventh transfer and thrust from the sixth engagement from long distance with
 – a step forward and lunge, or
 – flèche.
The action should be carried out in accordance with the principles described in the case of the fourth and second transfer.

The parries to be adopted are as follows: simple seventh and change second.

The exercises of parry and thrust, counter-riposte and stop thrust are identical with those of the seventh bind thrust.

*On the low line*

*Fourth transfer and thrust from the second (eighth) bind*

Performing the transfer and thrust from medium distance

This is an action used rather infrequently in practice because of the risk in the opponent's blade moved inwards and closer to the target offered by the fencer from preliminary second type of engagement. It presents a formidable threat to the attacker. In carrying out this transfer the fencer must exercise the maximum care to ensure that the adversary's blade is prevented from breaking away from the engagement. To this end the opponent's weapon should be transferred from a completely finished second engagement with a rapid and firm semicircular movement performed powerfully from the wrist and backed up by the forearm so that there should be no interruption in the continuity of the movement as the opponent's blade is passed across the face of the target.

Following completion of the transfer the fencer can adopt any of a wide variety of thrusts. Depending on whether he is to perform his thrust high or low it can be a thrust as in foil fencing, one of opposition, angular thrust, high bind thrust or flanconade.

Performing the transfer and thrust from long distance with
  – a step forward and lunge, or
  – flèche.

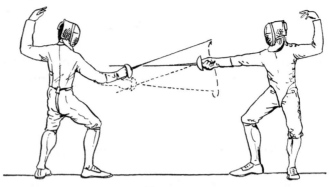

Fig. 71

Figure 71 shows the semicircular fourth transfer performed from the fencer's own eighth engagement and at close quarters.

Normally, the attack is introduced by an eighth bind. The engagement is prolonged with a step forward. The transfer is carried out by the arm moved from the shoulder, and the thrust is advanced either by the lunge or by the flèche, with the point of the blade directed to the adversary's shoulder. At the finish, opposition is adopted by the fist to the left so that the opponent's blade is totally deflected. No other form of thrust is advisable in this case.

The parries to be adopted are as follows:

in high line: simple fourth and change sixth (third); in low line: opposition second, ceding fourth and change seventh.

*Exercises of parry, thrust and riposte*

When the movement is carried out high, the exercises are identical with those of the fourth bind thrust. If performed low, they correspond to those of the fourth flanconade.

The exercises of thrust, parry and thrust and of counter-riposte are much the same as those discussed in connection with the fourth engagement and fourth flanconade.

## Counter-attacks

Counter-attacks can take the form of thrusts of the following types:

1. No time degagement thrust is adopted.
2. Change thrust should be performed high and outside to the inside part of the outside target, and angular thrust can also be used.
3. Stop thrust carried out in the final cadence.
The latter can be performed
in high line: inquartata and angular thrust executed inside instead of a simple fourth time thrust carried out outside and low, angular thrust instead of a change sixth;
in low line: imbroccata and angular thrust instead of the opposition second,
inquartata and angular thrust instead of the ceding fourth,
time thrust executed inside and low instead of change seventh thrust.

## From the sixth engagement sixth (third) transfer and thrust

From medium distance

This is a very useful and frequently adopted action. The attack should be started from the completed seventh engagement by the wrist which is moved outwards to the right. This will cause the opponent's blade to glide to the guard of the

Fig. 72

fencer's own weapon. The adversary's épée thus fixed is then transferred into sixth or third bind with a semicircular movement performed with the forearm. The finish can be low or high bind thrust.

The semicircular sixth transfer executed from the fencer's own seventh engagement and at close quarters is shown in figure 72. Performing the transfer and thrust from long distance with
 – a step forward and lunge, or
 – flèche.
 Performance of this action is generally successful irrespective of the kind of execution adopted.
 The following parries can be adopted:
in low line: simple second (eighth) and change seventh;
in high line: simple opposition sixth (third), change fourth and ceding first.

If the finish is executed low, the exercises are identical with those of the sixth bind thrust.

If the finish is performed high, they are the same as those of the sixth bind thrust.

## Counter-attacks

Counter-attacks can take the form of thrusts of the following types:

1. There is no time degagement thrust.
2. Change thrust should be performed high and inside to the inside upper opening of the target and to the opponent's arm.
3. Stop thrust executed in the final cadence.

The latter can be carried out:

in high line: sixth time thrust instead of simple opposition, sixth inquartata instead of change fourth, time thrust executed inside and low instead of ceding first; in low line: imbroccata instead of simple second and time thrust performed inside instead of change seventh.

# 2. Circular transfers

In the case of circular transfers the fencer's blade is moved back into the starting position after describing a complete circle. Contact between the two blades is maintained throughout the circular movement.

The material of circular transfers will not be discussed in detail because the action subsequent to the transfer and the exercises that can be performed from the individual positions are identical with those considered in connection with the semi-circular transfers. There is no difference at all between the two systems.

*Circular fourth transfer and thrust carried out from fourth engagement*

The parries to be adopted and the counter-attacks are the same as those of the semicircular transfers from second into fourth engagement.

*Circular second transfer and thrust from second (eighth) engagement*

The parries and the counter-attacks are identical with the corresponding actions of semicircular transfers from fourth into second engagement.

*Circular sixth (third) transfer and thrust from sixth (third) engagement*

The parries and the counter-attacks are the same as those of the semicircular transfers from seventh into sixth engagement.

*Circular seventh transfer and thrust from seventh engagement*

The parries to be adopted and the counter-attacks are identical with the corresponding semicircular transfers from sixth into seventh engagement.

# IX. BEATS

Beat can be defined as an attack on the blade with the objective of forcing the adversary's weapon out of line. An additional object of the beat is to cause the opponent to loosen his hold on the weapon, thus making it more difficult for him to perform a parry.

The beat should be powerful, short, limited and dry.

A beat is powerful if it achieves the objective of moving the opponent's weapon out of line or causes the adversary to loosen his hold. It is short if it cannot be avoided. It is limited if the fencer's weapon comes to a stop at the point where the opponent's blade was positioned before the beat. It is "dry" when the two blades meet at one point only.

Beats are named according to the invitos on which they are performed. There are fourth, sixth (third), second (eighth) and seventh (first) beats.

Regarding the relations between the two blades, beats can be carried out

*(a)* on a blade held in line,

*(b)* on a blade outside the line.

In the course of instruction the exercises belonging to points *(a)* and *(b)* can run parallel since they are related exercises. It is common to both of them that the exercises of parry, parry and thrust and counter-riposte are identical in both types of attack.

## Beats on a blade held in line

They can be performed
1. from invito on a blade held in line,
2. with a semicircular movement,
3. with a circular movement,
4. from the fencer's own engagement on an engaged blade (simple and change beats),
5. from line on a blade held in line.

## Beats on a blade held outside the line

They can be performed
6. from the opponent's engagement on a blade about to engage,
7. from invito and from line on a blade held in invito.

From medium distance the beats are carried out from on guard position and the lunge is performed simultaneously with thrust following the beat. When the attack is performed from long distance, the beat is executed as the fencer's right leg is straightened out for the step forward.

Beat attacks on the blade are much less frequent in épée than in foil fencing. The underlying reason is that the grip with which the blade is held in épée is much firmer than the hold adopted in foil fencing. Beats are generally used with the purpose of loosening the opponent's grip, preparing or introducing attacks. They serve as a kind of reconnaissance. Bind is a more frequent method of executing attacks.

The beat induces a rapid defensive reflex on the part of the adversary. This fact can be used to maximum advantage in the course of tactical preparation.

There are several similarities between beats and binds. These will be referred to from time to time during further discussion.

# 1. Simple beats from invito on the blade held in line

*Simple beats from invito on a blade held in high line*

*Performing fourth beat thrust from sixth (third) invito*

From medium distance

The fencer should rotate the plane of his weapon into the fifth position of the hand and in the direction of the fourth. While rotating his épée, the fencer should execute a brief, limited and energetic beat on the middle of his adversary's blade. The movement should be performed from the forearm and the weapon should be conducted powerfully by the wrist. The épée directed for the thrust and positioned shoulder high is then advanced with the lunge towards the inside upper opening of the target, and towards the upper arm of the opponent after he has widened the distance by retreating from the attack. At the finish the fencer's fist should be held high on the left-hand side.

The parries to be adopted are as follows:
in high line: simple fourth and change sixth;
in low line: simple second and change seventh.

The parries listed above are identical with those used in the case of fourth bind thrust. The general technique of execution is also the same as the method described in the chapter on Parries. However, it must be noted here that executions different from the general technique but corresponding to the special character of the beat are frequently adopted and successfully so if they are suited to the competitor's individual talent and reflexes. Such parries should be followed straight away by the riposte so that the thrust can be completed before the adversary recovers from the beat's effect in loosening his grip.

The fencer is advised to carry out his riposte along the shortest path and in the direction of the part of the target left open from every kind of parry executed with beat. The finish can be the same as in foil fencing, or one of opposition or an angular thrust.

Every version and form of finish can be applied from what are described as gliding parries.

The exercises of parry, thrust, riposte and counter-riposte are almost completely identical with those discussed in connection with the fourth bind thrust. They differ from one another in respect of certain special features that must be taken into account.

*Counter-attacks*

Counter-attacks can take the form of thrusts of the following types:
1. Time degagement thrust in order to avoid the beat.
2. Stop thrust performed on the opponent's closing thrust in the final cadence.
The latter can be carried out
in high line: inside or outside in the event of the thrust, directed to the upper part;
in low line: inside or outside in the case of thrusts directed towards the lower opening of the target.

*Performing sixth (third) beat thrust from the fourth invito*

*Performing sixth (third) beat thrust from the second (eighth) invito*

In both cases the beat is directed outside to the right-hand side. During the movement the fencer's fist can be in fourth position, that is with his palm pointing upwards, but a more powerful beat can be achieved in the direction of the third with the fist held in the sixth position. The main force necessary for rotating the wrist both rapidly and powerfully is supplied by the forearm. The thrust subsequent to the beat is directed towards the outside lower opening of the target. Sometimes when the thrust is an indirect one, the blade is directed to the outside upper opening. After the completed thrust the fist is positioned high on the right-hand side.

The following parries can be adopted:
in low line: simple second and change seventh;
in high line: simple sixth and change fourth.

The exercises of parry, thrust and riposte, thrust, parry and thrust and counter-riposte are completely identical with those of the sixth bind thrust.

Obviously modifications are necessary if the attack finishes on the upper side.


## Counter-attacks

Counter-attacks can take the form of thrusts of the following types:
1. Time degagement thrust in order to avoid a sixth beat.
2. Stop thrust executed on the adversary's concluding thrust in the last cadence.

The latter can be carried out
in low line: outside or inside in the case of low finishes;
in high line: outside or inside if the thrust is high and "indirect".

*Simple beats from invito on a blade held in low line*

*Performing second (eighth) beat thrust from sixth (third) invito*

*Performing second (eighth) beat thrust from seventh invito*

From medium distance

The beat is directed downwards and outwards to the right-hand side and the fencer's fist is held in second or fifth position. The thrust proper can be completed with the hand in second or fourth position. It can be performed outside and low to the adversary's hip or thigh corresponding to the hand holding the weapon, or it can be executed in the same manner as in the event of engagement: high to the inside upper opening of the target, that is the upper part of the opponent's trunk or the upper surface of his arm holding the épée. After the finish the fencer's fist should be held high on the right-hand side.
The following parries can be adopted:
in low line: simple second (eighth), change seventh and change first;
in high line: simple sixth (third) and change fourth.

*Exercises of parry, thrust and riposte*

In the event of low finish the exercises are the same as those in connection with the sixth bind thrust or beat thrust.

When the finish is a high one, the exercises are identical with those of the sixth bind thrust.

The exercises of thrust, parry and thrust and counter-riposte are much the same as those described in connection with the sixth bind thrust and the bind thrust.

## Counter-attacks

Counter-attacks can take the form of thrusts of the following types:

1. Time degagement thrust in order to avoid second (eighth) beat.
2. Stop thrust performed in the final cadence on the opponent's concluding thrust.

The latter can be carried out

in high line: outside or inside on the concluding thrust executed high;

in low line: outside or inside on the concluding thrust performed low.


### Performing seventh beat thrust from second (eighth) type invito

The plane of the blade should be rotated into fourth or fifth position. The adversary's weapon should be forced out of the line with a beat directed upwards to the left-hand side from below and performed with an arm held loose. The thrust should be carried out to the inside low opening of the target or the opponent's thigh in front, and then to the lower surface of the wrist lying below the guard of the épée. The fencer should conduct his blade on the left-hand side along a medium high or high plane compared to the adversary's weapon.

The following parries can be adopted: simple seventh and change second (eighth).

The exercises of parry, thrust, riposte and thrust, parry and thrust and counter-riposte are identical with the corresponding exercises of the seventh bind thrust.

Counter-attacks can take the form of thrusts of the following types:

1. Time degagement thrust in order to avoid seventh beat.
2. Stop thrust executed in the final cadence low and outside or inside on the opponent's low concluding thrust.

Performing the beat thrust from long distance with a step forward and lunge

When this movement is exercised from long distance the beat should take place simultaneously with the forward movement of the fencer's right foot. The final directing of the blade for the thrust should be effected at the moment the left foot makes contact with the piste as the concluding stage of the step forward. The finish should be performed in the same manner as when the thrust is carried out from medium distance.

Performing the beat thrust from long distance with flèche

If the flèche is introduced with a step forward, the beat is somewhat delayed, that is it should be performed at the moment, preceding the flèche, which is actually the ultimate stage of reducing the distance.

When the flèche is launched from on guard position, the beat should be executed at the moment the advance of the body's point of gravity is being completed. In this case the blade should be directed towards well visible surfaces instead of a particular point.

## 2. Semicircular beats from invito on the blade held in line

*Semicircular beats can be performed on a blade held against the low line:*

– semicircular seventh beat thrust from the sixth (third) invito,
– semicircular second (eighth) beat thrust from the fourth invito;

*against the upper line:*

– semicircular sixth (third) beat thrust from the seventh invito,
– semicircular fourth beat thrust from the second invito.
The above movements can be carried out
1. From medium distance
Technically speaking, the exercises should be performed in the same manner as those of the simple beats. The direction is a semicircular one irrespective of the final position the beat is carried out from.
2. From long distance
– with a step forward and lunge,
– with flèche.

They should be performed in the same manner as described in the corresponding paragraphs on simple beats. Parries and counter-attacks are similar to those used in the case of simple beats.

## 3. Circular beats from invito on the blade held in line

*Circular beats can be performed on a blade held in high line:*

– circular fourth beat thrust from the fourth invito,
– circular sixth (third) beat thrust from the sixth (third) invito;

– circular second (eighth) bind thrust from the second (eighth) invito,

– circular seventh beat thrust from the seventh invito.

The above movements can be carried out

1. From medium distance

As the beat is completed the fencer's blade, which has described a circle as a result of a circular movement performed from the wrist, is back in the initial position from which the action started.

2. From long distance

– with a step forward and lunge,

– with flèche.

Execution of these exercises does not involve any element other than those described in previous paragraphs.

Both the parries and counter-attacks are identical with those discussed in the chapter on Simple Beats.

## 4. Change beats from the fencer's own bind on the blade engaged

*Change beats can be performed on a blade held*

*in high line:*

– change sixth (third) beat thrust from the fourth engagement,

– change fourth beat thrust from the sixth (third) engagement;

*in low line:*

– change seventh beat thrust from the second (eighth) engagement,
– change second (eighth) beat thrust from the seventh engagement.

The above movements can be carried out

1. From medium distance

All the above types of change beats can be performed on the same side as that of the engagement. In this case the engagement is interrupted by lifting the blade with a movement from the wrist and the beat is carried out on the line thus left open to attack in the same manner as when the beat is executed from invito on a blade held in line.

The bind preceding the change can be performed in a manner identical with the execution of the engagement in the case of attacks with change bind. The engagement is interrupted as the blade is conducted by the wrist from the engagement and around the opponent's blade in the direction of the beat. The adversary's weapon is forced out of the line by adopting the technique described in the case of simple beats in order to create an opening for the finish of the attack.

2. From long distance
– with a step forward and lunge,
– with flèche.

In both cases the opponent's blade should be engaged from on guard position and the beat should be performed simultaneously with the inclining forward of the body to facilitate the step forward or the flèche as the case may be. The finish is identical with that adopted in the case of simple beat attacks.

The parries to be used are also the same as those of simple beat attacks.

Counter-attacks can take the form of thrusts of the following types:

1. Time degagement thrust on the change.
2. Stop thrust carried out in the final cadence on the opponent's concluding thrust.

## 5. Simple and change beats from the line on the blade held in line

*From upper line on a blade held in upper line:*

It can be of the following types:
– simple fourth beat thrust,
– change sixth (third) beat thrust.

*From upper line on a blade held in low line:*

It can be of the following types:
– simple second (eighth) beat thrust,
– change seventh beat thrust.

*From low line on a blade held in low line:*

– simple seventh beat thrust,
– change second (eighth) beat thrust.

*From low line on a blade held in upper line:*

- simple sixth (third) beat thrust,
- change fourth beat thrust.

From medium distance

When an attack is performed from the line on a blade held in line, there are no new exercises from a technical point of view because the relevant parrying system is identical with the system of attacks on the line, a question considered earlier.

The only minor new element to be detected is the position of the blade preceding the launching of an attack. But the line position of the fencer to be attacked renders the exercises identical with all the actions in which the defending fencer held his weapon in line, irrespective of the previous position of the attacker's épée.

The parries to be adopted are the same as those corresponding to the plane of the line concerned. This point was also discussed earlier.

The exercises of parry, thrust and riposte and those of the counter-riposte are identical with those of attacks on a blade held in line.

*Counter-attacks*

Counter-attacks can take the form of thrusts of the following types:
1. Time degagement thrust which can be used on every occasion.
2. Stop thrust carried out in the final cadence. It can be performed high or low, depending on the opponent's concluding thrust.
Performing the attacks listed previously from long distance

– with a step forward and lunge,
– with flèche.

From a technical aspect their execution is identical with that adopted in the event of attacks introduced by simple and semi-circular beats.

## 6. Change beats from the opponent's engagement on the engaging blade

*Attacks performed from high line*

*Performing change sixth (third) beat thrust on the fourth bind*

From medium distance

The relative position of the blades is much the same as in the case of binds when the fencer was recommended to adopt change bind in reply to his opponent's flat, line-type of engagement. In the present case the attack with change beat is used on a steep blade whose button points upwards.

The change or more exactly the rounding of the plane of the binding blade is carried out from the opponent's preliminary fourth engagement in the same manner as in bind attacks. The favourable angle for executing the beat is provided by the adversary's weapon that points upwards. As a rule, the outside upper part of the target is most vulnerable for the concluding thrust, but sometimes it is possible to carry out the thrust on the lower section of the target. The parries are adopted accordingly.

The following parries can be adopted:

in high line: simple sixth (third), circular fourth and ceding first;

in low line: semicircular second (eighth) and destructing seventh.

*Exercises of parry, thrust and riposte*

If they are performed high, they are identical with those of sixth bind thrust.

When they are executed low, they are the same as the exercises of the sixth bind thrust.

The exercises of thrust, parry and thrust and counter-riposte are also identical with those of the sixth bind thrust and bind thrust.

*Counter-attacks*

Counter-attacks can take the form of thrusts of the following types:

1. Time degagement thrust on the change carried out high and inside.

2. Stop thrust performed in the final cadence.

It can be executed

in high line: time thrust carried out inside or outside on the opponent's concluding thrust;

in low line: time thrust carried out inside or outside on the opponent's concluding thrust.

*Performing change fourth beat and thrust from the sixth (third) engagement*

This is a highly rational and effective movement and as such is frequently adopted. The change should be performed as if it were executed from the fencer's own sixth engagement. The angle for the beat is more favourable than when the attack is carried out on the line. Following the beat the thrust should be directed towards the inside upper opening of the target and the opponent's arm corresponding to the weapon. The thrust can be as in foil fencing, either an opposition or an angular thrust.

The parries to be adopted are as follows: simple fourth, circular sixth (third) and semicircular seventh.

The exercises of parry, thrust and riposte and thrust followed by parry, thrust and counter-riposte are completely identical with those of the fourth bind and thrust.


### Counter-attacks

Counter-attacks can take the form of thrusts of the following types:
1. Time degagement thrust performed high and outside on the change.
2. Stop thrust carried out in the final cadence.
The latter can be executed
in high line: time thrust performed inside or outside;
in low line: time thrust performed inside or outside.


### Attacks performed from low line

*Performing change seventh beat and thrust from the second (eighth) engagement*

The change beat should be performed in the same manner as from the fencer's own second bind. The finish is also identical with the concluding stage of the seventh beat and thrust carried out from the fencer's own engagement.

The parries to be adopted are as follows: simple seventh and circular second (eighth).

The exercises of parry, thrust and riposte and thrust followed by parry, thrust and counter-riposte are the same as those of the seventh beat thrust performed from the fencer's own engagement, the only difference being that in the present case the defending fencer should adopt circular second parry instead of a change second.

*Counter-attacks*

Counter-attacks can take the form of thrusts of the following types:
1. Time degagement thrust executed low on the opponent's hand.
2. Stop thrust carried out in the final cadence.

*Performing change second (eighth) beat thrust to the opponent's seventh engagement*

This type of movement is recommended only in case the opponent binds the blade held in low line deep in the plane of the low line and, as a result, an angle favourable for the beat is offered.

The beat should be carried out in the same manner as from the fencer's own seventh engagement. Following the attack on the blade the thrust can be performed high or low on the part of the target left open. The parries to be adopted by the defending fencer depend on the adversary's concluding thrust.

The following parries can be used:
in high line: semicircular sixth (third) and destructing fourth;
in low line: simple second and circular seventh.

| Pupil | Coach |
|---|---|

*Exercises of parry, thrust and riposte*

*First exercise*

| | |
|---|---|
| Binds with seventh engagement the coach's blade held in low line | Performs change second beat thrust to the inside upper opening of the target |

Adopts semicircular sixth or destructing fourth parry in on guard position or while taking a step backward. For the concluding thrust from every type of parry the most practical form should be selected

*Second exercise*

| | |
|---|---|
| Binds coach's blade held in low line with the seventh engagement | Performs change second beat thrust low to the outside low opening of the target |

Adopts simple opposition second or circular seventh parry in on guard position or while taking a step backward. The most practical form should be selected for the finish

214

| Coach | Pupil |
|---|---|

*Exercises of thrust, parry and thrust and counter-riposte*

### First exercise

| | |
|---|---|
| Binds pupil's blade held in low line with seventh engagement | Performs change second beat thrust to the upper opening of the target |
| Parries semicircular sixth and ripostes to the low opening | Adopts simple second or change seventh parry. Selects the most practical form of finish |

### Second exercise

| | |
|---|---|
| Binds pupil's blade held with seventh engagement in low line | Carries out change second beat thrust to the outside upper opening of the target |
| Performs high bind thrust from semicircular sixth parry | Adopts simple opposition sixth, change fourth or ceding first parry. Selects the most convenient form of finish |

### Third exercise

| | |
|---|---|
| Binds with seventh engagement pupil's blade held in low line | Carries out change second beat thrust into the outside high opening of the target |

215

| Coach | Pupil |
|---|---|
| Performs high riposte from destructing fourth parry | Parries the thrust with simple fourth or change sixth. Selects the most practical form of finish |

## Fourth exercise

| Coach | Pupil |
|---|---|
| Binds pupil's blade held in low line with the seventh engagement | Performs change second beat thrust to the outside upper opening of the target |
| Carries out a low riposte with flanconade from the fourth destructing parry | Adopts simple opposition second, change seventh or ceding fourth parry. Selects the most practical form of finish |

## Fifth exercise

| Coach | Pupil |
|---|---|
| Binds pupil's blade held in low line with seventh engagement | Performs change second beat thrust to the outside lower opening of the target |
| Parries the thrust with simple second opposition parry and performs a riposte to the higher part of the target | Adopts simple sixth or change fourth parry. Selects the most convenient solution for the finish |

| Coach | Pupil |
|---|---|

*Sixth exercise*

| | |
|---|---|
| Binds pupil's blade held in low line with seventh engagement | Performs change second beat thrust to the outside lower opening of the target |
| From simple second parry executes a low bind thrust | Adopts simple opposition second, change seventh or ceding fourth parry. Selects the most practical type of thrust for the finish |

*Seventh exercise*

| | |
|---|---|
| Binds pupil's blade held in low line with seventh engagement | Carries out change second beat thrust to the outside low opening of the target |
| Performs a low thrust from circular seventh parry | Parries the thrust with simple seventh or change. Selects the most practical form of finish |

*Counter-attacks*

Counter-attacks can take the form of thrusts of the following type:
1. Time degagement thrust performed high on the change beat.
2. Stop thrust on the adversary's concluding thrust in the final cadence.

217

The latter can be executed
in high line: outside or inside in the case of high finishes;
in low line: outside or inside in the event of low finishes.

## 7. Beats from invito (or on guard position) and from the line on the blade held in invito (on guard position)

All the exercises in which the opponent is in a position lying outside the line are related exercises and as such they can be regarded as parallel ones from the point of view of analysing the action, irrespective of the preceding position of the attacker's blade. The parrying system is determined in every case by the position of the defending fencer's weapon outside the line prior to the attack.

The exercises listed in the title of the present chapter according to the preceding position of the attacker's blade can be of a novel character only from the point of view of launching an attack. The fundamental exercises of the fencing lesson from the different positions, however, are identical with those discussed in the chapter on Change beats from the opponent's engagement on the engaging blade, where the weapon of the fencer subject to attack is forced out of the line as a result of preliminary bind.

Here the same thing is valid as for instance in the case of attacks carried out on a blade held in high line. The essence of the exercise is not altered by the fact that the attack is performed from the sixth on guard position, invito, second, fourth position, high or low line or perhaps from the fencer's own engagement. The parrying system to be adopted is determined exclusively by the previous position of the defending fencer's blade and the direction in which the attack is performed. This has been proved by all the exercises that have been adopted to date.

Only the versions that result in a different position of the blade from the point of view of launching an attack compared to the given line position will be discussed in the present chapter.

*Performing beats on the sixth (third) invito (or on guard position)*

They can be of the following types:
– simple sixth beat and thrust from the fourth invito,
– semicircular fourth beat and thrust from the eighth invito,
– destructing fourth beat and thrust from the seventh invito,
– simple fourth beat and thrust from the sixth invito,
– simple fourth beat and thrust from high line,
– change, fourth beat and thrust from low line.

*Performing beats on the fourth invito (or on guard position)*

They can be of the following types:
– simple sixth beat and thrust from the fourth invito,
– simple sixth beat and thrust from the eighth invito,
– semicircular sixth beat and thrust from the seventh invito,
– circular sixth beat and thrust from the sixth invito,
– simple sixth beat and thrust from low line,
– simple sixth beat and thrust from high line.

*Performing beats on the second (eighth) invito (or on guard position)*

They can be of the following types:

- semicircular second (eighth) beat and thrust from the fourth invito,
- simple seventh beat and thrust from the eighth invito,
- circular second beat and thrust from the second invito,
- simple second beat and thrust from the seventh invito,
- simple second beat and thrust from the sixth invito,
- simple second beat and thrust from high line,
- change second beat and thrust from low line.

*Performing beats on the seventh invito (or on guard position)*

They can be the following:
- semicircular sixth beat and thrust from the fourth invito,
- simple sixth beat and thrust from the eighth invito,
- simple second beat and thrust from the seventh invito,
- simple second beat and thrust from the sixth invito,
- change sixth beat and thrust from high line,
- simple sixth beat and thrust from low line.

While considering attacks initiated with a beat on the blade positioned outside the line no mention will be made of the exercises designed to cause the opponent's weapon lying outside the line to move back to the line while an attack is being performed. Any activity of this kind would be diametrically opposed to the previous definition according to which the primary objective of the beat is to deflect the adversary's épée held in line.

The correct thing to do is to widen the existing opening with the beat on the blade and to cause the opponent to loosen his hold on the weapon. To this end the beat should always be performed in the direction in which the opponent's weapon outside the line is moving. The variations of the finish are identical with those described in the chapter on Change beats from the opponent's engagement on the engaging blade.

The exercises of parries, parry and thrust, riposte, thrust, parry and thrust and counter-riposte are also the same as those given in the chapter referred to above. The coach is advised to conduct parallel exercises as early as at the initial stages of instruction.


*Counter-attacks*

They should be adjusted to the opponent's concluding thrust and therefore identical in every case with the stop thrust exercises carried out on the opponent's bind.


From long distance with
– a step forward and lunge,
– flèche.
Inclusion of the novel element discussed in the present chapter is not only made possible by the special character of the épée but it is also a necessity. Performance of attacks of this type is both rational and promising from every distance.

# X. TIME DEGAGEMENT THRUSTS

Time degagement thrust can be defined as a movement of the blade designed to avoid (go round) the adversary's weapon about to bind or beat the fencer's own blade before contact is made and to perform a thrust to the nearest opening target. The method of execution is completely identical with that of the change thrust. This serves as a preliminary exercise for feint attacks since feint can be termed as the indication of a thrust followed by circumvention of one or more subsequent parries. That is why it is advisable to practise this movement immediately before instruction in feint attacks.

So far time degagement thrusts have been considered in connection with counter-attacks performed in the course of attacks on the blade. Execution has been analysed at length in foil fencing so it is unnecessary to deal with them in any detail in épée fencing.

# 1. Time degagement thrusts on simple binds

*Time degagement thrusts from high line*

*Performing time degagement thrust on the fourth beat or bind*

From medium distance

The parries used can be: simple sixth (third), circular fourth and destructing seventh.

The exercises of parry, thrust, riposte and counter-riposte are identical with those of change thrust carried out from the fourth engagement.

*Counter-attacks*

They can be time thrusts performed in the final cadence (from fourth position), high or low, outside or inside, depending on the adversary's concluding thrust.

*Performing time degagement thrust on the sixth (eighth) bind or beat*

The parries adopted can be: simple fourth, semicircular seventh, circular sixth (third) and simple second.

The exercises of parry and thrust, riposte and counter-riposte are identical with those of the change thrust carried out from the sixth engagement.

*Counter-attacks*

They can be time thrusts executed in the final cadence, high or low, outside or inside, depending on the opponent's finishing thrust.


*Time degagement thrusts from low line*

*Performing time degagement thrust on the seventh bind or beat*

The parries used can be: simple second (eighth), circular seventh and destructing fourth.

The exercises of parry and thrust, riposte and counter-riposte are the same as those of the disengage thrust performed from the seventh engagement.


*Counter-attacks*

They can be stop thrusts carried out in the final cadence low, outside or inside on the adversary's finish.


*Performing time degagement thrust on the second (eighth) bind or beat*

The parries adopted can be: simple seventh, simple sixth (third), semicircular fourth and circular second (eighth).

The exercises of parry and thrust, riposte and counter-riposte are completely identical with those of the disengage thrust carried out from the second engagement.

They can be carried out high, outside or inside on the adversary's finishing thrust.

Performing time degagement thrust on the second (eighth) bind or beat from long distance with

– a step forward and lunge,
– flèche.

In both cases the adversary's blade about to engage should be rounded already from a long distance. This leaves the opponent with a comparatively long time to parry the attack before the finish. That is why in the overwhelming majority of cases only a time degagement thrust combined with a feint can be successful when the attack is carried out from long distance.

The finish of every attack executed with change thrust can be the same as in foil fencing, one of opposition or an angular thrust.

Bind thrusts can also be applied if they are built up on the fundamental exercises of the fencing lesson.

## 2. Time degagement thrusts on circular and semicircular binds

*Time degagement thrusts from high line*

They can be performed on
– circular fourth bind or beat,
– semicircular sixth (third) bind or beat.

*Time degagement thrusts from low line*

They can be performed on
– semicircular second (eighth) bind or beat,
– semicircular seventh bind or beat.


*Time degagement thrusts from high line*

They can be performed on
– circular fourth bind or beat,
– semicircular sixth (third) bind or beat.


*Time degagement thrusts from low line*

They can be performed on
– circular second (eighth) bind or beat,
– circular seventh bind or beat.

The exercises of parries and parry and thrust, riposte and counter-riposte are the same as those of the time degagement thrusts performed on the simple attacks on the blade.

The system of counter-attacks is identical with the types of time degagement thrusts that can be carried out on simple binds. The types of finish are the same as the time degagement thrusts performed on the simple attacks on the blade.


## 3. Time degagement thrusts on change binds and beats

The exercises denoted by the title of this chapter are extremely useful elements of épée fencing. While the two fencers seek opportunities for the most favourable action, their blades are engaged several times in succession. The favourable moment which should be seized by the fencer in line position is the opportunity for time degagement thrust carried out on the opponent's change from preliminary engagement. The disengage thrust from the fencer's own engagement and on his adversary's change engagement should be performed in the same manner as if the fencer were in line position.

The related exercises can be performed from

*high line:*

– time degagement thrust from the fourth engagement on change second bind or beat,
– time degagement thrust from the sixth (third) engagement on change fourth bind or beat; or

*low line:*

– time degagement thrust from the seventh engagement on change second bind or beat,
– time degagement thrust from the second (eighth) engagement on change seventh bind or beat.

The methods of parrying the attacks, the exercises that can be based on them and the system of counter-attacks and stop thrusts all follow necessarily from the prevailing relations between the two blades.

Only in the launching of attack do we find a new element.

# XI. FEINTS

The material considered so far comprises exercises of the basic level that should be regarded as the foundations of épée fencing. The superstructure of the sport can be built up on this basis.

The feints contain, as a rule, all the elements that have been acquired by the pupil in the course of receiving instruction on the basic level. They will invariably occur in connection with the launching of attacks, taking the form of the methods of introduction.

The parrying systems can be moulded and shaped by the fencer himself at will from the cohesive system of and relations between the parries discussed so far. Naturally, they can only be moulded within certain limits.

The system of feints arises from the parrying system adopted by the opponent and recognized by the attacker who outwits it.

A quotation from the passage on the definition of feints from The Handbook of Fencing by the late fencing master Gellér will complete the general introduction given above and provide a more accurate definition:

"The feint is a movement designed to mislead the opponent. The fencer forces his opponent to perform a parry (or parries) in reply to the indication of a thrust (or thrusts) with the real intention of rounding it (them) and performing a thrust to that part of the target left open."

*Classification of feints*

Feints can be classified on the basis of the
*(a)* method of introduction,
*(b)* quality of parries rounded,
*(c)* number of parries rounded.


*Under* (a) *the following feints can be distinguished*

Feints introduced by
- straight thrust,
- change thrust,
- bind and thrust,
- filo,
- beat and thrust,
- time degagement thrust.


*Under* (b) *there are*

- simple feints designed to round simple parries,
- circular feints designed to round circular, semicircular or change parries,
- mixed feints designed to round a complex parrying system composed of simple, circular, semicircular and change parries.


*Under* (c) *there can be*

- single feints designed to round one parry,
- double feints designed to round two parries,
- multiple feints designed to round several parries.

Any accurate definition of a feint attack is thus required to contain the three basic factors listed above.


*Examples*

Indication of straight thrust followed by single simple feint (it commences with a straight thrust and is designed to round one simple parry).

Indication of change thrust followed by circular single feint (the first stage is a change thrust followed by the rounding of one circular parry).

Indication of bind (or beat) followed by a simple single feint thrust.

Circular single feint introduced by bind thrust.

Circular single feint introduced by time degagement thrust.

In the case of double feints the variations of parries lead to the same number of changes (denominations).


*In the case of double feints the parries rounded can be of the following types:*

– both parries are simple,

– the first parry is a simple one followed by a circular (or semicircular) one,

– the first parry is of the change type followed by a simple one,

– the first parry is of the change type followed by a circular (semicircular) one,

– the first parry is a circular (semicircular) one followed by a circular (semicircular) one,

– the first parry is a circular (semicircular) one followed by a simple one.

230

Simple double feint introduced by straight thrust.

Simple and circular double feint introduced by change thrust.

Circular and simple double feint introduced by bind and thrust.

Circular double feint introduced by bind thrust.

Time degagement circular double feint thrust.

Circular and simple double feint introduced by beat thrust.

The cadencing of a feint depends on the distance, the method of introduction and, above all, on the opponent's parrying cadence. The different methods of cadencing will be considered during the detailed analysis of the material in the subsequent chapters.

The launching of attacks is determined by the methods of introduction which, in respect of the relations between the two blades, are identical with the variations discussed in the case of the basic exercises.

In the present chapter the fencing material is classified according to the principle of parallelism. This means that all the exercises that reveal differences in the phase of launching the attack but are completely identical with regard to the technical form of attack, the parry, the parry and thrust (riposte), the thrust, parry and thrust (counter-riposte) and the stop thrust, are classified in the same group.

The finish of the different actions is completed with thrust executed as in foil fencing, the opposition and angular thrust, all of them carried out with a feint.

It follows from the special character of épée fencing that the range of feints is much wider than in foil fencing in which there are two fundamental forms: *(a)* the so-called foil feint of a straight plane which is the most general form and *(b)* the feint with bind thrust (filo). Both of these forms are applied in épée fencing, but in addition angular feints and those of opposition are frequently employed.

*The technical forms of executing a feint are as follows:*

In the case of single feints the feint can be one
- as in foil fencing,
- of the opposition type,
- of angular thrust,
- of bind thrust (filo).

The finish can be
- as in foil fencing,
- one of opposition,
- an angular thrust.

The above scheme can be applied to the variations of double feints.

# Simple single feints

## 1. Straight thrust followed by simple single feints

The essence of the attack is accurately defined by the title of the chapter, that is
- the method of introduction is one of straight thrust,
- the feint is a simple one because it rounds a simple parry and
- it is a single feint because it rounds one parry only.

The related exercises need to be discussed separately because there is no group of exercises as regards simple single feints that could run parallel with them under identical conditions.

*Performing simple single feints introduced by straight thrust on the sixth (third) invito*

From medium distance

In the process of the feint the blade is conducted in the same manner as if a real straight thrust were being carried out. According to the general forms of feints discussed in the introductory part, the feint can be directed to the opponent's body over the whole surface opened up by the sixth invito, from the head down to the leg and the arm holding to the weapon.

The most frequent and most general type of feint is the one directed to the inside upper opening of the target and the surface of the arm holding the épée. The exercises will be analysed from this angle.

The parry forced by a definite feint is rounded from below and the concluding thrust is performed in the same manner as described in the case of time degagement thrusts.

*Parries*

The following parries can be performed
in the case of high finish:
– simple fourth–sixth (third),
– simple fourth–circular fourth,
in the case of low finish:
– simple fourth–destructing seventh,
– simple fourth–semicircular second.

*Exercises of parry and thrust and riposte*

The exercises are performed from the final position of the parries listed above. The number of versions comes from the high and low possibilities of concluding thrusts and from the forms of feint thrust (riposte) conducted freely or with the blade engaged.

*Exercises of thrust, parry and thrust and counter-riposte*

The exercises of parrying attacks can serve as a basis for analysing and conducting the ones indicated in the title of this paragraph. The riposte possibilities arise from the parries performed by the defending fencer. It can be concluded from this that the thrust carried out from any of the parries is of two directions: high and low. The exercises (of a thrust and parry alternatively) are built up on these ripostes which, depending on the given riposte, can be simple or change thrusts, or opposition, change or ceding parries on a riposte of the bind thrust type. The versions of the concluding thrust (counter-riposte) are left to the fencer to choose at his own will.

In order to facilitate complete understanding of the material involved, the exercises of the attack under discussion are analysed below.

| Pupil | Coach |
|---|---|
| | *First exercise* |
| Performs simple single feint attack introduced by a straight thrust on the coach's sixth invito | Parries with simple fourth and sixth and carries out riposte low as in foil fencing |

| Pupil | Coach |
|---|---|
| Adopts simple second or change seventh parry and chooses from the following types of riposte: a thrust as in foil fencing, one of the opposition type, angular thrust, bind thrust, simple single feint or simple single feint bind thrust | |

*Second exercise*

| Pupil | Coach |
|---|---|
| Carries out simple single feint attack introduced by a straight thrust on the coach's sixth invito | Performs bind riposte high from the sixth parry |
| Adopts simple opposition sixth, change fourth or ceding first parry<br>The method of the finish is selected freely | |

*Third exercise*

| Pupil | Coach |
|---|---|
| Executes simple single feint attack introduced by a straight thrust on the coach's sixth invito | Carries out a riposte with simple single feint from sixth parry |

| Pupil | Coach |
|---|---|
| Performs simple second sixth or simple second and semi-circular fourth parry | |
| The method of the finish is selected freely | |

*Fourth exercise*

| Pupil | Coach |
|---|---|
| Carries out simple single feint attack introduced by a straight thrust on the coach's sixth invito | From the sixth parry executes a bind thrust riposte with simple single feint |
| Parries the riposte with simple opposition sixth–fourth, simple opposition sixth–circular sixth or simple opposition sixth–semicircular | |
| Selects the type of finish freely | |

*Fifth exercise*

| Pupil | Coach |
|---|---|
| Performs simple single feint attack introduced by a straight thrust on the coach's sixth invito | Parries the attack with simple fourth–circular fourth parry and carries out a riposte high with a thrust like in foil fencing, one of opposition, bind thrust or angular one |

236

| Pupil | Coach |
|---|---|
| Carries out simple fourth, change sixth or half change seventh parry | |
| The finish to be adopted is up to the fencer | |

### Sixth exercise

| Pupil | Coach |
|---|---|
| Executes simple single feint attack by a straight thrust on the coach's sixth invito | Parries the attack with circular fourth, the riposte is a flanconade carried out low |
| Adopts simple opposition second, change seventh or ceding fourth parry and selects the finish freely | |

### Seventh exercise

| Pupil | Coach |
|---|---|
| Carries out simple single feint attack introduced by a straight thrust on the coach's sixth invito | Performs a riposte from circular fourth parry and with simple single (brief) feint |
| Uses simple fourth–sixth or simple fourth and circular fourth parry and adopts the finish he prefers | |

| Pupil | Coach |
|---|---|

*Eighth exercise*

| | |
|---|---|
| Performs simple single feint attack introduced by a straight thrust on the coach's sixth invito | Following a circular fourth parry he carries out a single feint flanconade riposte |
| Adopts simple (opposition) second and sixth or simple (opposition) second–semicircular fourth parry and uses the type of finish he prefers | |

The exercises of parry and thrust (or riposte) and thrust, parry and thrust (or counter-riposte) can be conducted along the scheme outlined above in the case of performing simple single feint attacks on any other invito.

*Counter-attacks*

Counter-attacks can take the form of stop thrusts of the following types:
1. Stop thrust carried out in the first cadence high and inside instead of the fourth parry.
2. Stop thrust in final cadence on the opponent's concluding thrust.
The latter can be performed
in high line: stop thrust executed high and outside instead of the sixth parry, or stop thrust executed high and inside instead of the circular fourth parry;

in low line: stop thrust executed inside and low instead of destructing seventh parry, stop thrust executed outside and low instead of the semicircular second parry, or any other-so-called "tempo" stop thrust identical with the direction of the corresponding parry and used instead of any of them performed to the adversary's arm or hand. This method can be adopted accordingly in the case of any other action.

From long distance with

– a step forward and lunge,
– flèche.

In both cases the feint is indicated in the course of the initial stage of advance (step forward). It is recommended that the finish be effected either with a lunge or a flèche.

*The feint can be cadenced in the following two ways:*

*(a)* A longer feint should be shown to the calm type of adversary whose parries are unhurried. As a result, the feint will tend to overlap the initial stage of the lunge. The concluding thrust should be of brief cadence. Thus the pattern of cadence will be one of "long and short".

*(b)* The shorter feint is shown the adversary who reacts quickly and nervously to any of the fencer's movements. The two successive cadences should be identical. The feint should be performed simultaneously with the step forward, the parry should be rounded at the moment the rear foot concludes the step forward by stamping on the piste and the thrust proper should be carried out with the lunge or flèche.

*Performing simple single feints introduced by straight thrust on the fourth invito*

From medium distance

The feint should be directed towards the outside upper opening of the target or the outside surface of the opponent's arm corresponding to the weapon.

*Parries*

The following parries can be used:
– simple sixth (third)–fourth,
– simple sixth (third)–semicircular seventh,
– simple sixth (third)–circular sixth,
– simple sixth (third)–simple second.
The exercises of parry and thrust (riposte) and thrust, parry and thrust (counter-riposte) can be conducted on the basis of the above types of parries and according to the system described in the examples given in connection with feint attacks on the sixth invito.

*Counter-attacks*

Counter-attacks can take the form of stop thrusts of the following types:
1. Stop thrust in the first cadence executed outside and low instead of the simple sixth parry.
2. Stop thrust in the final cadence executed on the adversary's concluding thrust.
The latter can be performed
– high and inside instead of the simple fourth parry and

– high and outside instead of the circular sixth parry
in the case of high finishes, or
    – low and inside instead of the semicircular seventh parry and
    – low and outside instead of simple second parry
in the case of low finishes.


*Performing simple single feints introduced by straight thrust on the second (eighth) invito*

From medium distance

The feint should be directed towards the inside upper part of the target or the upper surface of the adversary's arm.


Parries

The following parries can be adopted:
- simple seventh–second,
- simple sixth–second,
- simple seventh–circular seventh,
- simple sixth–circular sixth,
- simple sixth–fourth.

Both the sixth and seventh parries carried out from the second or eighth position are regarded as simple parries. Thus the range of parries is expanded.

The exercises of parry and thrust (riposte) and thrust, parry and thrust (counter-riposte) can be performed from the final positions of the parries listed above by adopting any of the forms (including feints) applied so far.

Counter-attacks can take the form of stop thrusts of the following types:

1. Stop thrust in the first cadence, executed outside and low instead of the simple sixth, and inside and low instead of the simple seventh parry.

2. Stop thrust in the final cadence executed on the adversary's concluding thrust.

The latter can be performed

– outside and low instead of the simple second parry,

– inside and low instead of the circular seventh parry

in the case of low finishes, or

– inside and high instead of the simple fourth parry,

– outside and high instead of the circular sixth parry

in the case of high finishes.

The execution of these types of feint attack from long distance with a step forward and lunge or with flèche is based on the principles discussed in connection with simple single feint attacks on the sixth invito.


*Performing simple single feints introduced by straight thrust on the seventh invito*

From medium distance

In this case the feint should be directed either towards the surface of the hand lying below the guard and pointing downwards or towards the adversary's knee or foot lying closest to the fencer.

*Parries*

The following parries can be adopted:
– simple second–sixth,
– simple second–circular second,
– simple second–semicircular fourth,
– simple second–simple seventh.
The exercises of parry and thrust (riposte) and thrust, parry and thrust (counter-riposte) are based on the types of parries listed above.

*Counter-attacks*

Counter-attacks can take the form of stop thrusts of the following types:
1. Stop thrust in the first cadence executed high and inside instead of the simple second parry.
2. Stop thrust in the final cadence, executed on the adversary's concluding thrust.
The latter can be performed
in high line: outside and high instead of the simple sixth parry, or inside and high instead of the semicircular fourth parry;
in low line: inside and low instead of the simple seventh parry, or outside and low instead of the circular parry.
The execution of this type of feint attack from long distance with a step forward and lunge or with flèche contains no new element compared to the previous types of feint attacks.

## 2. Disengage thrust followed by simple single feints

The disengage thrust was considered in detail during the description of instruction in performing simple attacks. In the case of every feint attack introduced by disengage thrust the first cadence of the movement (indication of the feint) is a disengage thrust and the action is concluded with a rounding thrust (*trompement*).

There can be two types of cadencing the feint from medium distance.

In the first type the two cadences are identical.

In the second type the feint takes a longer time and so it overlaps the lunge.

When the attack is carried out from long distance, the feint should be indicated well in advance if the first type is adopted, that is when the fencer is wide apart from his opponent, whose blade should be rounded, as a rule, simultaneously with the rear foot concluding the step forward by stamping on the piste. When using the second type, the feint should be delayed, commencing only as late as during the approach work. Thus the cadencing of the feint and the concluding thrust will be shorter.

When the feint is parried, the first parry is identical with that of the rounded thrust at the conclusion of the attack.

The second parry that can be simple, semicircular or circular is presented in the subsequent system.

The exercises of the fencing lesson are identical with those of simple single feint attacks introduced by straight thrust and carried out on invitos, irrespective of the kind of engagement from which they are performed.

Counter-attacks which take the form of time thrusts practically in every case are carried out in the first and final cadence.

The system of parries and counter-attacks listed below is given as a basic material.

244

*Performing simple single feint indicated by change thrust from the sixth (third) engagement*

*Parries*

The following parries can be adopted:
– simple fourth–sixth (third),
– simple fourth–circular fourth,
– simple fourth–destructing seventh,
– simple fourth–semicircular second.


*Counter-attacks*

Counter-attacks can take the form of stop thrusts of the following types:
1. Stop thrust in the first cadence executed high and inside instead of the simple fourth parry.
2. Stop thrust performed in the final cadence on the adversary's concluding thrust.
The latter can be performed
in high line: stop thrust executed high and outside instead of the simple sixth parry, or stop thrust executed instead of the circular fourth parry;
in low line: stop thrust executed inside and low instead of destructing seventh parry, or stop thrust performed outside and low instead of the semicircular second parry.


*Performing simple single feint indicated by change thrust from the fourth engagement*

*Parries*

The following parries can be used:
– simple sixth (third)–fourth,
– simple sixth (third)–circular sixth,
– simple sixth (third)–semicircular seventh,
– simple sixth (third)–simple second.


*Counter-attacks*

Counter-attacks can take the form of stop thrusts of the following types:
1. Stop thrust executed in the first cadence outside and low instead of the simple sixth parry.
2. Stop thrust executed in the final cadence on the opponent's concluding thrust.
The latter can be performed
in high line: inside and high instead of the simple fourth parry, or outside and high instead of the circular sixth parry;
in low line: inside and low instead of the semicircular seventh parry, or outside and low instead of the simple second parry.


*Performing simple single feint indicated by disengage thrust from the second (eighth) type of engagement*

*Parries*

The following parries can be adopted:
– simple seventh–second,
– simple seventh–circular seventh,
– simple sixth–second,

- simple sixth-circular sixth,
- simple sixth-circular seventh,
- simple sixth-fourth.

*Counter-attacks*

Counter-attacks can take the form of stop thrusts of the following types:
1. Stop thrust carried out in the first cadence, inside and low instead of the simple seventh parry,
   and
outside and low instead of the simple sixth parry.
2. Stop thrust performed in the final cadence on the adversary's concluding thrust.
The latter can be executed
in low line: outside and low instead of the simple second parry, or inside and low instead of the semicircular and circular seventh parry;
in high line: inside and high instead of the simple fourth parry, or outside and high instead of the circular sixth parry.

*Performing simple single feint indicated by change thrust from the seventh engagement*

*Parries*

The following parries can be adopted:
- simple second–seventh,
- simple second–circular second,
- simple second–semicircular fourth,
- simple second–simple sixth.

Counter-attacks can take the form of stop thrusts of the following types:

1. Stop thrust carried out high in the first cadence instead of the simple second parry.
2. Stop thrust performed in the final cadence.

The latter can be executed

in high line: outside and high instead of the simple sixth parry, or inside and high instead of the semicircular fourth parry;

in low line: inside and low instead of the simple seventh parry, or outside and low instead of the circular second parry.

## 3. Bind and thrust followed by simple single feint attacks on the opponent's blade held in line

It can be stated right at the outset that in case the attack is performed on the adversary's blade held in low or high line the technique of the execution of the attack and the exercises of parry and thrust (riposte), thrust, parry and thrust (counter-riposte) and stop thrust will be identical with those previously described irrespective of the methods of introduction applied by the attacker. Thus it is not necessary to discuss them separately in the present chapter.

The methods of introducing attacks on the opponent's blade held in line can be of the following types:

  – simple engagement from invito or on guard position,
  – semicircular engagement from invito or on guard position,
  – circular engagement from invito or on guard position,
  – simple engagement from the line,
  – change engagement from the line,
  – change engagement from the fencer's own bind,

– change engagement following transfer *(trasporto)*.

While giving instruction the method of parallel exercises should again be adopted.

Regardless of the type of introduction the first stage of the attack comprises making contact with the adversary's blade: that is a sort of bind.

The second stage is made up of the feint proper. The third, which is very closely linked to the second, consists of the rounding of the opponent's parrying blade.

The fourth stage is the concluding thrust.

Two types of cadencing can be distinguished in the execution of feints:

– the feint is indicated very markedly subsequent to the second and seventh binds;

– following the fourth and seventh engagement it is unnecessary to indicate the feint at all because the reflex parry is brought about so suddenly by the pressure exercised on the adversary's weapon that virtually all the attacker can do is to perform a brief passing feint.

The first parry will be a simple one forced by the feint movement.

The second one that can be simple, semicircular or circular is given in the system presented in the following lines.

The riposte following the parry can be of any type up to the simple single feints.

In conducting the exercises of the fencing lesson due consideration should be given to the fundamental principles outlined here.

In the case of counter-attacks the first possibility (avoiding the opponent's bind) is omitted. The second possibility is a stop thrust carried out in the first cadence. It is adopted as a time thrust instead of the first parry. This solution should be used according to the scheme concerning simple parries.

The ultimate possibility is a stop thrust executed in the final cadence on the adversary's finish. In this case the feint is reacted to by a simple parry and, depending on the direction of the thrust (whether it is high or low), the stop thrust is carried out inside or outside.

The counter-attack can take the form of
- time thrust, or
- tempo stop thrust

executed to that part of the body lying closest to the fencer.


*Performing bind and thrust simple single feint attacks on a blade held in high line*

*Fourth bind followed by simple single feint attack*

From medium distance

The attack can be performed from
- sixth (third) invito: simple fourth bind followed by simple single feint,
- second (eighth) invito: semicircular fourth bind followed by simple single feint,
- fourth invito: circular fourth bind followed by simple single feint,
- high line: simple fourth bind followed by simple single feint,
- low line: change fourth bind followed by simple single feint,
- the fencer's own sixth engagement: change fourth bind followed by simple single feint,
- seventh engagement: semicircular fourth bind followed by simple single feint.

*Parries*

The following parries can be adopted:
– simple fourth–sixth,
– simple fourth–circular fourth.

The parries listed above are identical with those discussed in connection with simple single feints carried out on the sixth invito. From this the obvious conclusion can be drawn that the exercises of the fencing lesson will also be identical. The relevant examples can thus be applied here, too.

The parries mentioned hold only good for parrying the concluding thrusts of attacks performed with the most usual type of form.

It was emphasized during the discussion of the exercises of the basic level (engagements) that the free character of the épée makes it possible to use forms that are different from those common to foil fencing. In the present case, provided the attacks are concluded with a thrust directed towards the lower openings of the expanded fencing target (for example, the adversary's thigh), both the parries and the exercises of the fencing lesson are built up on the low parries. In this case the first parry is, here too, the fourth, while the second one is a semicircular second or destructing seventh.

*Counter-attacks*

Counter-attacks can take the form of stop thrusts of the following types:
1. Stop thrust performed inside and high in the first cadence instead of the simple fourth parry.
2. Stop thrust executed outside and high in the final cadence.
The latter can be performed

– outside and high instead of the simple sixth parry, or
– inside and high instead of the circular fourth parry.
Performing the action from long distance
– with a step forward and lunge,
– with flèche.
This is a highly reasonable and, for that matter, extremely frequent action.

The attack proper can only be launched after contact has been made with the opponent's blade. Here again the feint is also of a passing nature because the rounding movement must commence without delay right after the parrying reflex induced by the engagement. As the rounding is completed the fencer's fist should be positioned high on the right-hand side in order to render a possible counter-thrust by the opponent harmless.

It was pointed out in the chapter on the relevant parries that the attack can be concluded also to the adversary's thigh placed in the front. In this case, however, the parries of the low plane should be adopted.

*Sixth (third) bind followed by simple single feint attacks*

From medium distance

The attack can be performed from
– fourth invito: simple sixth bind followed by simple single feint,
– second invito: simple sixth bind followed by simple single feint,
– seventh invito: semicircular sixth bind followed by simple single feint,
– sixth invito: circular sixth bind followed by simple single feint,

– high line: change sixth bind followed by simple single feint,
– low line: simple sixth bind followed by simple single feint,
– the fencer's own fourth engagement: change sixth bind followed by simple single feint,
– the fencer's own seventh engagement: semicircular sixth transfer followed by simple single feint.

## Parries

The following parries can be adopted:
– simple second-sixth (third),
– simple second-circular second,
– simple second-simple seventh,
– simple second-semicircular fourth.
The parries are thus identical with those of simple single feint attacks carried out on the seventh invito.
The exercises of parry and thrust (riposte) and thrust, parry and thrust (counter-riposte) are based on the parries listed above.

## Counter-attacks

Counter-attacks can take the form of stop thrusts of the following types:
1. Stop thrust performed outside and high in the first cadence and instead of the simple second parry.
2. Stop thrust carried out in the final cadence.
The latter can be executed
in high line: outside and high instead of the simple sixth parry, or inside and high instead of the semicircular fourth parry;
in low line: inside and low instead of the simple seventh parry, or outside and low instead of the circular parry.

Sixth (third) bind followed by simple single feint attacks from long distance:

– with a step forward and lunge,
– with flèche.

The feint is a real one in this case, too, and as such it must be indicated. The rounding movement employed depends on the opponent's cadence of parrying.

*Performing bind thrust simple single feint attacks on a blade held in low line*

From medium distance

The attack can be performed from
– sixth invito: simple second bind followed by simple single feint,
– seventh invito: simple second bind followed by simple single feint,
– fourth invito: semicircular second bind followed by simple single feint,
– second invito: circular second bind followed by simple single feint,
– high line: simple second bind followed by simple single feint,
– low line: change second bind followed by simple single feint,
– the fencer's own seventh engagement: change second bind followed by simple single feint,
– fourth engagement: semicircular second transfer followed by simple single feint.

The feint used in this type of attack is a real one and, for that matter, it should be indicated towards the inside upper part of the target or the opponent's upper arm after the blade has been bound.

The cadencing of the rest of the movement depends on the adversary's cadence of parrying.

*Parries*

The following parries can be used:
– simple sixth (third)–second (eighth),
– simple sixth (third)–circular sixth,
– simple sixth (third)–semicircular seventh,
– simple sixth (third)–fourth.

The parries given above and adjusted to the concluding thrust reveal certain differences compared to those of simple single feints performed on the fourth invito. There is no difference as to the first stage because the feint is reacted to by sixth as the first parry, but, depending on the direction of the thrust, simple second or semicircular seventh parry can, above all, be applied. Circular sixth is rarely used while the fourth parry cannot be adopted at all.

The exercises of the fencing lesson are in line with the movements described in the preceding paragraph.

*Counter-attacks*

Counter-attacks can take the form of stop thrusts of the following types:
1. Stop thrust performed outside and low in the first cadence instead of the simple sixth parry.
2. Stop thrust executed in the last cadence on the opponent's concluding thrust.

The latter can be performed
in high line: inside and high instead of the simple fourth parry, or
outside and high instead of the circular sixth parry;
in low line: outside and low instead of the simple second parry, or
inside and low instead of the semicircular seventh parry.
Bind thrust simple single feint attacks on a blade held in low line from long distance:
- with a step forward and lunge,
- with flèche.

Both types should be performed in accordance with the general principles described in connection with the attack carried out from medium distance.

*Seventh bind followed by simple single feint*

From medium distance

The attack can be performed from
- second (eighth) invito: simple seventh bind followed by simple single feint,
- sixth (third) invito: semicircular seventh bind followed by simple single feint,
- seventh invito: circular seventh bind followed by simple single feint,
- low line: simple seventh bind followed by simple single feint,
- high line: change seventh bind followed by simple single feint,
- the fencer's own second engagement: change seventh bind followed by simple single feint,

– the fencer's own sixth engagement: semicircular seventh transfer followed by simple single feint.

The feint in the above-listed attacks should be a passing one because the reflex induced in the opponent makes it impossible for the fencer to indicate the feint. The rounding of the adversary's weapon must, therefore, be started straight away in reply to the pressure exercised by his blade. The concluding thrust is directed, in the majority of cases, towards the lower part of the hand or wrist.

## Parries

The following parries can be adopted:
– simple seventh–second,
– simple seventh–circular seventh.

It follows from the character of the attack that the exercises of parry and thrust (riposte) and thrust, parry and thrust (counter-riposte) can be built only on the parries listed above. Here the exercises of the fencing lesson can be identical with those of simple single feint attacks on the second invito only with the combination of the above parries.

## Counter-attacks

Counter-attacks may be stop thrusts of the following types:
1. Stop thrust performed inside and low in the first cadence instead of the simple seventh parry.
2. Stop thrust carried out in the last cadence.
   The latter can be executed
   – outside and low instead of simple second parry, or
   – inside and low instead of circular seventh parry.

Execution of the seventh bind followed by simple single feint from long distance with a step forward and lunge or with flèche should be based on the principles discussed in the case of an attack carried out from medium distance.

## 4. Change bind from the opponent's engagement followed by simple single feint attacks on the engaging blade

Considering the adversary's preliminary engagement this type of attack is carried out on a blade positioned outside the line.

There is no essential difference between this type of movement and the fencing material discussed in the preceding chapter concerning the technique of executing the attack. Regarding the simple single feints identification of the parries, however, is only possible in the case of change fourth and change seventh bind feints applicable to the adversary's sixth and second engagement respectively.

Feint attacks carried out on the opponent's fourth and seventh engagement can be applied only as bind thrust simple or circular feints. The feint attacks occurring here will be considered in the chapter on Bind thrust and circular feint attacks.

The attack can be performed:

*1. On the adversary's sixth engagement change fourth bind followed by simple single feint*

Both the change and the attack that follows contact between the two blades should be performed in the same manner as though the movement were executed from the fencer's own sixth engagement.

The exercises of parries, parry and thrust (riposte), thrust, parry and thrust (counter-riposte) and stop thrusts are completely identical with the corresponding material of performing change fourth bind from the fencer's own sixth engagement followed by simple single feint attack.

*2. On the adversary's second (eighth) engagement as follows: change seventh bind followed by simple single feint*

The change should be performed and the catching of the blade should be made in the same manner as described in the case of executing the movement from the fencer's own second (eighth) engagement. As in the event of the fourth bind discussed in preceding paragraphs the feint is a passing one.

The exercises of parries, parry and thrust (riposte), thrust, parry and thrust (counter-riposte) and stop thrusts are the same as the corresponding material of performing change seventh bind from the fencer's own eighth type of engagement followed by simple single feint attack.

## 5. Simple single feint attacks introduced by bind thrust

The relevant fencing material is discussed separately from feint attacks introduced by engagement. The forms of introducing the attack completed with the change bind performed on the opponent's engagement are completely identical with the methods of introducing bind thrust followed by simple single feint attacks on the adversary's blade held in line.

The technical solution (the fencing) subsequent to the engagement reveals essential differences bringing about fundamental changes in the corresponding parrying system. This coincides with a change in the exercises of the fencing lesson as well. Both the similarities and dissimilarities will be considered in detail during discussion of the material. It must be mentioned in advance, however, that the simple single feints occurring here are built up on the opposition parries exclusively.

*Fourth engagement followed by bind thrust simple single feint*

From medium distance

Technically speaking, the execution of the action given in the above title is based on the bind thrust feint that gives the impression of being a real thrust. In the course of the bind thrust contact between the two blades should be maintained as long as the opponent is forced to perform a reflex parry as a result of continuous pressure exercised on his blade.

The adversary's fourth parry should be rounded in the same manner as described in the case of "passing" feints.

The thrust concluding the movement should be directed towards the outside upper opening of the target or the opponent's upper arm. The thigh can also serve as a target when the thrust is carried out with a half *cavazione*.

*Parries*

The following parries can be adopted:
in high line: simple opposition fourth–sixth, simple opposition fourth–circular fourth;
in low line: simple opposition fourth–semicircular second, simple opposition fourth–destructing seventh.

The exercises of parry and thrust (riposte), thrust, parry and thrust (counter-riposte) and the system of stop thrusts are built up on the parries listed above.

When the fourth engagement followed by bind thrust with simple single feint is performed from long distance either with a step forward and lunge or with flèche, the principles of execution are much the same as those of bind feint attacks.

*Fourth bind flanconade, simple single feint*

From medium distance

The methods of introducing this type of attack are the same as those considered in the preceding paragraphs. The only difference is that here a flanconade feint is performed. This circumstance, however, leads to a change in the parrying system, because if this type of attack is carried out, the simple feint is based on the opposition second parry. The subsequent stages are determined by this fact.

*Parries*

The following parries can be used:
– simple opposition second–sixth,
– simple opposition second-seventh,
– simple opposition second-semicircular fourth,
– simple opposition second–circular second.

The exercises of parry and thrust (riposte), thrust, parry and thrust (counter-riposte) and stop thrusts are built on the parries listed above.

Fourth bind flanconade, simple single feint is very rare to

occur from long distance either with a step forward and lunge or with flèche because the introduction of the attack is extremely complex.

*Second (eighth) engagement bind thrust simple single feint*

The character of this kind of attack is very similar to the flanconade feint action considered above. The difference in terms of the technique of execution is that while in the case of the flanconade the feint takes place in the low plane of the fourth with the fencer's fist held on the left-hand side, here the fist is positioned on the right-hand side in the plane of the second. As for the rest, they are completely identical in respect of both the parries and stop thrusts. The exercises of the fencing lesson are the same as those of the preceding type of attack.

*Sixth (third) engagement bind thrust simple single feint*

From medium distance

The methods of introducing this kind of attack (completed with the change sixth engagement followed by bind thrust with simple single feint on the opponent's fourth engagement) are identical with those of the sixth (third) bind simple single feint attack.

The feint is performed with a bind thrust indicated towards the outside upper part of the target so that the adversary's blade is held engaged so long as the opposition sixth type of parry is brought about. Then the parry is rounded from below and the thrust can be performed into the inside upper opening of the target, the inside of the opponent's arm, his wrist, leg or foot.

*Parries*

The following parries can be adopted:
– simple opposition sixth-fourth,
– simple opposition sixth–second,
– simple opposition sixth–circular sixth,
– simple opposition sixth–semicircular seventh.

The exercises of parry and thrust (riposte), thrust, parry and thrust (counter-riposte) and stop thrusts are built up on the parries given above.

Sixth (third) engagement followed by bind thrust with simple single feint from long distance is a highly reasonable and frequently adopted attack both with a step forward and lunge or with flèche. It is very often adopted by attacking types of épée-ists whose pace is fast.

*Seventh engagement bind thrust simple single feint*

From medium distance

This characteristic form which was established in épée fencing was considered in the section dealing with attacks introduced by bind as a flanconade performed from the seventh engagement. This exercise is, therefore, very different from the normal material of foil fencing because the attack is directed towards the inside low part of the target and so the feint is also indicated accordingly.

The attack can be introduced with all the forms used in the case of the seventh engagement followed by simple single feint, but it must be completed with those of the change seventh bind carried out on the adversary's eighth engagement. The related exercises of the fencing lesson are in essence identical with those of the seventh bind followed by simple single feint.

The parries to be used are the same as those of the simple single feint and so are the counter-attacks.

It is unreasonable to carry out this type of attack from long distance because the adversary's blade can be brought under control from medium distance only.

## 6. Simple single feint attacks introduced by beat

When we discussed in a basic sense the highly complex technical material of fencing composed of thousands of elements the psychological aspects were ignored because the overriding objective was to convey knowledge of the technical material and establish the necessary connections among its different elements.

The wide variety of the exercises and the diverse possibilities of execution are likely to induce the expert to pose the question whether or not it would be more reasonable to discard analysis on a high level altogether and establish instead a simplified fencing theory containing the essentials. It could be argued that the system evolved within the narrower limits of such a framework would enable the coach to reduce to a remarkable degree the required period of training.

However attractive this idea may be, the truth is that such an approach would lead not only to stagnation but to a decline in standards. Such a system would necessarily deprive both the coach and his pupils of the possibility of keeping abreast with world-wide developments in the sport professionally and in respect of efficiency.

This justifies the idea that wherever practical and wise, the psychological influence of the mechanical technical material should be given due consideration in the different phases of competitive fencing, and comparison should be made between the effects exercised by related yet different materials from the point of view of the attacking and defending fencer.

This method of examination concerns attacks that can be introduced by bind and beat, movements that belong to the category of attacks on the blade. The ultimate objective of both attacks is the same, yet there are differences in the technical methods of execution.

According to the old concept the performance of one or the other type of attack depends merely on the manner (rigid or loose) in which the opponent holds his weapon in line. The more up-to-date approach, however, suggests that bind or beat can be performed on the blade irrespective of the manner in which it is held. The relative looseness or rigidity of the adversary's blade determines only the dynamism, strength or perhaps looseness recommended for execution of the attack.

More important than this is the psychological stimulus induced in the fencer under attack by the movement itself in the course of its execution, that is during the launching of the attack, the intermittent period and the subsequent stages.

It can be stated that the movement with which engagement is performed at the moment the attack commences (contact between the two blades) fails to bring about rapid opposition type of reflex in the adversary because the real intention of the attacker remains concealed to a certain extent behind the restrained initial movement. Psychologically, no feeling of immediate threat is induced in the opponent at this stage. Provided the attacker feels the psychological tempo correctly, he can carry out a successful attack (even a straight one, that is without feint) even from long distance, following preparation of the kind described above. When the attacker adopts a feint causing the opponent to react to it for fear of immediate danger, he stands a good chance of completing his movement successfully.

The reaction displayed by the adversary to an action introduced by beat is somewhat different. The beat is a movement of a more drastic nature, and this characteristic is enhanced by the coincidental sharp sound. The nervous system tends to register the stimuli of a beat much faster than those of a bind. The opponent is thus inclined to reach to the beat more rapidly and sensitively, so that very often his reaction is controlled. With this in mind it can be said that the beat is extremely effective in disturbing the opponent's ability to act, in concealing the fencer's intention and preparing his attack. It must also be remembered, however, that only an action of the feint type is likely to succeed if the attack is carried out from long distance. High action speed and accurate conducting of the blade are the principal requirements when the movement is performed from medium distance.

Two types of exercises can be distinguished in the case of beats followed by simple single feint attacks.

*(a)* The first is performed, as in the case of bind, with a passing feint subsequent to fourth and seventh beat. Here the opponent's parrying reflex is induced by a powerful beat and the thrust that follows should be carried out after rounding the parrying blade. This is also similar to the movement adopted with binds.

*(b)* These are beats of the sixth and second type in the case of feint attacks where the feint must be definitely indicated so that the beat need not be so powerful as in the preceding case.

In the case of attacks that can be executed with a beat the determination of the relation between the two blades should be confined to the one prevailing prior to the moment at which the attack is launched. The variations of the exercises are independent of the relation between the blades, for they stem from the direction of the attack and the particular parrying system adopted.

The system of parries, parry and thrust (riposte), thrust, parry and thrust (counter-riposte) and counter-attacks are the same as those used in the case of bind thrust followed by simple single feint.

The principal positions from which attacks are launched are as follows:

(a) *In the case of attack on a blade held in line*

– from invito on a blade held in line: simple beat followed by simple single feint attack,
– from invito on a blade held in line: semicircular beat followed by simple single feint attack,
– from invito on a blade held in line: circular beat followed by simple single feint attack,
– from the fencer's own engagement on a blade engaged: change beat followed by simple single feint attack,
– from line on a blade held in line: simple or change beat followed by simple single feint attack.

(b) *In the case of attack on a blade held outside the line*

– from the opponent's engagement on the engaging blade: change beat followed by simple single feint attack.
– from invito or line on a blade held in invito: simple beat followed by simple single feint attack.

## 7. Simple single feint attacks introduced by time degagement thrust

The time degagement thrust was dealt with as an independent group of exercises when the basic exercises were considered.

This type of thrust can be found in every exercise of the feint attacks as the essential element of the finish. The first stage (the feint proper) is initiated with time degagement thrust. This follows from the attempt on the part of the opponent to carry out an attack on the fencer's blade held in line.

The second stage, that is the finish of the attack, is another time degagement thrust, as in the case of every other feint attack.

The system of parries and stop thrusts and the ripostes that can be performed following the parry of an attack are identical with those of the change thrusts.

*The major positions from which attacks are performed are as follows:*

– time degagement thrust on simple bind or beat followed by simple single feint attack,
– time degagement thrust, on semicircular bind or beat followed by simple single feint attack,
– time degagement thrust, on circular bind or beat followed by simple single feint attack,
– time degagement thrust, on change bind or beat followed by simple single feint attack.

# Circular single feints

A circular feint is performed when the opponent's reaction to the indication of the feint is a semicircular, circular, destructing or change parry.

The first stage of the exercise is composed of the same methods of introduction as were discussed in connection with the simple single feint attacks.

The second stage, that is the indication of the feint, takes place close to the adversary's blade because it is followed by the rounding of the weapon with time degagement thrust (which is the third stage), a movement possible to execute in the direction of the opponent's épée.

The fourth stage, that is the finish, is effected in the same manner as with the simple single feints.

In the case of parrying circular feint attacks performed on invito and when the circular feint is executed from engagement, the first parry is of semicircular, destructing or circular type, while if the attack is carried out on a blade held in line with circular feint, the first is a change parry type.

The second one that is designed to parry the attacker's concluding thrust can be a simple, semicircular or circular one.

Counter-attacks and ripostes that are possible to perform from the parries are in general the same as those adopted in the event of parrying simple feint attacks. Since the circular feint brings about essential changes in the exercises, the relevant system will be described in detail with every type of exercise.

## 1. Straight thrust followed by circular single feint attacks on invitos

*Circular single feint attack on the sixth (third) invito*

*Parries*

The following parries can be adopted:
– circular sixth (third)–circular sixth (third),
– circular sixth (third)–semicircular seventh,
– circular sixth (third)–fourth,
– circular sixth–second.

*Counter-attacks*

Counter-attacks can take the form of stop thrusts of the following types:
1. Stop thrust performed high and outside in the first cadence instead of circular sixth parry.
2. Stop thrust in the final cadence.
The latter can be performed
in high line: outside and high instead of the circular sixth parry, inside and high instead of the simple fourth parry;
in low line: low and outside instead of the simple second parry, low and inside instead of the semicircular seventh parry.


*Circular single feint attack on the fourth invito*

*Parries*

The following parries can be adopted:
– circular fourth–circular fourth,
– circular fourth–sixth (third),
– circular fourth–destructing seventh,
– circular fourth–semicircular second.


*Counter-attacks*

Counter-attacks can take the form of stop thrusts of the following types:
1. Stop thrust performed outside and low in the first cadence instead of circular fourth parry.
2. Stop thrust in the final cadence.
The latter can be performed

270

in high line: inside and high instead of the circular fourth parry,
outside and high instead of the simple sixth parry,
in low line: inside and low instead of the destructing seventh parry,
outside and low instead of the semicircular second parry.


*Circular single feint attack on the second (eighth) invito*

*Parries*

The following parries can be adopted:
– circular second (eighth)–circular second (eighth),
– circular second (eighth)–semicircular fourth,
– circular second (eighth)–seventh,
– circular second–sixth (third).


*Counter-attacks*

Counter-attacks can take the form of stop thrusts of the following types:
1. Stop thrust performed outside and low in the first cadence instead of the circular second parry.
2. Stop thrust in the final cadence.
The latter can be performed
in low line: outside and low instead of the circular second parry,
inside and low instead of the simple seventh parry,
in high line: outside and high instead of the simple fourth parry,
inside and high instead of the semicircular fourth parry.

*Parries*

The following parries can be adopted:
– circular seventh–circular seventh,
– circular seventh–second (eighth).


*Counter-attacks*

Counter-attacks can take the form of stop thrusts of the following types:
1. Stop thrust executed inside and high in the final cadence instead of the circular seventh parry.
2. Stop thrust in the final cadence.
   The latter can be performed low:
   – inside and low instead of the circular seventh parry,
   – outside and low instead of the simple second parry.


## 2. Change thrust followed by circular single feint attacks from the opponent's engagement

Conditions for performing the feint are created as the adversary engages the fencer's blade held in line. The feint should be indicated from engagement (by change thrust) in the same manner as in the case of simple feints or as if the fencer were to carry out a real attack. The concluding thrust should be carried out by rounding the semicircular, circular or destructing parry performed by the adversary under pressure. As elsewhere, the finish can be a thrust as in foil fencing, one of opposition or angular thrust.

*Circular single feint attack performed from the opponent's sixth (third) engagement*

*Parries*

The following parries can be adopted:
– circular sixth (third)–circular sixth (third),
– circular sixth (third)–seventh,
– circular sixth (third)–second (eighth),
– circular sixth (third)–fourth,
– semicircular seventh–circular seventh,
– semicircular seventh–second,
– semicircular seventh–destructing fourth or sixth.


*Counter-attacks*

Counter-attacks can take the form of stop thrusts of the following types:
1. Stop thrust in the first cadence.
It can be performed
– outside and high instead of the circular sixth parry,
– inside and high instead of the semicircular seventh parry.
2. Stop thrust in the final cadence.
It can be performed
in high line: outside or inside instead of the high parries,
in low line: outside or inside instead of the low parries.

*Circular single feint attack performed from the opponent's fourth engagement*

*Parries*

The following parries can be adopted:
– circular fourth–circular fourth,
– circular fourth–sixth (third),
– circular fourth–semicircular second,
– circular fourth–destructing seventh.

*Counter-attacks*

Counter-attacks can take the form of stop thrusts such as:
1. Stop thrust performed outside and low in the first cadence instead of the circular fourth parry.
2. Stop thrust in the final cadence.
The latter can be performed
in high line: inside or outside instead of the high parries,
in low line: outside or inside instead of the low parries.

*Circular single feint attack performed from the opponent's seventh engagement*

*Parries*

The following parries can be adopted:
– circular seventh–circular seventh,
– circular seventh–second (eighth),
– circular seventh–destructing fourth,
– circular seventh–semicircular sixth.

## Counter-attacks

Counter-attacks can take the form of stop thrusts such as:
1. Stop thrust performed outside and high in the first cadence instead of the circular seventh parry.
2. Stop thrust executed in the final cadence.
The latter can be performed
in high line: inside or outside instead of the high parries,
in low line: outside or inside instead of the low parries.


## Circular single feint attack performed from the opponent's second (eighth) engagement

### Parries
The following parries can be adopted:
– circular second (eighth)–circular second (eighth),
– circular second (eighth)–fourth,
– circular second (eighth)–seventh,
– semicircular fourth–circular fourth,
– semicircular fourth–second (eighth).


## Counter-attacks

Counter-attacks can take the form of stop thrusts of the following types:
1. Stop thrust executed inside and low in the first cadence instead of the circular second parry.
2. Stop thrust in the final cadence.
The latter can be performed
in high line: inside or outside instead of the high parries,
in low line: inside or outside instead of the low parries.

## 3. Bind and thrust followed by circular single feint attacks

(a) *Attack from invito on the opponent's blade held in line*

All the principles considered in connection with the introduction of the movement in the case of simple single feint attacks introduced by bind are valid for the circular feint attacks as well. The only essential difference between them lies in the fact that in the event of circular feint attacks the thrust is completed after the adversary's change parry has been rounded subsequent to the indication of the feint.

When the circular feint attack is introduced by engagement or bind thrust, the first parry will always be one of the change type. The second parry can be simple, semicircular, circular or destructing. This circumstance results in an extremely wide variety of exercises assuming the form of a bout.

*Circular single feint attack on a blade held in high line*

*From sixth (third) invito fourth bind followed by circular single feint*

*Parries*

The following parries can be adopted:
– change sixth (third)–circular sixth (third),
– change sixth (third)–semicircular seventh,
– change sixth (third)–fourth,
– change sixth (third)–second (eighth).

*Counter-attacks*

Counter-attacks can take the form of stop thrusts of the following types:
1. Stop thrust carried out inside and high in the first cadence instead of the change sixth parry.
2. Stop thrust in the final cadence.
The latter can be performed
in high line: inside or outside instead of the high parries,
in low line: outside or inside instead of the low parries.

*From fourth invito sixth (third) bind followed by circular single feint*

*From second (eighth) invito sixth (third) bind followed by circular single feint*

*Parries*

The following parries can be adopted:
– change seventh–circular seventh,
– change seventh–second (eighth),
– change seventh–semicircular sixth,
– change seventh–destructing fourth.

*Counter-attacks*

Counter-attacks can take the form of stop thrusts of the following types:
1. Stop thrust executed outside and high in the first cadence instead of the change seventh parry.
2. Stop thrust in the final cadence.

The latter can be performed
in high line: outside or inside instead of the high parries,
in low line: outside or inside instead of the low parries.


*Circular single feint attack on a blade held in low line*

*From second (eighth) invito seventh bind followed by circular single feint*

*Parries*

The following parries can be adopted:
– change second (eighth)–circular second (eighth),
– change second (eighth)–semicircular fourth,
– change second (eighth)–seventh,
– change second (eighth)–sixth (third).


*Counter-attacks*

Counter-attacks can take the form of stop thrusts of the following types:
1. Stop thrust executed inside and low in the first cadence instead of the change second parry.
2. Stop thrust in the final cadence.
The latter can be performed
in low line: outside or inside instead of the low parries,
in high line: outside or inside instead of the high parries.

*From seventh invito second (eighth) bind followed by circular
single feint*

*Parries*

The following parries can be adopted:
– change fourth–circular fourth,
– change fourth–sixth (third).


*Counter-attacks*

Counter-attacks can take the form of stop thrusts of the following types:
1. Stop thrust performed outside and low in the first cadence instead of the change fourth parry.
2. Stop thrust in the final cadence.
   The latter can be performed
   – inside and high instead of the circular fourth parry,
   – outside and high instead of the simple sixth parry.


*Further possibilities of bind and thrust, circular single feints*

(b) *Semicircular bind, circular single feint attacks.*
(c) *Circular bind from invito followed by circular single feint attacks
on the opponent's blade held in line.*
(d) *Change bind from the fencer's own engagement followed by circular
single feint attacks on the engaged blade.*
(e) *Simple and change bind from the line followed by circular single
feint attacks on a blade held in line.*
(f) *Transfer from the fencer's own engagement followed by circular single
feint attacks.*

*(g) Change bind from the opponent's engagement followed by circular single feint attack on the engaging blade.*

The exercises of the fencing lesson and counter-attacks of the actions listed from *(b)* to *(g)* are identical with those of bind thrust followed by circular single feint attacks from invito on the opponent's blade held in line, a movement discussed in point *(a)*.

## 4. Bind thrust followed by circular single feint attacks carried out with bind thrust feints

Circular single feint introduced by bind thrust describes the action when the opponent reacts to the indication of the bind thrust feint by performing change parry instead of the simple opposition parry adopted in the case of simple feints. This corresponds to the given situation, in contrast to the simple parry.

For example, change fourth parry is adopted instead of the simple opposition sixth in the event of the sixth bind thrust (filo).

The circular feints of the seventh and fourth flanconade are identical with the exercises of circular single feint attacks with the seventh and second bind thrust.

The parries adopted to counter the circular single feints introduced by the above-listed attacks on the blade and the system of stop thrusts are naturally built up on the parries of the actions mentioned above.

## 5. Beat and thrust followed by circular single feint attacks

Every exercise of the type covered by the title is composed of the indication of beat thrust followed by the rounding of a change parry and a concluding thrust adopted so far in the event of feints.

These types of feint attacks should be practised against every kind of invito, from every sort of engagement and on every type of bind. Every possible type of beat should be used.

The parries and the system of counter-attacks and the ripostes that can be performed after parrying the attacks are identical with the relevant types of exercises analysed in the chapter on Bind thrust followed by circular single feint. There is no difference even in the methods of introducing the attacks.


*The methods of introduction are as follows:*

(*a*) Simple beat thrust followed by circular single feint from invito and on a blade held in line.

(*b*) Semicircular beat followed by circular single feint from invito and on a blade held in line.

(*c*) Circular beat followed by circular single feint from invito and on a blade held in line.

(*d*) Change beat followed by circular single feint from the fencer's own engagement and on the engaged blade.

(*e*) Change beat followed by circular single feint from line and on a blade held in line.

(*f*) Change beat followed by circular single feint from the opponent's engagement and on the engaging blade.

(*g*) Simple, semicircular, circular and change beats performed from invito and line on a blade held in invito.

## 6. Time degagement thrust followed by circular single feint attacks

The definition given in connection with the time degagement thrust followed by simple single feint is also valid for circular single feints introduced by time degagement thrust.

In the first cadence of the attack a time degagement thrust feint is carried out on the opponent's simple, semicircular, circular or change beat or bind.

This is followed in the second cadence by the rounding of the opponent's semicircular or circular parry with a time degagement thrust.

The third cadence is the finish when the thrust proper is carried out to the opening of the target lying closest to the fencer.

Apart from the first degagement the system of parries is identical with the one adopted in the case of circular single feint attacks introduced by change thrust.

The range of counter-attacks and ripostes that can be adopted after parrying the attack is the same as that of the corresponding exercises of attacks introduced by change thrust.

*The attacks can be carried out on*

*(a)* the opponent's simple bind or beat,
*(b)* the opponent's semicircular bind or beat,
*(c)* the opponent's circular bind or beat,
*(d)* the opponent's change bind or beat.

# Double feint attacks

A knowledge of the practical material of épée fencing we have discussed so far will enable both coach and fencer to exercise successfully over a comparatively wide range. The constant development of épée fencing, however, demands that both coach and fencer should base their knowledge on the broadest possible foundation.

The ability to constantly show new ideas, techniques and actions is absolutely vital for the fencer who wants to do well in international competition for a prolonged period of time.

For the épéeist of exceptional talent and skill or the fencer who wishes to rise above those of average standards, even a sound knowledge of and ability to use the exercises discussed and analysed up to this stage is not enough. The fencer can only raise himself to higher standards by seeking new avenues and expansion of his arsenal of movements. In addition to mastering the actions and exercises analysed to the present stage, the épéeist must also practice complex feint movements of a multiple character. When selecting the relevant material, the individual's abilities and skill should be taken into consideration along with his psychological and physical capacities. The elements should be built up on one another and drilled to form an uninterrupted movement. The coaches and competitors capable of this type of effort are those prompted by the desire to acquire the maximum knowledge and ability.

The coach must be more than familiar with the material as a whole. Of course no competitor can be expected to meet the same demand especially because even a most talented competitor needs some four to six months of practice to master a key movement. The desire to achieve success within the shortest possible time, however, should not lead to the simplification of fencing. The key to prolonged success can be found in technical training of the highest level. Some six to eight years are necessary to achieve this standard. Both coach and his pupil must satisfy very high requirements in order to reach this objective. When working in this direction a number of factors must be taken into consideration in addition to the physical abilities and the acquisition of the technique and tactics of épée fencing. They include the development of psychological properties and will-power. The work performed to this end necessitates a sportsmanlike way of life and application of the most modern principles and methods of preparation.

In proceeding from the discussion of single to double feints, there has been a tendency for fencing literature to describe the diversity of methods of introducing attacks and parries as creating innumerable opportunities for the fencer.

This statement is not strictly accurate. It reflects the fact that there has been little serious attempt to really analyse and systematize the actual diversity of opportunities. However, the system of double feints does show that a very large number of linked exercises can be performed. After detailed analysis of the actions these can be incorporated in the fencer's arsenal of movements, depending of course on his abilities. The fact that there is an immense number of actions and movements to choose from means that even in his prime the fencer's technical development need never reach a deadlock. Any danger of deadlock can be eliminated by long-term conscious and planned co-operation between coach and fencer.

By contrast, the fencer who makes a sudden change of coach often suffers a halt to his development.

New practical and methodological guidance for the performance of the exercises of double feints is not necessary because these exercises follow from the further development of the basic and simple single feint attacks and from the systematic application of simple, semicircular, circular and change parries used during these types of attacking actions.

The system of stop thrusts is always dependent on the methods of introduction and the parries rounded. The difference between single and double feint movements arises simply from the essence of the two exercises, in other words, from the special possibility of execution which contains one plus element compared to the single feints and which can be delayed by one cadence.

Double feints are recommended to be adopted against opponents good at parrying single feints or against those reacting to every feint movement with a parry.

The execution comprises indication of a single feint and a thrust rounding the second parry.

The most frequent cadencing of double feint attacks carried out from long distance is as follows:

(*a*) Every movement of the hand or arm is accompanied by a foot exercise, that is the first feint is accompanied by the step forward, the second one by the forward movement of the rear foot, and the thrust is accompanied by the lunge or flèche.

(*b*) When the fencer faces a cool opponent, the first feint should be indicated for a longer spell (while the step forward is taken). This should be followed by a very brief second feint (which is the rounding of the second parry as the rear foot concludes the step forward by stamping on the piste), and the concluding stage is the thrust carried out with the lunge or flèche. The cadences are thus of the following pattern: long, brief, brief.

(*c*) When the adversary is an excitable type of fencer the first feint should be indicated from on guard position, and the step forward should be taken simultaneously with the rounding of his first parry and with the second feint performed well ahead of the fencer. The rounding of the second parry is followed by the finish: a thrust accompanied by the lunge or flèche. The pattern of the cadence is: brief, long, brief.

In a double feint it is very important that the parries be rounded with a movement from the wrist enabling the weapon to proceed in the direction of the opening of the pre-selected target with a continuous spiral forward movement.

Double feints are classified according to the system adopted with single feints. The denomination is also the same. The feints are distinguished on the basis of the methods of introduction, the number and type of parries to be rounded.

*The parries rounded can be the following:*

*(a)* Two simple parries (simple double feint).
*(b)* A simple parry followed by a circular one (simple and circular double feint).
*(c)* A change parry followed by a simple one (circular and simple double feint).
*(d)* A change parry followed by a circular one (double circular feint).
*(e)* Two circular parries (double circular feint).

# Simple double feints

As was mentioned earlier double feints should be adopted when the opponent is very good at parrying single feints.

An important precondition of the execution of the movement is technical preparation based on correct tactical considerations. The adversary should be forced to perform the movements (parries) in space and in time necessary for the successful execution of the fencer's own action as a result of conscious and reasonable preparation by the attacker. The preparatory movements can be identical with or different from the attack proper to follow. The type of movement employed depends on the plane of part of the target on which the fencer wishes to carry out his attack.

The simplest form of preparation is when the adversary (who has a good ability to parry and the fencer has made sure that he is good at parrying straight attacks) is forced to perform parries in reply to the indication of serious thrusts, while the real thrust comes with a feint (rounding a parry). The same method is employed when the oppnonet is forced to react to double feints. Thus he will be kept constantly uncertain as to the fencer's real intention even if no change is introduced in respect of the type of attack throughout the whole bout. This is the manner in which the way is paved for simple double feints arising from straight thrusts.

During the exercises the coach should always return to the single feints through the fundamental exercises of the fencing lesson, and the stage of double feints should be reached with the principle of gradual progress borne in mind. Exercises taking the form of bout fencing should always be preceded by the mechanical execution of movements.

## 1. Straight thrust followed by simple double feint attacks carried out on invitos

*Double feint attack on the sixth (third) invito*

*Parries*

The following parries can be adopted:
– fourth–sixth (third)–fourth,

– fourth–sixth (third)–circular sixth (third),
– fourth–sixth (third)–semicircular seventh,
– fourth–sixth (third)–second (eighth).

*Counter-attacks*

The first cadence is omitted; instead the first feint should be reacted to by the fourth parry.

1. Stop thrust carried out on the second feint in the second cadence outside and low instead of the sixth parry.

2. Stop thrust executed on the opponent's concluding thrust in the final cadence. The stop thrust should be performed high or low, or outside or inside, depending on the adversary's finish.

As in the case of every subsequent double feint, tempo stop thrusts can be carried out on the opponent's arm or hand corresponding to the weapon. They are dependent on the adversary's finish and are performed instead of the relevant parries in a direction identical with that of the parry concerned. In this case the opponent's concluding thrust must be anticipated in good time by our point.

*Counter-attacks*

The first cadence is omitted; instead the first feint should be reacted to by the second parry.

1. Stop thrust carried out on the second feint in the second cadence and the point conducted inside and high instead of the simple fourth parry.

2. Stop thrust performed on the opponent's concluding thrust in the final cadence. The stop thrust is dependent on the direction of the opponent's finish.

*Double feint attack on the fourth invito*

*Parries*

The following parries can be adopted:
– sixth (third)–fourth–sixth (third),
– sixth (third)–fourth–circular fourth,
– sixth (third)–fourth–semicircular second (eighth),
– sixth (third)–fourth–destructing seventh.


*Counter-attacks*

The first cadence is omitted; instead the first feint should be reacted to by the sixth parry.
1. Stop thrust performed on the second feint in the second cadence and the point conducted inside and high instead of the simple fourth parry.
2. Stop thrust on the opponent's finish in the final cadence.


*Double feint attack on the second (eighth) invito*

*Parries*

The following parries can be adopted:
– sixth (third)–second (eighth)–sixth (third),
– sixth (third)–second (eighth)–circular second (eighth),
– sixth (third)–second (eighth)–semicircular fourth,
– seventh–second (eighth)–seventh,
– seventh–second (eighth)–circular second (eighth),
– seventh–second (eighth)–semicircular fourth.

*Counter-attacks*

The first cadence is omitted; instead the first feint should be reacted to by the seventh parry.
1. Stop thrust carried out on the second feint in the second cadence and the point conducted outside and high instead of using the simple second parry.
2. Stop thrust executed on the opponent's concluding thrust (finish) in the final cadence.


*Double feint attack on the seventh invito*

*Parries*

The following parries can be adopted:
– second (eighth)–seventh–second (eighth),
– second (eighth)–seventh–circular seventh.


*Counter-attacks*

The first cadence is omitted; instead the first feint should be reacted to by the second parry.
1. Stop thrust performed on the second feint in the second cadence and the point conducted inside and low instead of the simple seventh parry.
2. Stop thrust on the opponent's finish in the final cadence.

## 2. Change thrust followed by simple double feint attacks carried out from the opponent's engagement

The change thrust is the predecessor and, at the same time, reasonable preparatory action of simple double feint introduced by change thrust. It is a precondition for the change thrust that the fencer's own blade which is engaged by his opponent should be held in line. In this position the fencer's primary objective is to break away from the engagement forced on him by his adversary and score a hit with a change thrust. The fencer has secondary security in the knowledge that provided the opponent carries out a riposte after parrying the thrust, he can reply with a counter-riposte.

The next stage is the single and then the double feint, provided there has been adequate preparation by the previously outlined method.

The fact that the elements of the action must be built on top of one another must always be borne in mind during the fencing lesson.

*Double feint attack carried out from the opponent's sixth (third) engagement*

*Parries*

The following parries can be adopted:
– fourth–sixth (third)–fourth,
– fourth–sixth (third)–circular sixth (third),
– fourth–sixth (third)–semicircular seventh,
– fourth–sixth (third)–second (eighth).

*Counter-attacks*

The first cadence is omitted; instead the first feint should be reacted to by the fourth parry.
1. Stop thrust carried out in the second cadence outside and low on the second feint instead of the simple sixth parry.
2. Stop thrust in the final cadence performed on the opponent's concluding thrust.


*Double feint attack from the opponent's fourth engagement*

*Parries*

The following parries can be adopted:
– sixth (third)–fourth–sixth (third),
– sixth (third)–fourth–circular fourth.


*Counter-attacks*

The first cadence is omitted; instead the first feint should be reacted to by the sixth parry.
1. Stop thrust executed inside and high on the opponent's second feint in the second cadence and instead of the simple fourth parry.
2. Stop thrust performed on the adversary's finish in the final cadence.

*Double feint attack from the opponent's second (eighth) engagement*

*Parries*

The following parries can be adopted:
– sixth (third)–second (eighth)–sixth (third),
– sixth (third)–second (eighth)–circular second (eighth),
– sixth (third)–second (eighth)–semicircular fourth,
– seventh–second (eighth)–seventh,
– seventh–second (eighth)–circular second (eighth),
– seventh–second (eighth)–semicircular fourth.

*Counter-attacks*

The first cadence is omitted; instead the first feint should be reacted to by the sixth or seventh parry.
1. Stop thrust carried out outside and low on the second feint in the second cadence and instead of the simple second parry.
2. Stop thrust executed on the adversary's concluding thrust in the final cadence.

*Double feint attack performed from the opponent's seventh engagement*

*Parries*

The following parries can be adopted:
– second (eighth)–seventh–second (eighth),
– second (eighth)–seventh–circular seventh.

The first cadence is omitted; instead the first feint should be reacted to by the second parry.

1. Stop thrust carried out inside and low on the opponent's second feint in the second cadence and instead of the simple seventh parry.

2. Stop thrust on the opponent's concluding thrust in the final cadence.

## 3. Bind and thrust followed by simple double feint attacks

*(a) Double feint attack performed with simple engagement from invito and on a blade held in line*

Attack with bind is the natural preliminary action of the simple double feint attack introduced by engagement. The very realistic character of attacks with bind was pointed out earlier during the discussion of actions of the basic level. The contact made between the blades in the course of engagement brings about the physical contact with the opponent which can tell the attacker through the blade the phase at which the adversary is realizing the forthcoming attack. Depending on this the final form to be assumed by the attack is established as the movement develops. If the opponent is found to have been taken by surprise, a straight thrust is carried out through the acceleration of the action. In this case the secondary possibility is to perform a counter-riposte and then a single or double feint attack can be applied by building up the movement on the reflex parries. The relation between the blades prior to the launching of the attack has an important part to play in the preparatory stage because it enables the fencer to carry out an attack from the side from which an offensive is not expected. This can be done not only by simple bind but also semicircular, circular and change types of engagement as well as transfers.

*Double feint attack on a blade held in high line*

*Fourth bind, simple double feint attack performed from the sixth (third) invito*

*Parries*

- fourth–sixth (third)–fourth,
- fourth–sixth (third)–circular sixth (third),
- fourth–sixth (third)–seventh,
- fourth–sixth (third)–second (eighth).

*Counter-attacks*

The first possibility, that is the time degagement thrust, and the second, that is the stop thrust to be carried out on the first feint in the first cadence, are omitted; instead the first feint should be reacted to by the fourth parry.

1. Stop thrust performed outside and low on the opponent's second feint in the second cadence and instead of the simple sixth parry.

2. Stop thrust carried out on the opponent's concluding thrust in the second cadence.

*Sixth (third) bind, simple double feint attack performed from the second (eighth) invito*

*Parries*

The following parries can be adopted:
– second (eighth)–sixth (third)–second (eighth),
– second (eighth)–sixth (third)–circular sixth (third),
– second (eighth)–sixth (third)–semicircular seventh.

*Counter-attacks*

The first possibility, that is to carry out a time degagement thrust, and the second, that is the performance of a stop thrust on the first feint in the first cadence, are omitted; instead the first feint should be reacted to by the second parry.
1. Stop thrust performed outside and low on the opponent's second feint in the second cadence and instead of the simple sixth parry.
2. Stop thrust carried out on the opponent's concluding thrust in the final cadence.

*Double feint attack on a blade held in low line*

*Second (eighth) bind, double feint attack from sixth (third) and seventh invito*

*Parries*

The following parries can be adopted:
– sixth (third)–second (eighth)–sixth (third),

– sixth (third)–second (eighth)–seventh,
– sixth (third)–second (eighth)–circular second (eighth),
– sixth (third)–second (eighth)–semicircular fourth.

### Counter-attacks

The time degagement thrust, which is the first possibility, and stop thrust carried out in the first cadence, which is the second one, are omitted; instead the first feint should be reacted to by adopting the second parry.
1. Stop thrust executed outside and high on the second feint in the second cadence and instead of the simple second parry.
2. Stop thrust carried out on the opponent's concluding thrust in the final cadence.

### *Seventh bind, double feint attack performed from the second (eighth) invito*

### Parries

The following parries can be adopted:
– seventh–second (eighth)–seventh,
– seventh–second (eighth)–circular second (eighth),
– seventh–second (eighth)–semicircular fourth,
– seventh–second (eighth)–simple sixth.

### Counter-attacks

The time degagement thrust (the first possibility) and stop thrust carried out in the first cadence (second possibility) are omitted; instead the first feint should be reacted to by using the seventh parry.

1. Stop thrust carried out outside and high on the second feint in the second cadence and instead of the simple second parry.

2. Stop thrust performed on the opponent's concluding thrust in the final cadence.

(b) *Double feint attack performed with semicircular bind from invito and on a blade held in line*

*Attack on a blade held in high line*

*Simple double feint, semicircular fourth bind from the second (eighth) invito.*

*Simple double feint, semicircular sixth (third) bind performed from the seventh invito.*

*Attack on a blade held in low line*

*Simple double feint introduced by semicircular second (eighth) bind and performed from the fourth invito.*

*Simple double feint introduced by the seventh bind and performed from the sixth (third) invito.*

*The parries and the exercises of counter-attacks* are identical with those of simple engagements.

(c) *Double feint attack performed with a circular bind from the invito and on a blade held in line*

*Attack on a blade held in high line*

*Simple double feint with circular fourth bind performed from the fourth invito.*

*Simple double feint with circular sixth (third) bind performed from the sixth (third) invito.*

*Attack on a blade held in low line*

*Simple double feint with circular second (eighth) bind performed from the second (eighth) invito.*

*Simple double feint with circular seventh bind and performed from the seventh invito.*

*The parries and the exercises of counter-attacks* are the same as those of double feints introduced by simple engagements.

(d) *Double feint attack with change bind on the engaged blade and performed from the fencer's own engagement*

*Attack on a blade held in high line*

*Simple double feint with change sixth (third) bind performed from the fourth engagement.*

*Simple double feint with change fourth bind performed from the sixth (third) engagement.*

*Attack on a blade held in low line*

*Simple double feint introduced by change second (eighth) bind performed from the seventh engagement.*

*Simple double feint introduced by change seventh bind performed from the second (eighth) engagement.*

*The parries and the exercises of counter-attacks* are identical with those of simple binds followed by double feint attacks.

(e) *Double feint attack with change bind on the engaging blade and performed from the opponent's engagement*

*Attack carried out from high line*

*Simple double feint introduced by change sixth (third) bind on the fourth engagement.*

*Simple double feint introduced by change fourth bind on the sixth (third) engagement.*

*Attack carried out from low line*

*Simple double feint introduced by change second (eighth) bind on the seventh engagement.*

*Simple double feint introduced by change seventh bind on the second (eighth) engagement.*

*The parries and the exercises of counter-attacks* are identical with those of double feints introduced by simple bind.

(f) *Double feint attack with simple and change binds performed from the line and on a blade held in line*

300

*Attack from high line on a blade held in high line*

*Simple double feint introduced by simple fourth bind.*

*Simple double feint introduced by change seventh bind.*

*Simple double feint introduced by change sixth (third) bind.*

*Attack from high line on a blade held in low line*

*Simple double feint introduced by simple second (eighth) bind.*

*Simple double feint introduced by change seventh bind.*

*Attack from low line on a blade held in low line*

*Simple double feint introduced by simple seventh bind.*

*Simple double feint introduced by change second (eighth) bind.*

*Attack from low line on a blade held in high line*

*Simple double feint introduced by simple sixth (third) bind.*

*Simple double feint introduced by half change fourth bind.*

*The parries and the exercises of counter-attacks* are the same as those
of simple double feints introduced by simple bind.

(g) *Transfer from the fencer's own engagement*

*Simple double feint introduced by transfer from the fourth engagement
into the second (eighth) bind.*

*Simple double feint introduced by transfer from the second (eighth) engagement into the fourth bind.*

*Simple double feint introduced by transfer from the seventh engagement into the sixth (third) bind.*

*Simple double feint introduced by transfer from the sixth (third) engagement into the seventh bind.*

*The parries and the exercises of counter-attacks* are identical with those of simple double feints introduced by simple binds.

## 4. Bind thrust followed by simple double feint attacks

Simple double feint attacks introduced by bind thrust can be deduced directly from the bind thrust, but they are related to every bind attack discussed so far.

Simple double feint introduced by the fourth flanconade, a section of the relevant material, is analysed below to serve as an example. The analysis is extended to the preliminary actions, which should be linked with one another in the course of bout fencing.

The attacker tries to score a hit by adopting the seventh bind and thrust. To this end he makes thorough preparations.

In the event of his attack having been parried by the opponent and followed by a riposte his reply is a counter-riposte. He might as well employ a stop thrust carried out on his adversary's riposte, or if the riposte fails to come, the fencer can perform a renewed attack *(remise)*.

The recommended method of developing this action is by adopting a simple feint followed by a double one designed to round the opponent's parry and parries.

Provided the adversary parries also the feint attack, he will follow with a counter-riposte or stop thrust on the opponent's action.

If the attacker finds that his attack on his adversary's seventh side promises little if any success, he should carry out change second bind from a preliminary light seventh contact made with the opponent's blade. He should then elaborate this action (simple feint, double feint, bind thrust and feint actions that can be performed from the bind thrust) in the same manner as in the case of simple attacks.

Where there is no hope of success with an attack on the adversary's seventh and second side, the fourth transfer from preliminary second engagement is available to create a new opportunity. All types of attacks that have been considered so far (from the fourth position) can be carried out from the new situation; they can be directed towards the high or low openings of the target and simple feints can be used to the best advantage.

The example analysed above is not given as some kind of hard and fast rule. The intention is simply to illustrate methods of preparing actions and of connecting them with one another.

The methods of introducing simple double feint attacks initiated by bind thrust can be of the following types:

*Attacks executed from invito on a blade held in line can be introduced by*

- simple bind,
- semicircular bind,
- circular bind.

*Attacks performed from engagement with change bind on a blade held in line can be carried out from*

- the fencer's own engagement,
- the opponent's engagement.


*Attacks from line on a blade held in line can be introduced by*

- simple bind,
- change bind.


*Attacks performed with transfer bind*

*Simple double feint with second (eighth) bind thrust*

*Simple double feint with fourth flanconade*

*Parries*

The following parries can be adopted:
- second (eighth)–seventh–second (eighth),
- seventh (eighth)–seventh–circular seventh,
- second (eighth)–sixth (third)–second (eighth),
- second (eighth)–sixth (third)–circular sixth (third),
- second (eighth)–sixth (third)–and semicircular seventh.


*Counter-attacks*

Counter-attacks can take the form of stop thrusts of the following types:

1. Stop thrust performed on the second feint in the second cadence.
It can be executed
 – inside and low instead of the simple seventh parry, or
 – outside and low instead of the simple sixth parry.
2. Stop thrust on the opponent's concluding thrust in the final cadence.
It can be carried out
 – high in the case of high finishes, or
 – low, inside or outside in the event of low finishes.


*Simple double feint introduced by the seventh bind thrust*

*Parries*

The following parries can be adopted:
 – seventh–second (eighth)–seventh,
 – seventh–second (eighth)–circular second,
 – seventh–second (eighth)–sixth (third),
 – seventh–second (eighth)–semicircular fourth.


*Counter-attacks*

Counter-attacks can take the form of stop thrusts such as:
1. Stop thrust performed outside and high on the second feint in the second cadence and instead of the simple second parry.
2. Stop thrust on the opponent's concluding thrust in the final cadence.
It can be performed
 – high, inside or outside in the case of high finishes, or
 – low, inside and outside in the event of low finishes.

## 5. Beat and thrust followed by simple double feint attacks

During the discussion of simple single feint attacks introduced by bind a comparison was made between the identical and different characteristics of binds and beats. It was stated, among other things, that while the objectives of binds and beats are similar they exercise very different influences on the opponent.

The beat accelerates the action and causes a faster reflex parry by the opponent. This is what justifies the method of adopting feints in the overwhelming majority of bind attacks. Parrying reflex brought about fairly early gives priority, especially in case the attack is to be performed from long distance, to the application of double feints.

When preparing an attack of this type, the fencer must constantly bear in mind that the action should be launched in as varied a manner as possible and from different blade relations. Compared to attacks with bind, the methods of introduction are of a shorter range because the possibility of adopting transfer is ruled out.

The methods of performing simple double feint attacks with beat thrust are as follows:

*(a)* Simple double feint attacks with beat thrust from invito and carried out on a blade held in line.

*(b)* Simple double feint attacks with semicircular binds from invito and carried out on a blade held in line.

*(c)* Simple double feint attacks with circular beats from invito and carried out on a blade held in line.

*(d)* Simple double feint attacks with change beats from the opponent's engagement and carried out on the engaging blade.

*(e)* Simple double feint attacks with simple and change beats from line and carried out on a blade held in line.

*(f)* Simple double feint attacks with change beats from the opponent's engagement and carried out on the engaging blade.

*(g)* Simple double feint attacks with beats from invito and line and carried out on a blade held in line.

The parries and the counter-attacks are identical with those of simple double feint attacks introduced by bind.

## 6. Time degagement thrust followed by simple double feint attacks

Simple double feint attacks introduced by time degagement thrust should be prepared and commenced in the same manner as simple double feint attacks introduced by change thrust. The only difference between the two methods is that the attack is started by time degagement thrust, and the opponent's blade must be avoided when his first bind is attempted.

*The attacks can be performed on*

– simple bind or beat,
– semicircular bind or beat,
– circular bind or beat,
– change bind or beat.

*The parries and the exercises of counter-attacks* are identical with those of simple double feint attacks started with change thrust.

# Circular double feints

When giving general definitions referring to feints it was pointed out that the type (quality) of feint is dependent on three principal factors:

(a) *The methods of introduction*. For example, straight thrust, change or time degagement thrust, bind, bind thrust, transfer, beat and the variations of their combinations. This applies to circular double feints to the same extent as to simple single, circular single and simple double feints, points discussed earlier. The methods already listed should be taken as the basic introduction to the material and to instruction in circular double feints.

(b) *The number of parries rounded*. The circular double feint rounds two parries.

(c) *The type (quality) of parries rounded*. In the latter case three variations can be distinguished.

In the first case: the first parry is a simple one, while the second is a circular, semicircular or destructing parry.
In the second case: the first is a circular, semicircular, destructing or change parry, while the second parry is a simple one.

The relevant actions are classified under the group of double circular feints, but it would be more accurate to describe them as mixed feints.

Their character is only too easy to recognize from the definition of the feint because the sequence of the parries rounded is given.

For example, "simple and circular" double feint or "circular or simple" double feint introduced by the fourth engagement.

In the third case: both are circular, semicircular or destructing parries or the first parry is a change one, the second parry is circular, semicircular or destructing.

The latter combination frequently occurs in the event of attack carried out on a blade held in line.

During the analysis of the material the scheme of parries outlined above is applied.

The principal points of launching an attack which determine the preceding relation between the blades should be given special emphasis in the practical material. Naturally there are no new elements to be encountered here. The parrying system from which the basic exercises of the fencing lesson can be conducted is determined, and in the knowledge of the preliminaries of all the types of attacks the basis can be found on which the exercises can be built up to the highest level, that is to the counter-riposte ending in circular double feint.

This will be followed by the analysis of a concrete version of the different types of actions to serve as an example. All possible exercises are subject to detailed and complete analysis as a result of which all possible variations of the two parries that can be rounded are given within the three basic variations along with the possibility of parrying the action as the third (concluding) parry.

Such concrete material is supplied in the analysis of
– simple and circular double feints introduced by straight thrust,
– circular and simple double feints introduced by straight thrust,
– double circular feints introduced by straight thrust
and carried out on the sixth invito.

If the material we have discussed up to now has analysed in detail the possibilities and forms of finish from the final position of all the four parries, and from a consideration of the material it can be seen that at the present stage of épée fencing innumerable variations of exercises can be applied by coach and pupil. To attempt to calculate just how many even only approximately would be to go well beyond our objective. In what may seem to be a labyrinth of actions there exist certain basic central actions, and these are brought within easy reach by the reduction of the innumerable variations to the basic ones. These basic centres are, for example, the four on guard and two line positions, the final position of the four parries and the mutual relation between the two blades prior to the launching of an attack. Every action invariably starts out from these basic points and returns to them.

It is an essential means of and condition for understanding and then acquiring the material now under consideration that every action given can be reduced to the basic. This solution renders it unnecessary to describe the process of elaboration from every position and in every variation, since the individual examples analysed in detail are sufficient to indicate that they become identical at the relevant focuses, they are limited and as such they do not result in new variations for they are only repeated.

The association to one another of the variations analysed at the stage of fundamental exercises is central to the material we are about to consider.

Concerning the system of stop thrusts it is important to repeatedly point out that in the case of double feints the first cadence is omitted (in order to give prominence to the feint), and so the "stop thrust in the second cadence" is performed–as a primary movement–only in the second stage instead of the second parry that is to be rounded.

If the fencer is well versed in the rules, this is also a standard centre. A secondary stop thrust possibility in the final cadence in the execution of both parries is to rule out the attack, depending on the direction of the attack, high or low.

# 1. Straight thrust followed by circular double feint attacks carried out on every type of invito

*Attacks on the sixth (third) invito*

*Straight thrust, simple and circular double feints*

*Parries*

The following parries can be adopted:
- fourth–circular fourth–sixth (third),
- fourth–circular fourth–circular fourth,
- fourth–circular fourth–semicircular second,
- fourth–circular fourth–destructing disengage seventh,
- fourth–semicircular second (eighth)–sixth (third),
- fourth–semicircular second (eighth)–seventh,
- fourth–semicircular second (eighth)–circular second (eighth),
- fourth–semicircular second (eighth)–circular second (eighth),
- fourth–semicircular second (eighth)–semicircular fourth,
- fourth–destructing seventh–second (eighth),
- fourth–destructing seventh–circular seventh,
- fourth–destructing seventh–semicircular sixth (third),
- fourth–destructing seventh–destructing fourth,
- second (eighth)–circular second (eighth)–seventh,
- second (eighth)–circular second (eighth)–sixth (third),
- second (eighth)–circular second (eighth)–circular second (eighth),
- second (eighth)–circular second (eighth)–semicircular fourth,
- second (eighth)–semicircular fourth–sixth (third),
- second (eighth)–semicircular fourth–circular fourth,
- second (eighth)–semicircular fourth–semicircular second (eighth),
- second (eighth)–semicircular fourth–destructing seventh.

*Counter-attacks*

Counter-attacks can take the form of stop thrusts of the following types:
1. Stop thrust performed low on the second feint in the second cadence and instead of circular fourth, semicircular seventh, destructing seventh, circular second or semicircular fourth parry.
2. Stop thrust carried out low or high in the final cadence, time thrust executed on the opponent's concluding thrust.

*Straight thrust, circular and simple double feints*

*Parries*

The following parries can be adopted:
– circular sixth (third)–fourth–sixth (third),
– circular sixth (third)–fourth–circular fourth,
– circular sixth (third)–fourth–semicircular second,
– circular sixth (third)–fourth–destructing seventh,
– circular sixth (third)–second (eighth)–sixth (third),
– circular sixth (third)–second (eighth)–seventh,
– circular sixth (third)–second (eighth)–circular second (eighth),
– circular sixth (third)–second (eighth)–semicircular fourth,
– semicircular seventh–second (eighth)–seventh,
– semicircular seventh–second (eighth)–sixth (third),
– semicircular seventh–second (eighth)–circular second (eighth),
– semicircular seventh–second (eighth)–semicircular fourth.

## Counter-attacks

Counter-attacks can take the form of stop thrusts of the following–types:
1. Stop thrust carried out high on the second feint in the second
cadence and instead of a simple fourth and second parry.
2. Stop thrust performed high or low in the final cadence. It is
actually a time thrust on the opponent's finish.

## Double circular feints

### Parries

The following can be adopted:
– circular sixth (third)–circular sixth (third)–fourth,
– circular sixth (third)–circular sixth (third)–second (eighth),
– circular sixth (third)–circular sixth (third)–circular sixth
(third),
– circular sixth (third)–circular sixth (third)–semicircular seventh,
– circular sixth (third)–semicircular seventh–second (eighth),
– circular sixth (third)–semicircular seventh–circular seventh,
– circular sixth (third)–semicircular seventh–semicircular
sixth (third),
– circular sixth (third)–semicircular seventh–destructing fourth,
– semicircular seventh–circular seventh–second (eighth),
– semicircular seventh–circular seventh–semicircular sixth
(third),
  – semicircular seventh–circular seventh–destructing fourth,
  – semicircular seventh–semicircular sixth (third)–fourth,
  – semicircular seventh–semicircular sixth (third)–second
(eighth),

– semicircular seventh–semicircular sixth (third)–circular sixth (third),

– semicircular seventh–semicircular sixth (third)–semicircular seventh,

– semicircular seventh–destructing fourth–sixth (third),

– semicircular seventh–destructing fourth–circular fourth,

– semicircular seventh–destructing fourth–semicircular second,

– semicircular seventh–destructing fourth–disengage seventh.

*Counter-attacks*

Counter-attacks can take the form of stop thrusts of the following types:

1. Stop thrust carried out high on the second feint in the second cadence and instead of the circular sixth, semicircular seventh, semicircular sixth and circular seventh parry.

2. Stop thrust performed low or high on the opponent's concluding thrust in the final cadence.

*Attacks on the fourth invito*

*Straight thrust simple and circular double feints*

*Parries*

The following parries can be adopted:
– sixth (third)–circular sixth (third),
– sixth (third)–semicircular seventh.

*Counter-attacks*

Counter-attacks can take the form of stop thrusts of the following types:
1. Stop thrust performed in the second cadence instead of the second parry.
2. Stop thrust carried out low or high on the opponent's concluding thrust in the final cadence.

*Straight thrust, circular and simple double feints*

*Parries*

The following parries can be adopted:
– circular fourth–sixth (third),
– semicircular second (eighth)–sixth (third),
– semicircular second (eighth)–seventh,
– destructing seventh–second (eighth).

*Counter-attacks*

Counter-attacks can take the form of stop thrusts of the following types:
1. Stop thrust executed low or high on the second feint in the second cadence and instead of the second parry.
2. Stop thrust carried out low or high on the opponent's concluding thrust in the final cadence.

*Straight thrust, double circular feint*

*Parries*

The following parries can be adopted:
– circular fourth–sixth (third),
– semicircular second (eighth)–sixth (third),
– semicircular second (eighth)–seventh,
– destructing seventh–second (eighth).

*Counter-attacks*

Counter-attacks can take the form of stop thrusts such as:
1. Stop thrust executed low or high on the second feint in the second cadence and instead of the second parry.
2. Stop thrust carried out low or high on the opponent's concluding thrust in the final cadence.

*Straight thrust, double circular feint*

*Parries*

The following parries can be adopted:
– circular fourth–circular fourth,
– circular fourth–semicircular second (eighth),
– circular fourth–destructing seventh,
– semicircular second (eighth)–circular second (eighth),
– semicircular second (eighth)–semicircular fourth,
– destructing seventh–circular seventh,
– destructing seventh–semicircular sixth–circular sixth,
– destructing seventh–disengage fourth.

316

## Counter-attacks

Counter-attacks can take the form of stop thrusts of the following types:

1. Stop thrust carried out low or high on the second feint in the second cadence and instead of the second parry.

2. Stop thrust performed low or high on the opponent's concluding thrust in the final cadence.

It can be observed that in the case of the exercises analysed so far the system of stop thrusts is identical with that of the material considered earlier in every situation that occurs. For this reason analysis of this system will be omitted.

### Attacks on the second invito

### Straight thrust, simple and circular double feints

### Parries

The following parries can be adopted:
– sixth (third)–circular sixth (third),
– sixth (third)–semicircular seventh,
– seventh–circular seventh,
– seventh–semicircular sixth (third),
– seventh–destruction fourth.

*Straight thrust, circular and simple double feints*

*Parries*

The following parries can be adopted:
– circular second (eighth)–sixth (third),
– circular second (eighth)–seventh,
– semicircular fourth–sixth (third).


*Double circular feints*

*Parries*

The following parries can be adopted:
– circular second (eighth)–circular second (eighth),
– circular second (eighth)–semicircular fourth,
– semicircular fourth–circular fourth,
– semicircular fourth–semicircular second (eighth),
– semicircular fourth–destructing seventh.


*Attacks on the seventh invito*

*Straight thrust, simple and circular feints*

*Parries*

The following parries can be adopted:
– second (eighth)–circular second (eighth),
– second (eighth)–semicircular fourth.

*Straight thrust, circular and simple double feints*

*Parries*

The following parries can be adopted:
– circular seventh–second (eighth),
– semicircular sixth (third)–second (eighth),
– semicircular sixth (third)–fourth,
– destructing fourth–sixth (third).

*Double circular feints*

*Parries*

The following parries can be adopted:
– circular seventh–circular seventh,
– circular seventh–semicircular sixth (third),
– circular seventh–destructing fourth,
– semicircular sixth (third)–circular sixth (third),
– semicircular sixth (third)–semicircular seventh,
– destructing fourth–circular fourth,
– destructing fourth–semicircular second (eighth),
– destructing fourth–destructing fourth.

## 2. Change thrust followed by circular double feint attacks

The movement that precedes this action is engagement performed by the adversary.

In the material considered so far the change thrust has been described as

– an independent group of exercises,
– simple single feint,
– circular single feint,
– simple double feint.

The material denoted by the title of the present chapter is based on the previous material which, at the same time, comprises the elements of which double circular feints are composed. As in the case of circular double feints introduced by straight thrust all the three types of circular double feints can be found here. Analysis of the relevant material is unnecessary because the variations occurring here are identical in both attack and defence with those of circular double feints introduced by straight thrust. For example, the exercises introduced by change thrust and carried out from the sixth engagement are the same as those that can be performed on the sixth invito. The only new and different element occurs in the relative position of the blades prior to the launching of the attack.

## 3. Bind and thrust followed by circular double feint attacks

Attack performed with engagement serves as a basis for the material to be considered in the present chapter. In the case of single feint attacks introduced by bind thrust the possibilities of launching an attack on every position of the blade is considered from every possible situation. They are exactly the same in the present type of attack, too.

In the course of the discussion of circular single feint attacks it was stated that when the attack is performed on a blade held in line (in the event of a circular feint) the parry rounded should be qualified as a change parry.

In the case of double feints there are again three possibilities taking into account the sequence of parries rounded. They are as follows:

*(a)* The first parry is a simple one as in the case of a simple feint whereas the second one is circular as in the case of the circular feint.

*(b)* The first is a change parry as in the case of circular feint whereas the second is a simple one as in the case of the simple feint.

*(c)* The first is a change parry as in the case of the circular feint while the second one is circular as in the case of the circular feint.

It is obvious from the above that the exercises of this kind of attack are based on the variations established as a combination of simple and circular single feints introduced by bind. The parrying system is adjusted accordingly.

As earlier, the complete parrying system is given in detail only in the case of one attack: the circular double feint started with the fourth bind, because all the four types of parries can be found in the final position of parrying an attack that can be performed from any of the sides. Further elaboration of the actions from the individual parries always offers identical possibilities.

*Attack on a blade held in high line*

*Fourth bind, circular double feint attacks*

*Fourth bind, simple and circular doublef eints*

*Parries*

The following parries can be adopted:
– fourth–circular fourth–sixth (third),
– fourth–fourth–circular fourth,

- fourth–circular fourth–semicircular second (eighth),
- fourth–circular fourth–destructing seventh,
- fourth–semicircular second (eighth)–sixth (third),
- fourth–semicircular second (eighth)–seventh,
- fourth–semicircular second (eighth)–circular second (eighth),
- fourth–semicircular second (eighth)–semicircular fourth,
- fourth–destructing seventh–second (eighth),
- fourth–destructing seventh–circular seventh,
- fourth–destructing seventh–semicircular sixth (third),
- fourth–destructing seventh–disengage fourth.


*Counter-attacks*

Counter-attacks can take the form of stop thrusts of the following types:
1. Stop thrust carried out low on the second feint in the second cadence and instead of the second parry (which can be a circular fourth, semicircular second [eighth] or destructing seventh).
2. Stop thrust performed low or high on the opponent's concluding thrust in the final cadence.


*Fourth bind, circular and simple double feints*

*Parries*

The following parries can be adopted:
- change sixth (third)–fourth–sixth (third),
- change sixth (third)–fourth–circular fourth,
- change sixth (third)–fourth–semicircular second,
- change sixth (third)–fourth–destructing seventh,
- change sixth (third)–second–sixth (third),

– change sixth (third)–second (eighth)–seventh,
– change sixth (third)–second (eighth)–circular second (eighth),
– change sixth (third)–second (eighth)–semicircular fourth,
– change seventh–second (eighth)–sixth (third),
– change seventh–second (eighth)–seventh,
– change seventh–second (eighth)–circular second (eighth),
– change seventh–second (eighth)–semicircular fourth.

## Counter-attacks

Counter-attacks can take the form of stop thrusts of the following types:
1. Stop thrust executed high on the second feint in the second cadence and instead of the second parry that can be a fourth or second.
2. Stop thrust carried out high or low on the opponent's concluding thrust in the final cadence.

## Fourth bind, double circular feint

### Parries

The following parries can be adopted:
– change sixth (third)–circular sixth (third)–fourth,
– change sixth (third)–circular sixth (third)–second (eighth),
– change sixth (third)–circular sixth (third)–circular sixth (third),
– change sixth (third)–circular sixth (third)–semicircular seventh,
– change sixth (third)–semicircular seventh–circular seventh,

– change sixth (third)–semicircular seventh–semicircular sixth (third),

– change sixth (third)–semicircular seventh–destructing fourth,

– change seventh–circular seventh–second (eighth),

– change seventh–circular seventh–circular seventh,

– change seventh–circular seventh–semicircular sixth (third),

– change seventh–circular seventh–destructing fourth,

– change seventh–semicircular sixth (third)–fourth,

– change seventh–semicircular sixth (third)–second (eighth),

– change seventh–semicircular sixth (third)–circular sixth (third),

– change seventh–semicircular sixth (third)–semicircular seventh,

– change seventh–destructing fourth–sixth (third),

– change seventh–destructing fourth–circular fourth,

– change seventh–destructing fourth–semicircular second (eighth),

– change seventh–destructing fourth–destructing seventh.


*Counter-attacks*

Counter-attacks can take the form of stop thrusts of the following types:

1. Stop thrust carried out on the second feint in the second cadence and instead of the second parry that can be circular sixth, semicircular and circular seventh, semicircular sixth and destructing fourth.

2. Stop thrust performed low or high on the opponent's concluding thrust in the final cadence.

The paragraphs that follow contain circular double feint attacks introduced by the sixth, second or seventh bind, but only the first two parries rounded by the attacker will be given in accordance with the sequence outlined above.

The system of stop thrusts whether they are carried out in the second or final cadence is identical with that discussed so far.


*Attack on a blade held in high line*

*Sixth bind, circular double feints*

*Sixth bind, simple and circular double feints*

*Parries*

The following parries can be adopted:
– second (eighth)–circular second (eighth),
– second (eighth)–semicircular fourth.


*Sixth bind, circular and simple double feints*

*Parry*

The following parry can be adopted:
– change seventh–second (eighth).


*Sixth bind, double circular feint*

*Parries*

The following parries can be adopted:
– change seventh–circular seventh,

- change seventh–semicircular sixth (third),
- change seventh–destructing fourth.


*Attacks on a blade held in low line*

*Second bind, circular double feint attacks*

*Second bind, simple and circular double feints*

*Parries*

The following parries can be adopted:
- sixth (third)–circular sixth (third),
- sixth (third)–semicircular seventh,
- seventh–circular seventh,
- seventh–semicircular sixth (third),
- seventh–destructing fourth.


*Second bind, circular and simple double feints*

*Parries*

The following parries can be adopted:
- change fourth–sixth (third),
- sixth (third)–circular sixth (third),
- sixth (third)–semicircular seventh.

*Second bind, double circular feint*

*Parries*

The following parries can be adopted:
– change fourth–circular fourth,
– change fourth–semicircular second (eighth),
– change fourth–destructing seventh,
– change second (eighth)–circular second (eighth),
– change second (eighth)–semicircular fourth.


*Attacks on a blade held in low line*

*Seventh bind, simple and circular double feints*

*Parries*

The following parries can be adopted:
– seventh–circular seventh,
– seventh–semicircular sixth (third),
– seventh–destructing fourth.


*Seventh bind, circular and simple double feints*

*Parries*

The following parries can be adopted:
– change second (eighth)–sixth (third),
– change second (eighth)–sixth (third),
– change fourth–sixth (third).

*Parries*

The following parries can be adopted:
- change second (eighth)–circular second (eighth),
- change second (eighth)–semicircular fourth,
- change fourth–circular fourth,
- change fourth–semicircular second (eighth),
- change fourth–destructing seventh.

# 4. Bind thrust followed by circular double feint attacks

The foundations of the material were discussed in detail in connection with bind thrust followed by simple and circular double feints. Among other things the difference arising from the direction of the attack compared to attacks introduced by a bind was also pointed out.

The direction of the attack brings about fundamental changes in the parrying system.

In contrast to attacks with bind the simple parries act as opposition and ceding parries. Parry performed on the opposite side is termed as change parry here, too. The name and part played by the parry rounded by the second feint is the same as those in case of attacks introduced by bind.

Where necessary the system of the material will be analysed below in appropriate detail.

*Attacks on a blade held in high line*

*Circular double feints introduced by sixth engagement and bind thrust*

*Simple and circular double feints introduced by sixth engagement and bind thrust*

*Parries*

The following parries can be adopted:
– simple opposition sixth (third)–circular sixth (third),
– simple opposition sixth (third)–semicircular seventh,
– simple ceding first–circular first.

*Circular and simple double feint introduced by sixth engagement and bind thrust*

In this case the parry is confined to
– change fourth–sixth (third).

*Double circular feint introduced by sixth engagement and bind thrust*

*Parries*

The following parries can be adopted:
– change fourth–circular fourth,
– change fourth–semicircular second (eighth),
– change fourth–destructing seventh.

*Attacks on a blade held in high line*

*Circular double feints introduced by the fourth engagement and bind thrust*

*Simple and circular double feints introduced by the fourth engagement and bind thrust*

*Parries*

The following parries can be adopted:
– simple opposition fourth–circular fourth,
– simple opposition fourth–semicircular second (eighth),
– simple opposition fourth–destructing seventh,
– simple ceding seventh (this is only a theoretical definition).

*Circular and simple double feints introduced by the fourth engagement and bind thrust*

*Parries*

The following parries can be adopted:
– change sixth (third)–fourth,
– change sixth (third)–second (eighth),
– change seventh–second (eighth).

*Double circular feint introduced by the fourth engagement and bind thrust*

*Parries*

The following parries can be adopted:
– change sixth (third)–circular sixth (third),
– change sixth (third)–semicircular seventh,
– change seventh–circular seventh,
– change seventh–semicircular sixth (third),
– change seventh–destructing fourth.

*Attacks on a blade held in high line*

*Circular double feints introduced by the fourth engagement and flanconade*

In the material denoted by the title the direction of the attack changes as compared to the previous exercises. At the same time the whole parrying system is adjusted to the attack.

*Simple circular double feint introduced by the fourth engagement and flanconade*

*Parries*

The following parries can be adopted:
– simple opposition second (eighth)–circular second (eighth),
– simple opposition second (eighth)–semicircular fourth,
– simple ceding fourth–circular fourth,
– simple ceding fourth–semicircular second,
– simple ceding fourth–destructing seventh.

*Circular and simple double feint introduced by the fourth engagement and flanconade*

In this case the parry is confined to
– change seventh–second (eighth).

*Double circular feint introduced by the fourth engagement and flanconade*

*Parries*

The following parries can be adopted:
– change seventh–circular seventh,
– change seventh–semicircular sixth,
– change seventh–destructing fourth.

*Attack on a blade held in low line*

*Second engagement and bind thrust, circular double feints*

Each of the exercises is identical with those of circular double feint introduced by the fourth flanconade, a point considered earlier.

*Seventh bind–flanconade, circular double feint*

*Seventh bind–flanconade, circular double feint*

The parrying system of both groups of exercises is identical with that of circular double feint attacks introduced by the seventh bind thrust. The formal differences arising from the special character of the attack were considered in connection with the simple feints.

No mention has been made of the concluding (third) parry and the stop thrust throughout the discussion of the whole material because they repeatedly occur (assuming the same form) in the material of the feint attacks considered earlier.

## 5. Beat and thrust followed by circular double feint attacks

The methods of introduction can be:
- beat thrust followed by simple and circular double feints,
- beat thrust followed by circular and simple double feints,
- beat thrust followed by double circular feints.

The exercises of this type of attack are grouped around the above-listed movements. The material concerning the preliminaries and introduction of the relevant exercises was discussed at length in connection with the simple double feints and in the corresponding paragraphs on simple single and circular single feint attacks. The material of the present chapter stems from the connection to one another in an appropriate sequence of the exercises discussed in detail in the chapter mentioned above. The system of parries and counter-attacks is identical with that of circular double feint attacks introduced by bind thrust.

## 6. Time degagement thrust followed by circular double feint attacks

Like the preceding chapters, this one also contains the three types of exercises discussed earlier. Every previous exercise that commences with time degagement thrust must be regarded as an antecedent of the group of exercises denoted in this chapter's title. Apart from this, analysis of the relevant exercises is rendered unnecessary by the fact that the exercises occurring here are identical with those of circular double feints introduced by change thrust and straight thrust.

Obviously the particular form of launching attacks must be taken into consideration here. The special feature of the action lies in the fact that establishment of the position of the blade resembling invito or preliminary engagement is delayed by one cadence (following degagement). The subsequent movements from this position are completely identical (in both attack and defence, including counter-attacks) with those of the exercises of circular double feints introduced by change thrust and straight thrust.

# XII. RENEWED
# ATTACKS

The preliminary conditions for the performance of renewed attacks arise from the positive initiative of the attacker. While causing the opponent to carry out parry or parries, or retreat in the course of the preparation of the attack, he can be forced into a defensive situation from which he will find it impossible to take the initiative or execute a riposte from the parry performed. Instead he will make every effort to withdraw from the range of attack either by carrying out parries in on guard position or by retreating.

Renewed attacks can be introduced by any version of the actions studied so far, or they can be prepared by complex repeated initiatives that follow from these actions.

The most general and frequently adopted tactical method of introduction is the beat because it is likely to bring about a rapid defensive reflex in the adversary.

*The technical forms of carrying out renewed attacks*

Like any other type of attack, renewed attacks can be performed as in foil fencing, with opposition or with angular thrust.

*Renewed attacks can take the form of*

(*a*) straight thrust,
(*b*) change thrust,
(*c*) straight lengthening,
(*d*) engagement followed by bind thrust,
(*e*) beat thrust.

(*a*) Renewed attacks are carried out with straight thrust if the defending fencer does not parry the first (pseudo) attack; instead he retreats with an invito in an attempt to withdraw himself from the range of attack.

Renewed attacks can be performed with renewed lunge (*rad-doppio*) when the opponent retreats by taking a step backwards.

In this case the renewed attack should be carried out as follows: the attacker resumes on guard position from the lunge of the preceding attack by pulling his rear foot forward and performs a straight thrust from on guard

– with lunge or
– with flèche

directed towards the opening of the target selected before the first attack.

Fig. 73

The renewed attack executed with renewed lunge from the previous lunge on the opponent's sixth type of invito is illustrated in figure 73. The dotted line indicates the attacker in the first lunge followed by the resumption of on guard position, while the dotted line on the right-hand side indicates the defending fencer at the moment the attack is launched.

Renewed attacks can be carried out with attack renewed completely *(ripresa d'attacco)* when the defending fencer takes two steps backwards at the moment the attack is started. In this case the completely renewed attack takes the form of a repeated step forward and lunge.

Renewed attacks can be executed with flèche when the defending fencer retreats continually. In this case the renewed attack takes the form of flèche.

In addition, renewed attacks from the position described above can also be performed with

– straight thrust, simple single feint,
– straight thrust, circular single feint,
– straight thrust, simple double feint,
– straight thrust, circular double feint.


*Parries*


The system of parrying renewed attacks is identical with the parries adopted against attacks of the same type.


*Counter-attacks*


The system of counter-attacks is the same as that of counter-attacks carried out on straight thrusts and their combination with feints.

337

*(b)* Renewed attacks are carried out with change thrust if the defending fencer parries the first (pseudo) attack but is either too slow in the riposte or does not execute a return thrust at all.

Renewed attacks can be performed with appel when the defending fencer carries out the parry without retreating. In this case the renewed attack should be executed as follows:

While remaining in the lunge that concluded the first attack the fencer should adopt a change thrust and conduct his blade in the direction of the open part of the target. While doing so he should stamp the foot corresponding to the hand holding the weapon on the piste.

Renewed attack can be executed with renewed lunge *(raddoppio)* if the defending fencer parries the first (pseudo) attack but he is either too slow to riposte or does not carry out a return thrust at all. In this case the guard of the adversary's weapon is rounded after breaking away from the parry; simultaneously the fencer resumes on guard position by pulling his rear foot forward, the right foot keeping the original position a thrust. A brief flèche can also be used instead of he second lunge.

Renewed attacks can be carried out with attack renewed completely *(ripresa d'attacco)* when the defending fencer takes two steps backwards simultaneously with the parrying movement but he is either too slow to riposte or does not perform a return thrust at all. In this case on guard position is resumed by pulling the rear foot forward. The rest of the hand's movement and the foot exercise is identical with all the variations performable with change thrust from long distance and executed from the opponent's engagement.

Renewed attacks can be carried out with flèche if the defending fencer is continuously on the retreat and is either too slow to riposte or does not perform a return thrust at all. In this case the attack should be renewed with change thrust supported by flèche. Breaking away from the parry should be delayed as much as possible and it should be performed in accordance with the parrying reflex induced in the opponent.

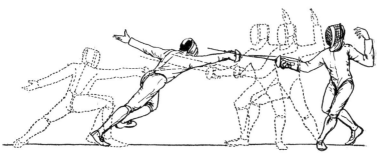

Fig. 74

Renewed attack executed with change thrust and flèche from the adversary's preliminary fourth parry is shown in figure 74. The position of the attacker and defending fencer prior to the attack is indicated by the dotted line.

In addition, renewed attacks from the positions described above can also be performed with

– change thrust, simple single feint,
– change thrust, circular single feint,
– change thrust, simple double feint,
– change thrust, circular double feint.

The system of parries and counter-attacks is identical with the system of parries and counter-attacks performed on change thrusts and their combination with feint.

*(c)* Renewed attacks are carried out with straight lengthening if the defending fencer displays uncertainty by parrying the first (pseudo) attack with a half parry or his parry is belated. In this case favourable tempo is provided for the attacker who can carry out a successful renewed attack on the partly undefended

section of the target as a result of appropriate co-ordination of time and fencing distance. The most reasonable method of renewal is, in this case, what is termed as straight lengthening.

The decisive factors of the success of renewal are time and speed. That is why it is imperative for the attacker to renew his movement without delay and at the very moment his adversary is found to be in a most uncertain position, that is when he is already on the retreat and his blade has been deadlocked in the unfinished parry.

Practically only the flèche is suitable for carrying out the action successfully.

In several cases the first attack (which acts as the introduction or preparation of the renewed one) is performed with flèche.

The action outlined above proved to be the key to the success of the Polish team in the final of the Gdansk World Championship. Irrespective of whether the host nation's squad applied this method consciously or only on the spur of the moment, it actually led to the defeat of both the Hungarian and French team.

This movement is neither a classic one nor a new one; nevertheless its highly successful application at a major international fencing tournament indicates its increasing importance. A study of the fencing methods of the top competitors shows that they have not adopted this action, yet those who have adopted it have had considerable success as a result.

*Parries*

It follows from the essence of the attack that virtually the simple opposition parry is the only rational action to adopt, because any movement involving the attacking weapon moving apart from the adversary's blade (such as rounding, circling or change) constitutes increased danger for the attacker.

340

*Riposte*

It is wrong to riposte mechanically. As long as the point of the opponent's blade is kept immediately in front of the target the fencer offers, the riposte is fraught with great danger. It is therefore advisable to maintain the weapon in the parry until the adversary's blade moves past the fencing target. This process can be accelerated if the defending fencer takes a step forward simultaneously with the parry and performs a riposte possibly of the bind type with a sort of turn outside in the opening stages of fencing at close quarters as the opponent is moving past him.

*Counter-attacks*

The counter-attack can take the form of stop thrust to be performed only at the moment the renewed attack is started, in other words, in the first cadence.

*(d)* Renewed attacks are carried out with engagement followed by bind thrust if, in reply to the first attack or the preparatory movement, the defending fencer holds his weapon in line or retreats while performing an uncertain, prolonged and line-like parry.

Depending on the distance, the foot exercise can be
– renewed lunge *(raddoppio)* or brief flèche,
– attack completely renewed *(ripresa d'attacco)* with a step forward and lunge or with flèche.

The bind should be performed simultaneously with the rear foot being pulled forward to enable the fencer to resume on guard position. The subsequent stages of the attack are identical with the basic exercises connected with bind and thrust performed from line on a blade held in line, or bind and thrust carried out from the opponent's engagement on the engaging blade.

341

The technical and formal versions of the thrust are also the same as those applied in the case of engagement and bind thrust.

Accordingly, the renewed attack can be performed on the opponent's blade held in line with

– simple or change engagement followed by thrust or bind thrust,

– change thrust carried out from the fencer's own engagement and followed by thrust or bind thrust,

– transfer from the fencer's own engagement followed by thrust or bind thrust.

The engagement positions listed above can be combined with

– simple single feint,

– circular single feint,

– simple double feint,

– circular double feint.

In reply to the adversary's engagement (so-called lengthened parries) the following actions can be carried out:

– simple re-engagement of the opposition type,

– change engagement on the opposite side.

The methods listed in connection with attacks on the opponent's blade held in line can be adopted in both of the above cases.

The possibilities and variations of parries and counter-attacks (stop thrusts) are completely identical with those analysed in the case of the simple and feint versions of engagement followed by bind thrust.

*(e)* Renewed attacks can be carried out with beat and thrust in case the defencing fencer, in response to the first attack or preparatory action, retreats

– with his blade held in line,

– with a parry,

– with invito.

In all the above cases the renewed attack can be a movement

introduced by beat. The foot exercise to be adopted depends on the distance between the two fencers.

Depending on the relation between the fencer's blade and that of his adversary the beat can be carried out:

*On a blade held in line*

in the following manner:
- simple or change beat–straight thrust,
- simple or change beat,
- simple single feint,
- circular single feint,
- simple double feint,
- circular double feint.

*From the opponent's engagement on the engaging blade*

- change beat–thrust,
- change beat–simple single feint (in the case of change fourth and seventh only),
- change beat–simple double feint (in the case of change fourth and seventh only),
- change beat–circular single feint,
- change beat–circular double feint.

Renewed attacks introduced by beat can also be carried out on invito and on guard position, both of them ranked as blade positions lying outside the line.

The parries and the exercises of counter-attacks are identical with the corresponding ones discussed in connection with attacks on the blade performed with beat.

# XIII. SECOND INTENTION ATTACKS

Second intention attacks are ranked by the Competition Rules issued by the International Fencing Federation in the category of "counter-tempo". Irrespective of the official classification, they are classic elements of fencing, and in the process of instruction we shall examine them as attacks, for the attacking characteristic is undoubtedly their dominant element.

The starting move, which is not of first intention, is performed by the fencer who means to carry out the second intention action. This can be verified by the analysis of the actions.

With this in mind the following definition given by Gellér in his book "Foil Fencing" is recommended to be accepted:

"Second intention can be defined as counter-actions performed on the opponent's habitual movements and those recognized or induced by the fencer in advance."

It is obvious from what has been described above that the "counter-tempo" is actually a counter-attack carried out on the counter-attack (tempo movement) the opponent has been caused to perform as a result of the fully conscious initiative taken by the fencer. Those ancient manuals which put the so-called second intention parries executed on the usual ripostes and the subsequent counter-ripostes, in the same category as second intention attacks are wrong. The criterion, they argue, is a counter-riposte that should be performed straight away from the parry carried out from the lunge.

This position is outdated because while admitting that from a tactical aspect every action can take the form of a second intention move as a preparatory movement of an attack or even counter-attack, it must be made clear that this process results in a new type of action only in the technical execution of counter-attacks.

The response to the opponent's ripostes or habitual ripostes is a counter-riposte carried out after parrying the opponent's move. The cadence and composition of the parry performed and the subsequent finish (the process of the counter-riposte) and the foot exercise adopted are always dependent on the situation prevailing between the two fencers, but above all on the distance separating them. Concerning the movements carried out with the hand and arm corresponding to the weapon and the foot exercise this does not exclude any of the possibilities that were discussed in connection with the "counter-riposte", the exercise of the highest level in the actions built up on the basic exercises of the fencing lesson.

These actions have been attached to the individual types of attack, and have been related to every possible attack analysed in detail.

The second intention parry as a possibility of continuing or finishing a move brings us back to the sphere of actions studied up to now. From the parry adopted it is possible to perform the same simple and feint attacks as those which can be carried out from the final position of a parry stemming from any other action.

Depending on the relation between the two blades the parries are identical with the types of parries considered so far. That is, if the parry is introduced by a thrust:

– the straight thrust and the associated simple or circular feints,

– the change thrust and the associated simple or circular feints,

– time degagement thrust and the associated simple or circular feints,

– bind and thrust and the associated simple or circular feints,

– bind thrust and the associated simple or circular parries,

– beat and thrust and the associated simple or circular feints.

At the moment the counter-attack is carried out both fencers hold their blade in line. In this case the relation between the two blades determines the "quality" of the second intention attack.

If the movement is introduced by attack on the blade and the opponent avoids contact with the attacker's weapon:

bind–simple, semicircular, circular or change,

beat–simple, semicircular, circular or change.

At the moment the counter-attack is due if one fencer is in on guard position and the other is holding his weapon in line, the second intention parry can be:

simple, semicircular, circular or destructing.

It is vital to the success of second intention attacks that they be prepared adequately and appropriately. This means that the opponent should be made to believe in the indicated first intention while the second remains concealed. Failure to perform the action in this manner leads to the opponent recognizing in due time what the fencer is after.

The relation between the two blades determines the "quality" of the second intention attack.

Detailed analysis of the different types of exercises was made in the chapter on Counter-attacks. The possibilities of applying them were determined for every possible attack.

Here they are summarized briefly and then fitted into the framework of the new type of actions.

*Counter-attacks can be of the following types:*

*(a)* – time degagement thrusts (performed on attacks on the blade),

– change stop thrusts (carried out from effective engagement of the blades),

*(b)* – stop thrusts of the following types:

– stop thrust executed in the first cadence (on the single feint),

– stop thrust carried out in the second cadence (on the double feint),

– stop thrust performed in the final cadence (on the concluding thrust of any of the attacks carried out by the adversary).

Second intention attack is carried out on the actions listed above in case the opponent's intention to perform a counter-attack has been recognized in time or he has been made to execute one.

It should be executed as follows: in the first stage the attack is indicated simultaneously with the foot corresponding to the arm with the weapon moving forwards. In the second stage the parry is carried out as the rear foot is pulled forward.

Depending on the distance the concluding thrust can be performed

– from on guard position,

– with lunge

– with flèche.

It can be a simple or a compound action if combined with one or another of the possibilities.

*Second intention attacks carried out on counter-attacks*

*First exercise*

*Second intention attack on counter-attack with time degagement thrust*

Fourth bind thrust.

(The attack should be performed from long distance and the pupil should be allowed to score a hit occasionally.)

*Counter-attack*

Time degagement stop thrust executed to the outside upper part of the target, the shoulder, upper arm or wrist corresponding to the weapon.

Depending on the distance the exercise is carried out with a powerful half lunge performed from on guard position, or perhaps by taking a step backwards if the adversary attacks with a flèche.

*Second intention parry*

in high line: simple fourth–sixth,
simple fourth–circular fourth parry;
in low line: simple fourth–destructing seventh parry,
simple fourth–semicircular second parry.

When executing the action, the fourth parry should be feinted and performed simultaneously with the foot corresponding to the hand with the weapon gradually slowly moving forward, so that the adversary is forced to avoid the bind. As the rear foot is pulled forward and stamping on the floor the opponent's thrust is parried by one of the parries listed above (the type of parry used depends on the direction in which the adversary's blade is moving in an attempt to avoid contact). From the resulting final position of the parry a simple finish of only one cadence is the generally adopted action, and it is directed towards the part of the target lying closest to the fencer.

Fig. 75

Figures 75, 76 and 77 illustrate the individual elements of second intention attacks.

Fig. 76

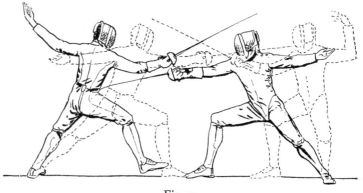

Fig. 77

Naturally the finish can be combined with a feint. This solution is recommended when the opponent seeks to take refuge in lengthening the distance and his reaction to the thrust is a rapid reflex-like move.

*Second exercise*

*Second intention attack on change stop thrust*

*Attack*

Sixth bind thrust to the low opening of the target performed from the fencer's own fourth engagement.

*Counter-attack*

Change stop thrust carried out
– low on the opponent's wrist or

– on the inside of his upper arm or on his shoulder corresponding to the weapon.

The action should be performed after the opponent's bind has been executed and at the moment contact is made between the two blades.

*Second intention parry*

It is performed
in low line: simple sixth–second parry,
simple sixth–semicircular seventh parry,
in high line: simple sixth–fourth parry,
simple sixth–circular sixth parry.

The technique of execution and the foot exercise are identical with the principles described in connection with the first exercise.

Of the parries listed above the most general and, at the same time, most effective one is the second (eighth), from which usually a bind time thrust of one cadence is performed as the finishing move of the action.

This type of thrust is effective even if one cadence is omitted, since the opponent's blade is completely under control throughout and it moves apart from the fencer's body during the thrust.

## Third exercise

*Second intention attack on a stop thrust executed in the first cadence*

*Attack*

A simple single feint (performed low or high) introduced by a change thrust and carried out from the opponent's second engagement.

*Counter-attack*

A stop thrust executed low and in the first cadence and instead of
– the simple sixth or
– the simple seventh parry.

In this case the fencer does not react to the feint. The parry is substituted by a stop thrust executed in accordance with the scheme analysed earlier.


*Second intention parry*

Performed with a
– high feint followed by simple second parry,
– high feint followed by change seventh parry,
– low feint followed by simple seventh parry,
– low feint followed by change seventh parry.

Simultaneously with the forward movement of the foot the change thrust feint is indicated and the opponent's counter-attack is parried in harmony with the reduction of the distance effected by the rear foot being pulled forwards.

The finish to be adopted is dependent on the final position of the parry, the distance and the fencer's own second intention.


*Fourth exercise*

*Second intention attack on a stop thrust performed in the second cadence*

*Attack*

Fourth beat on the opponent's blade held in high line, followed by circular and simple double feint.

352

*Counter-attack*

A stop thrust executed high in the second cadence and instead of
– the simple fourth or
– the simple second parry.
In the present case the first (circular) feint is reacted to by a
change sixth parry, while a stop thrust is carried out instead of
the second simple parry
– if the opponent indicates the second feint high, the stop
thrust should be carried out *high* instead of the simple fourth
parry,
– if the opponent indicates the second feint low, the stop
thrust should be executed *high* instead of the simple second
parry.


*Second intention parry*

It is performed with a
– beat–circular feint–simple fourth parry,
– beat–circular feint–change sixth parry.
In the case of a low feint
– the fourth parry is of the change type,
– the sixth parry is a simple one.
In the example analysed above and in the case of a second intention attack carried out on any of the stop thrusts executed in
the second cadence the attacker rounds his opponent's first parry
in every case, that is he actually performs one feint. This is the
movement with which the opponent is induced to carry out a
counter-attack. The second intention attack is executed on the
counter-attack by adopting any of the parries listed above.
For the finish the most convenient type of thrust should be
chosen.

*Fifth exercise*

*Second intention attack on a stop thrust performed in the final cadence*

*Attack*

It is a fourth flanconade combined with circular simple double feint.

*Counter-attack*

It is a stop thrust carried out in the final cadence.
The direction of the finish is a high one here, and
– inquartata or
– the sixth time thrust
is applied instead of the high parries so that both feints are reacted to; change seventh parry is performed in response to the flanconade feint and a simple second is carried out to the second (simple) feint.
The stop thrust is executed in the final cadence from the situation thus created and it is dependent on the direction of the opponent's closing thrust which, in the present case, is a high one.

*Second intention parry*

It is executed with
– flanconade circular and simple double feint–simple sixth parry,
– flanconade circular and simple double feint–change fourth parry.

In the exercises analysed above the fencer should perform the first phase of his own action, which is the approach comprising the forward movement of the foot corresponding to the hand with the weapon, so that the opponent's stop thrust in the final cadence is caused to be executed on the second feint following the rounding of both of the adversary's parries. The second intention parry should be performed on this stop thrust after the approach work (reduction of the distance) has been completed.

The form of finish to be adopted can be chosen freely.

All of the five exercises discussed in the foregoing are complete in themselves, only the question of differences between the counter-attacks has been considered within the framework of concrete action.

The examples can be applied in any attack of the same type, so no detailed descriptions to this effect are given here.

In the individual chapters of this book we have included detailed discussion of every type of counter-attacks carried out as determined by the specific character of the attack concerned. Second intention attacks on these counter-attacks should be executed in accordance with the technical and methodological principles described in the examples.

# XIV. FEINT COUNTER-ATTACKS (FINTA IN TEMPO)

Feint counter-attacks are regarded as belonging to the category of classic actions of the thrusting weapons. They should be adopted against opponents who use second intention attack on one or another type of counter-attack. In this case the counter-attack should be only a feint and the thrust should be carried out after rounding the opponent's induced second intention parry.

Depending on the quality (type) of the parry that has been rounded, the feint counter-attack can be

– simple or
– circular

according to the type of parry the fencer executing a second intention attack adopts in response to the indication of the feint.

All the actions discussed in the preceding chapter are also convenient and suitable for use as introductory moves of feint counter-attacks *(finta in tempo)*. However, it must be pointed out that feint counter-attacks are, as a rule, carried out consciously, that is following adequate preparation on second intention attacks introduced by simple attacks (bind or beat) on the blade.

These are the attacks enabling the best possible observation of the opponent's manipulation of the blade outside the line, the type or quality of the parries (simple or circular) he performs and their cadencing. It is a point of considerable importance that a blade moving outside the line does not involve the threat of an immediate hit.

Irrespective of what has been said the feint counter-attack introduced by stop thrusts executed in the first, second or final cadence can also be a consciously performed move even in the case of top class competitors, but in most cases this is a "reflex movement" that develops in course of the action.

The exercises of "feint counter-attacks" must be performed with due consideration paid to the ideas outlined above.

### First exercise

*Attack*

Semicircular fourth bind thrust performed from the fencer's own second invito.

*Counter-attack*

Time degagement stop thrust carried out high and outside.

*Second intention parry*

Semicircular fourth followed by simple sixth.

*Feint counter-attack*

It is composed of a feint indicated outside followed by a thrust inside.

The time degagement stop thrust performed on the oppo-

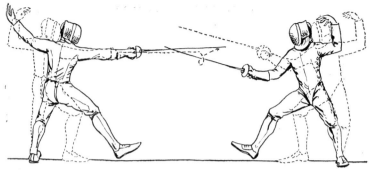

Fig. 78

The essential movements of the feint counter-attack *(finta in tempo)* are presented in figures 78 and 79.

Fig. 79

nent's attack on the blade is indicated in on guard position with the foot making a powerful stamp on the piste. The adversary's fourth bind is rounded with this thrust, this causes him to carry out a second intention parry which, in the present case, is a "circular fourth". This parry is also rounded and the movement is concluded with a powerful half lunge.

Provided the action is performed correctly the opponent is trapped in a stationary position and the second parry put in "freeze" position.

*Second exercise*

*Attack*

Circular sixth bind followed by bind thrust.

*Counter-attack*

Change stop thrust carried out low on the opponent's wrist.

*Second intention parry*

Circular sixth followed by semicircular seventh.

*Feint counter-attack*

Low feint followed by a low thrust directed towards the adversary's wrist.

The principles along which this action should be performed are identical with those of the previous exercises. In this case, however, the feint counter-attack should not be carried out before contact between the two blades is made with a bind. In this as well as in all the other cases the foot exercise and the subsequent stages of the action are the same as those described in connection with the first exercise.

## Third exercise

*Attack*

Circular single feint introduced by straight thrust and performed on the opponent's fourth invito.

*Counter-attack*

Stop thrust performed low in the first cadence and instead of the circular fourth parry.

*Second intention parry*

Executed with a feint straight thrust followed by second parry.

*Feint counter-attack*

A feint carried out low and followed by a thrust performed high.

## Fourth exercise

*Attack*

Change sixth bind followed by bind thrust. The movement is combined with a simple single feint and is performed from the fencer's own fourth engagement.

*Counter-attack*

Stop thrust carried out in the final cadence.

The reaction by the fencer to his opponent's feint sixth thrust is a simple opposition sixth which is followed by a stop thrust carried out high instead of the simple fourth parry.

*Second intention parry*

"Simple fourth" parry is performed after the execution of a change sixth engagement followed by feint sixth bind thrust.

*Feint counter-attack*

Subsequent to the simple opposition sixth parry carried out in response to the adversary's feint attack executed with sixth filo thrust a stop thrust is indicated on the filo feint thrust. After rounding the second intention fourth parry the opponent has been induced to perform the fencer carries out a feint counter-attack outside and high.

## Fifth exercise

*Attack*

High straight thrust executed on the adversary's upper arm. The movement is carried out on the opponent's eighth invito.

*Counter-attack*

A stop thrust executed low in the first and at the same time in the final cadence and on the adversary's wrist. This action might well lead to misunderstanding in the outsider because the opponent executes his finish high and, as a result, high time stop thrusts are adopted instead of the simple sixth and change fourth parries. In connection with this, however, it is essential to take into account the rule applying to stop thrusts that in the final cadence not only stop thrusts excluding the opponent's thrust but also those of the "tempo" type can be applied.

The direction in which such thrusts are performed and the corresponding fencing target are identical with the direction of the parries adopted against the attack concerned and that of the concluding thrusts that can be carried out from them.

In the case outlined above, the sixth parry followed by a thrust on the lower part of the opponent's hand, a movement composed of two cadences, has been substituted by a one-cadence low thrust directed towards the hand.

*Second intention parry*

The feint is performed high simultaneously with the forward movement of the fencer's foot and the second parry is carried out as the rear foot is being pulled forward.

*Feint counter-attack*

The appel coincides with a feint performed low (stop thrust carried out in the final cadence) and the thrust is executed high (after rounding the second parry) simultaneously with the lunge.

# XV. RENEWED COUNTER-ATTACKS

The renewed counter-attack is frequently adopted in épée fencing. Among competitors not of the highest technical standards, it is a key but reflex action. Among fencers at a higher stage of development it is a conscious second intention tempo action.

The preconditions for execution of the movement are created when the attacker parries the defending fencer's simple counter-attack (stop thrust, time degagement thrust or change thrust) but his finish is delayed or he fails to keep the adversary's weapon under control during his riposte. In such a case the action is continued, as a rule, by a "renewed counter-attack" carried out on the opponent's finish while resuming on guard position from the lunge.

The renewed counter-attack can be performed on the side and part of the target selected for the first stop thrust, or it can be executed with a change thrust that follows yielding to the pressure exercised by the opponent's blade and rounding the guard of his weapon. This action ignores all conventions. It is based exclusively on the principle of the priority of hitting and so it corresponds to the rules governing épée fencing.

The motivation and justification of this action can be assessed and understood correctly if it is examined within the structure of fencing and the basic principle of seeking a counter-action to every existing group of actions. The theory of fencing cannot tolerate situations that are left open unclarified or unresolved. It discards such concepts as infallible attacks and parries of "general" application. These are survivals of traditions that dominated fencing thought from the Middle Ages onwards. Today, the search for counter-actions that can be set against movements of a higher level, is a paramount aim of fencing theory and practice. Experience has demonstrated the correctness of these concepts in the case of the basic exercises in both attack and defence.

This axiom has been verified by the establishment of the system of parries and counter-attacks created for use against any type of attack.

The system of second intention attacks has been elaborated as a method against that of counter-attacks. Feint counter-attacks have, in turn, been introduced as actions to be adopted against second intention attacks.

In the case of renewed counter-attacks we must set out from the presumption that the opponent has parried the counter-attack with a "second intention parry". In such a situation the attacker who dominates the counter-attacker's weapon as a result of his parry enjoys all the rights and privileges provided for the attacker by the rules of the conventional weapons. He is protected also by them to the extent of having a complete cadence in hand.

This, however, does not apply to épée fencing the practice and theory of which ignore these limits. As in other cases the rule of priority for the fencer hitting first, suggests the subsequent stage: the renewed counter-attack, a movement for which it is wisest to conduct the weapon along the plane of the line (that is within the range of the fencing target). The thrust proper should be performed on the opponent's finish.

When analysing renewed counter-attacks for the purpose of giving an example detailed elaboration of the actions will be

364

dispensed with. In other words, the composition of attacks which determines the system of counter-attacks that can be carried out on the actions will not be subject to examination. Here the vital factor is the relation between the two blades brought about by the adversary's second intention parry. This is what determines the subsequent move for both fencers. Based on the second intention action described briefly in the examples it is possible to draw retrospective conclusions as to the antecedents of the complete movement.

*First exercise*

*Second intention attack and the subsequent parry*

Straight thrust feint followed by simple fourth parry.

It is characteristic of this situation that the attacker has carried out a straight thrust feint simultaneously with a step forward and parried the opponent's stop thrust executed in the final cadence with the fourth parry. The counter-attacker performed a last cadence stop thrust assisted by a half lunge and found his blade to be bound by his opponent in the situation thus created.

*The movements to follow:*

- the attacker carries out a high riposte,
- the counter-attacker performs a renewed stop thrust from half lunge by lengthening his lunge and this is an
- inquartata if it is performed inside, or
- change stop thrust if it is carried out outside.

Fig. 80

Figures 80 and 81 illustrate the stages of renewed counter-attack.

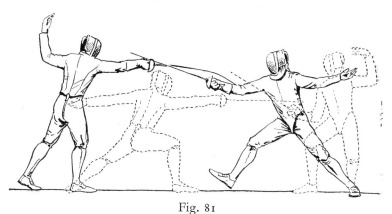

Fig. 81

*Second exercise*

*Second intention attack and the subsequent parry*

Change fourth beat executed from the fencer's own sixth engagement–simple sixth parry.

It is obvious from the description of the movement that the second intention sixth parry is directed against the "time degagement or change stop thrust" expected to be carried out by the adversary.

*Subsequent movements*

– the attacker: carries out a low riposte from sixth,
– the counter-attacker: performs a high renewed counter-attack (tempo stop thrust), or a low second time stop thrust *(imbroccata)* while resuming on guard position from the lunge.

The two examples elaborated are the basis for successful renewed counter-attacks from the relation between the blades brought about after parrying any of the counter-attacks.

# XVI. COUNTER-ATTACK CARRIED OUT ON A FEINT COUNTER-ATTACK
*(Counter-tempo)*

This action brings us to the closing chapter of the theoretical material we have examined and elaborated so far. It should be adopted against adversaries tending to carry out feint counter-attack on the second intention attack.

The technique of execution is as follows:

A is induced to perform a feint counter-attack on B's second intention attack in which the real intention must be adequately camouflaged. B consciously reacts to the feint, with a parry. Meanwhile A tries to score a hit after rounding B's parry.

Instead of performing a concluding parry B carries out a stop thrust or time stop thrust according to the scheme analysed in the chapter on Counter-attacks. The movement should be executed from on guard position or with a short step backwards.

The denomination of the action indicates the fact that it is a counter-action to be performed against a feint counter-attack *(finta in tempo)*. It follows that each of the actions discussed in the chapter on Feint counter-attacks can be adopted here, too. The requirements concerning the preparation and performance of the actions must be taken into account here, too, but from the attacker's viewpoint because the counter-tempo is always carried out by the fencer who has launched the attack. If it is easier to recognize the possibility of a *finta in tempo* in the case of simple actions introduced by an attack on the blade, it is certain that the fencer carrying out a second intention attack will find it most convenient (provided he is all out to adopt counter-tempo) to bring about a feint counter-attack on the part of his opponent by executing an attack above all on the blade.

It follows from the above that in this case the *finta in tempo* takes the form of a time degagement or change thrust with feint. This is the movement on which the attacker carries out his counter-tempo.

The examples that follow have been elaborated on the basis of the viewpoints discussed above. Each phase of the movement is analysed in the exercises.

### First exercise

*Attack* (it is performed by the attacker)

Second beat thrust carried out from the fencer's own sixth on guard position.

Counter-attack (it is performed by the defending fencer)

Time degagement stop thrust carried out high on the attacker's shoulder.

### Second intention attack (it is performed by the attacker)

Second beat followed by simple sixth parry executed on the defending fencer's time degagement thrust. The attacker is free to choose the finish.

*Feint counter-attack* (it is performed by the defending fencer)

A feint carried out high is followed by a low thrust after rounding the attacker's second and sixth parry, assisted by a half lunge.

*Counter-tempo* (it is performed by the attacker)

– attacker executes the second beat while stamping his foot corresponding to the arm with the weapon on the piste;
– defending fencer rounds the attacker's second beat simultaneously stamping on the floor with the foot corresponding to the arm holding the weapon and then indicates a high feint time degagement thrust;
– attacker: instead of the sixth parry he carries out a time stop thrust outside and low, accompanied by a powerful half lunge, on the defending fencer's concluding thrust (finish);
– defending fencer: his intention of following the feint counter-attack with a concluding movement aided by a half lunge has been frustrated by the counter-tempo to the lower part of the target.

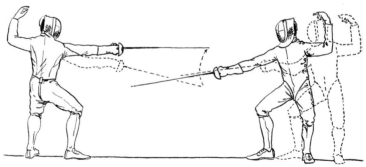

Fig. 82

In the exercises analysed above the feint counter-attack is based on simple parry. That is why the direction of the counter-tempo is determined by the preceding simple parry.

However, in the exercise which follows the second intention parry will be of the circular type. The direction of the counter-tempo will be adjusted to it.

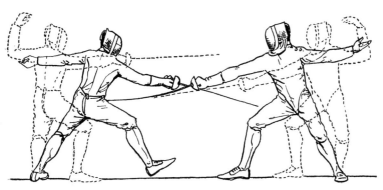

Fig. 83

The essential elements of the counter-tempo are illustrated in figures 82 and 83.

### Second exercise

*Attack* (it is performed by the attacker)

Simple fourth engagement followed by flanconade and parried out from the fencer's own sixth on guard position.

*Counter-attack* (it is performed by the defending fencer)

Change stop thrust executed high and outside on the attacker's upper arm with the weapon and from the attacker's fourth engagement.

*Second intention attack* (it is performed by the attacker)

Fourth engagement followed by circular fourth parry on the defending fencer's change stop thrust.

*Feint counter-attack* (it is performed by the defending fencer)

Feint change stop thrust carried out outside and high and by rounding the attacker's fourth engagement.
Following the rounding of the attacker's second intention circular fourth parry a thrust is executed outside and high on the attacker's upper arm. The movement is assisted by a half lunge.

*Counter-tempo* (it is performed by the attacker)

– attacker executes the fourth engagement simultaneously with his foot corresponding to the arm with the weapon stamping on the piste;
– defending fencer rounds the attacker's fourth bind with a feint move while stamping the floor with his foot corresponding to the hand with the weapon;
– attacker carries out a time stop thrust to the lower part of

the target and with a half lunge instead of second intention circular fourth parry;

– defending fencer attempts to execute his finish in the direction of the attacker's circular fourth, but his action assuming the form of the concluding move of the feint counter-attack, coinciding with a half lunge and designed to end on the lower part of the target, is rendered ineffective by the attacker's counter-tempo.

# XVII. PREPARATION OF BOUT (FREE) FENCING

## (a) *Linking up the component parts of the fencing material*

Only occasionally can an outsider or onlooker recognize that the individual actions of the fencers are related to one another. Each movement preceding the hit proper tends to dissolve and loses its importance to the eye as a result of the objective recognition of the fact of a hit having been scored. It must be borne in mind, however, that the hit itself is neither more nor less than the fullstop ending a sentence that has been properly constructed in respect of both content and style. The essence, style and content of fencing are to be found in the stages prior to the hit. The build-up shapes the bout in which two opponents try to convince one another of their superior knowledge, seeking to display the extent of that superiority on the piste within the framework of the competition rules and in a language and form that is both intelligible and convincing for expert observers.

If fencing as a whole is viewed from this angle the individual elements making up an action are like words. As in speech, these words can only result in continuous and fluent expression if the competitor is familiar not only with the sense and nuance of meaning associated with each word, but is also capable of linking them up as required by grammar and in a form enabling him to sustain continuous conversation on a high level when so required. He must be able to use the elements to argue, find a solution to problems and deliver a riposte to views raised by others. It is the fencer with the more convencing argument that will leave the piste with the debate won.

If the fencing coach has reached the stage of mastery of the fencing material, acquired the method of effective instruction, recognized the objective to be reached by his pupils and established a solid professional basis combined with a knowledge of modern sciences, he will certainly guide young people entrusted to his charge with a firm hand. The coach who has worked to meet these requirements should never experience a deadlock, or find himself short of new ideas. He will always be capable of recognizing and finding the direction in which his pupils' individual talent, abilities, bents, physical and psychological qualities can be developed most wisely. It is true that the above circumstances determine the direction in which a person can be developed and make it necessary for the coach to adjust himself to a certain extent, yet he will always remain the man in control, the creative individual moulding the material in his hands. Only the coach can undertake this task, and recognition of this fact, however flattering it may be, imposes very high demands on the coach himself. Two major demands are maximum dedication and the highest possible professional standards. Dedication exercises a decisive influence on a coach's career and results. Professional knowledge, the fruit of years of constant and continuous study, observation and practice constitute a basis which, if combined with appropriate pedagogical abilities, can lead to success in training the young generation of fencers.

The term "competitor" means a fencer who has had to cover a long path paved with tiring, dedicated, sometimes dull but purposeful work. At the beginning of a competitive career in any sport both the athlete and his coach confront quite new problems. At this stage the fencer must be capable of performing independent and continuous actions. This is the fact necessitating the establishment of a wide range of varied movements during the preliminary stages, enabling the épéeist to join to one another, in complete actions, elements that have been to some extent separated from one another during instruction and coaching.

Examination of the periods of a fencer's course of progress assists the coach in formulating the tasks he must perform at the different stages of development and classification.

When training young people in their lower teens, the major task confronting the coach is that of achieving an appropriately balanced development of his pupils' physical and psychological abilities, irrespective of whether the youngsters' primary interest is in fencing or not. In this period the coach should confine himself to instruction in the elements of fundamental movement, in other words, he should not go beyond the teaching of the épée alphabet. In this period the foil is the weapon used in training by all student fencers whether they intend to become foilists or épéeists.

With an age-group one grade higher, general training designed to develop the physique should continue. However, this should be done at a higher standard and it should be combined with the formation of special fencing abilities. The principal objective of training in fencing proper is to enable the pupils to acquire the basic exercises of the fencing lesson, develop fencing reflexes, co-ordinate the execution of their movements technically, establish harmony between the hand movements and the foot exercises, sense the tempo and cadence correctly, assess the actions in a realistic manner, select and co-ordinate in time the sequence of the values of movements and be familiar with the connections and relationship between technique and tactics. At this stage a line of distinction is gradually being drawn between the foilist and the épéeist. Specialized training is now under way.

Concerning the *attack*, the fencer should be trained in executing the simplest exercises (straight thrust) by adopting every possible form and method of introduction, as well as in linking up the most complex exercises in connection with the launching of attacks (such as the change engagement and bind thrust). These actions should be combined with simple and double feints, simple, circular and double feints. They should be carried out from different distances and every possible foot exercise should be adopted. Based on the single, double, simple and circular feint ripostes arising from the four basic parries executed by the opponent the individual actions should be built up to the stage of the counter-riposte. The foot exercises must be adjusted to the type and cadencing of the different actions and should include all the possibilities (in the phase of steady, half-steady and continuous movements) used in bout (free) fencing.

Regarding the *defence*, the pupils should be instructed in how to keep distance correctly and use this method as a means of defence. When training them in defending themselves with the weapon, they should be taught how to apply the parry best suited to match the adversary's move, selected in good time and carried out with a limited movement. This necessitates drilling the student fencers in all the types of parries within the framework of a parrying system to a level of reflex-like movements and joining them to one another; most expedient performance of the concluding thrust that is related or subsequent to the parry used so that it is limited in both space and time and is best suited to the prevailing situation; the ability to adopt foot exercises that are dependent on the changing distance.

There are examples for linking up the different elements in every group of the exercises of the fencing lesson. In the following paragraphs, each element is illustrated by one example. These examples are independent, and have nothing to do with one another.

## *Examples*

### *Attack*

1st element: Simple and circular double feint introduced by change thrust from the opponent's sixth engagement. The action is carried out from long distance.

### *Parry*

1st element: Simple fourth and circular fourth parry carried out with a step backwards in reply to the opponent's simple single feint attack introduced by change fourth beat.

### *Parrying the attack*

1st element: Simple single feint attack with change second bind performed from the fencer's own seventh engagement on the adversary's blade held in low line. The attack is carried out with a step forward and lunge.

2nd element: Simple fourth–circular fourth parry in response to the opponent's simple sixth–fourth parry followed by a simple *(passé)* feint thrust. The parry should be carried out while on guard position is being resumed from the lunge.

### *Parry and thrust*

1st element: Change seventh, circular seventh or simple second parry performed from high line in reply to the adversary's double circular feint attack introduced by the sixth bind. The parry should be carried out with a step back-wards.

2nd element: Simple single feint riposte executed with a brief flèche on a retreating opponent.


*Attack, parry and thrust*

1st element: Simple single feint attack introduced by a second beat on the opponent's blade held in low line.
The attack is carried out from long distance with flèche.
2nd element: Simple opposition sixth and fourth parry carried out on the adversary's simple single feint riposte intro-duced by simple sixth and circular sixth bind thrust. The parry is performed as the opponent is retreating.
3rd element: Counter-riposte with a fourth flanconade carry-ing on the flèche.


It is obvious from the above examples that the exercises are composed of three elements on the highest level. The material given here offers a solid basis not only for the representatives of the group of pupils in their late teens but also for those pupils for whom instruction has been accelerated to keep pace with their more rapid progress.

No hard or fast line of distinction can be drawn between ju-nior and adult fencers. Teenagers of outstanding talent are of-ten pushing at the heels of the leading adult fencers, and are entitled to join the leading group on merit based on their devel-opment and results. They need training on a higher level along with the widening of the range of actions. To meet this require-ment the counter-attack, second intention attack, feint counter-attack, counter-attack on the feint counter-attack, renewed at-tack and renewed counter-attack are introduced.

Each of the possibilities arising from these new elements are related individually and collectively to those of the exercises studied so far in both attack and defence. The result is a mass of exercises, so many that even after years of constant practice, observation and analysis of the material published on fencing the expert can still find something new waiting to be applied in practice, and to the enrichment of his own knowledge and the general advance of the sport.

The following types of exercises can be established from the linking up of "well-known" and "new" elements given as examples of the fundamental exercises of the fencing lesson.

## In attack

### Attack, renewed attack

1st element: Circular sixth beat followed by low angular thrust on the wrist of the opponent holding his blade in the high line. The attack is carried out from medium distance with half-lunge.

2nd element: Renewed attack executed with change thrust to the outside upper opening of the target. The attack on the opponent while he retreats by taking a step backwards and performs the eighth parry is carried out with a brief flèche.

### Attack, renewed attack and counter-riposte

1st element: Circular single feint attack introduced by time degagement thrust from high line and on the adversary's change fourth engagement. The attack is carried out from long distance with a step forward and by lunge.

2nd element: Renewed attack on the opponent's blade pausing in the position of circular fourth–sixth parry. The attack is carried out with renewed lunge.

3rd element: Simple double feint counter-riposte with an angular thrust executed inside from change fourth parry. The attack on the circular sixth parry followed by bind thrust riposte of the opponent retreating by taking a step backwards is carried out with a brief flèche.

*Attack and counter-attack on the opponent's counter-riposte*

1st element: Change sixth beat followed by thrust on the lower part of the hand. The attack from the opponent's fourth engagement is carried out with lunge.

2nd element: First cadence stop thrust on the lower part of the hand in response to the opponent's destructing seventh parry followed by simple single feint riposte. The counter-attack is carried out while resuming on guard position.

*Attack and counter-attack on the riposte and renewed counter-attack*

1st element: Simple single feint attack introduced by change fourth engagement on the opponent's blade held in high line. The attack from the fencer's own sixth engagement is carried out from medium distance with half-lunge.

2nd element: Final cadence stop thrust executed outside and high or inside and high on the opponent's simple opposition fourth–sixth bind thrust riposte. The counter-attack performed instead of simple opposition sixth or change fourth parry is carried out while on guard position is being resumed from the lunge.

3rd element: Renewed counter-attack outside and high with change thrust on the opponent's simple or change fourth parry. The renewed counter-attack is performed while the fencer continues to retreat.

*Attack and counter-attack on the riposte and counter-riposte*

1st element: Simple single feint attack introduced by change fourth bind on the opponent's blade held in high line. The attack from the fencer's own sixth engagement is carried out from medium distance with half-lunge.
2nd element: First and at the same time final cadence change stop thrust performed inside and high on the inside of the opponent's arm in response to his simple fourth–sixth parry followed by bind thrust riposte. The counter-attack is parried out while on guard position is being resumed from the lunge.
3rd element: Change sixth parry followed by sixth bind thrust and counter-riposte with simple single feint. The counter-riposte that is in reply to the opponent's simple fourth of parry–riposte is carried out with a brief flèche.

*Attack and counter-attack on the riposte and renewed counter-riposte*

1st element: Simple single feint attack introduced by time degagement thrust on the opponent's semicircular seventh bind. The attack from low line is carried out from long distance with a step forward and lunge.
2nd element: First cadence stop thrust executed outside and low on the lower part of the adversary's hand instead of the simple sixth parry. This follows the fencer's own oppo-

sition fourth parry performed on the opponent's circular single feint riposte subsequent to his simple second parry. The counter-attack is carried out while on guard position is being resumed from the lunge.

3rd element: Renewed counter-attack on the lower part of the opponent's hand with time degagement thrust executed on the change seventh parry. The renewed counter-attack is carried out as the fencer retreats continuously.

4th element: Seventh flanconade counter-riposte from the change seventh parry performed on the opponent's simple eighth parry–low bind riposte. The counter-riposte is carried out with flèche.


*Second intention attack executed on counter-attack*

1st element: The opponent carries out a counter-attack from the high line on the fencer's own simple fourth beat. The counter-attack that takes the form of time degagement thrust and is recognized in advance by the fencer is parried by circular fourth. While doing so he reduces the distance.

2nd element: Reduction of the distance is followed by a fourth bind thrust directed into the inside upper opening of the target. The second intention attack (thrust) is carried out from on guard position.


*Counter-attack performed on counter-attack*

1st element: The adversary executes a feint counter-attack on the fencer's own second intention circular fourth (sixth) parry.

383

2nd element: Subsequent to the fencer's own circular fourth parry a final cadence time stop thrust *(imbroccata)* is performed by the fencer outside and low on the opponent's feint counter-attack. The counter-attack (stop thrust), executed instead of the simple sixth parry, is carried out with a step taken backwards.

*In defence*

*Counter-attack*

1st element: Instead of the simple opposition second parry final cadence time stop thrust *(imbroccata)* is performed to the outside low opening of the target. The counter-attack on the opponent's attack executed with the second engagement followed by bind thrust is carried out with half-lunge.

*Counter-attack and counter-riposte*

1st element: Instead of the change fourth parry, final cadence stop thrust *(inquartata)* is performed from low line into the inside upper opening of the target. The action on the opponent's second bind thrust is carried out while a step is taken backwards.

2nd element: The response to the adversary's second intention change sixth parry and bind thrust (riposte) is a gliding beat *(froissement)*–counter-riposte to the outside upper opening of the target. This counter-riposte from ceding first parry is carried out with flèche. This is a type of movement in which the initiative is taken over.

1st element: Counter-attack from high line and from the opponent's fourth engagement on the inside of the upper arm. The counter-attack executed with time degagement angular thrust on the adversary's change sixth bind is carried out with a step taken backwards.

2nd element: Renewed counter-attack with change thrust on the opponent's head in response to his second intention simple second parry followed by bind thrust directed towards the leg corresponding to the arm with the weapon. The renewed counter-attack is carried out as the fencer's foot is being withdrawn.

*Counter-attack, renewed counter-attack and counter-riposte*

1st element: Instead of simple second parry a final cadence stop thrust is performed outside and high on the adversary's shoulder. The counter-attack on the opponent's sixth beat thrust directed towards the fencer's leg is carried out as a step is taken backwards with the foot corresponding to the arm with the weapon.

2nd element: Renewed counter-attack executed with time degagement thrust on the lower part of the opponent's hand. The renewed counter-attack on the adversary's second intention sixth parry is carried out with a step taken backwards.

3rd element: Counter-riposte with bind thrust from simple parry. The counter-riposte on the opponent's simple second parry followed by high thrust is carried out with a brief flèche.

*Feint counter-attack*

1st element: Feint is performed inside and high from high line on the opponent's feint thrust introduced by a fourth beat. The counter-attack carried out with lunge is directed towards the inside of the upper arm following the rounding of the adversary's second intention change sixth parry.

*Feint counter-attack and counter-riposte*

1st element: Feint counter-attack from high line executed by rounding the opponent's second intention circular sixth–simple fourth parries. The counter-attack is executed with half-lunge.
2nd element: Counter-riposte with bind thrust from change eighth parry in response to the adversary's destructing seventh parry followed by simple *(passé)* single feint thrust. The counter-riposte is carried out with lunge.

*Feint counter-attack and renewed counter-attack*

1st element: Feint counter-attack outside and low from low line on the opponent's shoulder. The feint counter-attack that rounds the adversary's second intention semicircular seventh–simple second parries is carried out with lunge.
2nd element: Instead of the change sixth parry a final cadence time sixth stop thrust is performed outside and high on the opponent's shoulder. This renewed counter-attack on the adversary's semicircular fourth parry followed by riposte is carried out while on guard position is resumed.

*Feint counter-attack, renewed counter-attack and counter-riposte*

1st element: Feint counter-attack on the inside of the opponent's arm bent from high line. The feint counter-attack rounds the opponent's second intention circular fourth and sixth parries performed from the fourth invito and is carried out with half-lunge.

2nd element: Instead of the simple opposition sixth parry low angular thrust is executed on the lower part of the opponent's wrist. The renewed counter-attack, which is in reply to the adversary's circular sixth followed by riposte with bind thrust, is carried out while on guard position is being resumed from the lunge.

3rd element: Counter-riposte with change fourth parry followed by circular single feint in response to the opponent's simple second type of parry followed by riposte. The counter-riposte is carried out with flèche.

*Note*

In respect of form or content the examples given above do not include all the possibilities of linking up the parts of the material considered in this book. My principal objective has been illustrative; I have tried to link what are often extreme and difficult elements, in order to widen the horizons of my fellow-coaches endeavouring to achieve higher technical standards necessary for the successful performance of future tasks.

## (b) *Practice in the form of bout*

The pupil was made familiar with the idea of the exercises taking the form of bout fencing as early as at the fencing lessons of foil fencing. The essence and methods of the application of this kind of exercise repeatedly occurred in the course of the acquisition of the foregoing material.

Unilateral bout-like conditions prevail at the stage when basic level instruction is given in the foot exercises and those with the hand where the pupil must perform the exercises as required by the coach's attitude, his movements, oral and other types of instruction. Before being introduced to bout fencing as a means of further instruction and training in some movements, the pupil should have progressed to the part where he is able to carry out that movement in two, three or more variations in order to reply to charges in the coach's movements.

Bilateral bout-like conditions based on the simplest exercises can be created at a later stage when the pupils are trained in the fundamental exercises of the fencing lesson. Here they should be given a choice of actions so that the lesson has bout-like conditions for the coach, too.

For example, the student fencer carries out a change thrust or a simple single feint with change thrust from the coach's sixth engagement.

The coach parries the thrust with a simple or circular parry and carries out a riposte thus developing the exercise into one of thrust, parry and riposte, or he can stop at the stage of allowing himself to be hit by the pupil's change thrust or change thrust with simple single feint.

The primary object of the exercises is to enable the pupils to acquire definite technical skills within the framework of standard forms or under conditions similar to those prevailing during actual bout fencing.

A secondary but equally important goal is to equip the pupil to be able to apply the acquired technical material according to general tactical principles and to develop his own individual tactics.

There are references in fencing literature to exercises involving bout-like conditions, or those designed to parry attacks either in the conventional manner or in pairs. The views expressed on this subject are often contradictory but in essence they agree on the need to ensure that already at the stage of giving instruction in the basic exercises of the fencing lesson, the coach must adopt methods that facilitate the linking up of the parts of the material by the pupil. These methods should also develop a realistic assessment of the applicability of the different actions. This is what is described as the gradual promotion of progress by graded exercises.

With this in mind it would be unwise to argue over the correctness of different views and contrast them with one another because graded exercises, that is the build-up of exercises in a logical manner (advancing from the easy to the difficult stages, from the simple to the complex) leads to balanced development.

As a competitive sport fencing is regulated by rules and conventions that are perhaps stricter than those of any other sport, because here the hits scored during individual combat are awarded according to a time sequence. That is why it is difficult to imagine such an action as could dispense with the bondage of conventions. Accordingly, every technical element is regarded as a conventional one irrespective of whether it is adopted in attack, defence or counter-attack. Exceptions to this rule can only be made to a limited extent even in the case of épée fencing. Here the principle of the priority of the hit is enforced and this, apparently, resolves the bondage of conventions to a certain extent.

During the development that has taken place over the past

two decades or so the practice of fencing has verified the view that the technical material of épée fencing is based on that of its related conventional weapon, the foil. It is impossible to reach high technical standards without command of the technical material of foil fencing. The special actions characteristic of the épée sprang up from this basis, and in some cases they reacted to it by bringing about changes in the forms and methods of applying the conventional actions. What are termed as "combat actions" enabling simple and faster hits have been formed to counter-balance the conventional actions.

At the present stage of development there is real harmony between the conventional and combat systems united impressively in the bout. The combination of these two systems is characteristic of the style of the top-class competitor. Very often we witness bouts in which fencers representing the same or opposite styles (combat and conventional) meet on the piste. It is beyond any doubt today that an épée (or even foil) fencer in the conventional style is bound to be inferior to an opponent adopting a combination of the two styles. What is more, he will very very often turn out to be the loser when facing a fencer using only the combat system.

Fencing lessons built up systematically, practice under bout-like conditions, exercises *"au mur"*, conventional exercises, exercises designed to parry attacks, bouts, systematic free fencing, unlimited bouts, bouts fenced until 5 or 10 hits and competitive fencing constitute the framework within which the fencer can grow to the stature of a competitor.

# CONCLUSION

The scattered, tiny mosaic pieces that I have attempted to mould into one big unit in respect of structure and content were mentioned in the Foreword.

I have endeavoured to achieve completeness in the discussion of the technical material, yet I do not assert that I have been able to give something that is final. The present stage of development is recorded in this book and the path of advance is left open. Development is a constant process opening up new vistas and possibilities in both theory and practice. Changes taking place in the theory and practice of fencing stretch the framework of the rules and these rules must be adjusted to the special nature of the weapons even if this process is generally somewhat belated. The weapons and the scoring device also undergo changes leading to alterations in fencing as well.

Fencers and experts must always adjust themselves to new conditions in good time. My reply to the question whether I have left consciously certain problems to be settled is positive. Systematization of the material on a higher level offered the possibility to consider renewed attacks, counter-attacks, second intention attacks and counter-attacks that can be performed on feint counter-attacks during the discussion of the fundamental exercises of the fencing lesson (in the case of every group of actions) as integral parts of the material and as counter-moves of a superior level. However, I resisted this temptation because at the present stage of knowledge and the technical standards of the competitors, the coach who attempted to do what is described above would find himself faced with such difficulties as would render it impossible for him to give instruction in the complete material of the range of actions without any gap. That is why during the discussion of the above-mentioned material and when referring to its antecedents I had to go back to the fundamental exercises of the fencing lesson. This explains how relations between elements of an identical type can be found but, of course, at a higher stage of development.

Comparison of the practical material arising from having left-handed fencers facing right-handed ones on the piste and of the relations between actions carried out by left and right-handed fencers is another question left open. The technical material on this issue, in the majority of cases, is identical with what has been considered in this book. However, judgement of each situation and different tactical approach required is something for the future.

The argument can be raised that no separate chapter has been devoted to tactics. In connection with this I wish to point out that the principle according to which instruction in technique is combined with the tactical application of the material already at the basic stage of training was emphasized at the outset. The individual features of training in tactics and the stages of development that have to be covered by the competitor during his career from fencing lesson to the victory rostrum have also been dealt with.